WRITING
ESSAYS
ABOUT
LITERATURE

WRITING ESSAYS ABOUT LITERATURE

A Literary Rhetoric

Joanne Cockelreas
Dorothy Logan

University of New Mexico

Holt, Rinehart and Winston, Inc.
New York   Chicago   San Francisco   Atlanta
Dallas   Montreal   Toronto

To Charles Cockelreas and Esther Redmond

who edited, proofread, and
made invaluable suggestions
for improving this book

Library of Congress Catalog Card Number: 74-126798

SBN: 03-076495-5

Printed in the United States of America

0123   40   9 8 7 6 5 4 3 2 1

Preface

Most students new to the study of literature agree that their greatest obstacle to writing essays of literary criticism is their inability to understand the works they read. Their problem resembles that of George Dane, the principal character in Henry James' story "The Great Good Place." After a life of tensions so great that he is near a breakdown, George suddenly finds himself in a place of great charm and contentment—a place of actual perfection. Immediately he and his companion feel compelled to analyze the source of such perfection. They examine the Great Good Place—what is there, what it resembles, what it might represent. In their analysis, they leave out nothing that might aid their total understanding of the *essence* of the place. Similarly, before the student can write effectively about the whole or any element of a work of literature, he must thoroughly understand the work. He must subject it to critical analysis.

Too often the student who finds himself powerless before those baffling questions "What does it mean?" and "What shall I write about?" imagines that those experienced in interpreting and writing about literature read a work once and are blessed with instantaneous and total comprehension. Admittedly, experienced analysts reach that "great good place" sooner than do the novices, but even they spend much time examining and re-examining evidence from the work to reach their conclusions. Analysis always precedes understanding.

We believe that every student can learn to analyze and write about literature, and in that belief we offer a plan that is valid for ana-

lyzing poems, plays, and fiction. Our plan is designed for the student of
introductory courses in literature; it has been tried on students and has
proved effective.

Our plan for learning to understand a work of literature contains
three steps:

1. Discovering the dramatic experience (what happens and to
whom)

2. Discovering the author's presentation of the dramatic experience
(the techniques the author employs to enrich with meaning the human experience he sets before the reader)

3. Synthesizing the two steps above to discover, narrowly, what the
author has to say about a particular human experience, or, more broadly,
what he has to say about the human condition in general

These three discoveries reveal what a work means—its theme, and,
in addition, the ways of its meaning.

Our plan for teaching the student to write about literature is also de-
velopmental. We introduce in the second section the form and theory of
writing critical analysis. We analyze and demonstrate with essays appropriate to the student's own writing assignments the various ways to approach and structure subject matter. In the three succeeding sections, devoted to fiction, poetry, and drama respectively, we explore the nature
of these major genre. Because concepts and terminology vary with each
genre, we define and explain those literary terms the student will need in
order to write with precision. Thus, we prepare the student to look for
the characteristic elements of works of different genre.

In the final part of our plan for teaching the student to write, we include representative works from each of the genre—"Araby" by James
Joyce, "Sonnet CXLVI" by Shakespeare, "The Rival" by Sylvia Plath,
and *The Leader* by Eugene Ionesco. We subject these works to the type of
analysis we expect from the student. Following each analysis we give sample essays of the kinds customarily assigned in literature courses. As a result, each section becomes an independent unit; it is not necessary for the
student to read the entire text before he is ready to write his first essay.

Throughout the text various approaches to criticism are acknowledged.
The instructor may be opposed to some of the critical approaches introduced, but these ways of getting at the meaning of works are common to
modern literary criticism and we believe that they should, and in some
cases must, be acknowledged for a full review of critical methods. Our approach, however, is usually that of explication of theme through close
textual analysis.

The Glossary at the back of the book includes literary terms that are
used but not discussed in the text. The first use of a literary term to be discussed or defined in the text or the Glossary will be boldfaced. If the textual

content does not permit a definition of the term at its first usage, however, the reader will be referred ahead to the definition by page number or the use of boldface will be postponed until a definition of the term becomes essential to the reader's understanding.

In this text we give the student both the tools and the patterns for study. When he subsequently finds himself in various "great good places" in literature, he will be able to explore them with order and reason.

Joanne Cockelreas   *Albuquerque, New Mexico*
Dorothy Logan   *August 1970*

Contents

CRITICAL
READING
OF
LITERATURE

READING WITH PERCEPTION

Before you can write effectively about a work of literature you must be able to read that work with perception—and critical analysis is the path to perception, to understanding, to appreciation. Critical analysis is not an attempt to discover what is wrong with a work, but rather a process by which the whole is separated into its parts and those parts examined to discover their nature, function, and relationship.

When you read a work of literature critically, your goal is to discover it: to find the broad outlines of its form, to pinpoint its areas of excellence, and to seek out those qualities that enrich it with meaning. Finally, critical reading is an attempt to see a work of literature in the light of certain enduring aspects of life: esthetics, religion, history, and philosophy.

But how does one read a work of literature critically? An analogy may help. Suppose that several of your friends—a historian, an architect, a moral philosopher, a psychologist, and an artist—have each suggested that you visit a certain town. Each has described the town as "worth seeing."

Now you are parked on a hillside with the town stretched out below you. You see only a few streets. Along the highway, the stores are unpainted, and toward the river, clustered between an unpaved road and a line of trees, you see fifty or sixty run-down houses. Why, you ask yourself, is this town worth seeing? Why did it interest my friends?

You drive down the hill into the town, explore its streets, stop by a hardware store and watch the townspeople going from one store to another. Whatever interest the town holds is not readily apparent. You begin to walk, to talk with the inhabitants, to observe, and to note—to examine the town critically, to analyze it, to discover it.

You learn that the town was founded in the mid-nineteenth century by runaway slaves who worked for nearby farmers until they could buy the land on which the town is built. That would explain the historian's interest. And your architect friend undoubtedly found the buildings interesting. Even though the town is in a midwestern state, the style of all the buildings is southern Colonial. The moral philosopher and the psychologist probably were interested to learn that the town has been free and self-supporting since its founding, and that today it is an integrated community where crime and violence are unknown. At sunset, as the grayness of the weathered buildings changes to shades of gold (giving reality for an instant to the vision of the original founders), you see the town through the eyes of your artist friend.

Obviously, there are many ways to view the town. The same is true of literature. An enduring work possesses a depth that invites much probing. In a critical sense, its multiple layers of meaning attract the literary equivalents of architects, philosophers, historians, psychologists, and artists— each of whom analyzes a work of literature from a special viewpoint.

For example, some works of literature present true and accurate pictures of the customs, fashions, and morals of the age in which they were written. Critical readers who are interested in sociology and history tend to analyze the relationship of art to society, to see them as endlessly interacting forces.

Other critical readers use the author's life to explain his works. They want to know an author's religious beliefs, whether his marriage was a happy one, whether he fought in a war, whether he held strong political beliefs. Readers who follow this line of inquiry believe that an author's biography reveals the concepts of his works.

There are also readers who believe that a work can reveal the author's personality, his mind, and his patterns of behavior. At base, those who approach literature in this way are psychoanalyzing the author; they are using his work as evidence that shows the unconscious workings of his mind. Needless to say, one needs to know much about psychology before attempting to interpret literature in this way.

Somewhat akin to the psychological approach, but differing from it in important respects, is the approach that attempts to discover not the author's personal unconscious, but rather the revelation in his work of what is called the "collective unconscious" of the human race. This approach shows the importance of myth as the artist's mind uses it in the act of creation.

Another way readers arrive at an understanding of literature, the one that forms the basis of our approach to critical reading, considers a work of literature an entity. We advocate examining a work quite apart from its author's life and times, his psychological behavior, or his unconscious employment of myth. In our method, we assume that the work itself contains all the information necessary for understanding and evaluating it, and further, that the author has used his creative powers deliberately to shape and perfect his work as an object of art.

Although we acknowledge the other methods of literary inquiry as valid aids to illuminating special facets of a work, we believe that true depth of understanding comes from confronting the work as a complete artistic experience. This kind of confrontation is actually a study of the shaping process, the means by which the author produces his work of art. To understand how he did it, you must separate the whole into its parts and examine their nature, their function, and their relationship to the whole. This book is an attempt to help you recognize the *means* an author uses to develop a work. This will help you read with greater sensitivity and, consequently, with greater enjoyment. When you understand the methods an author uses to shape his work, the work itself will yield to your understanding.

Before describing our plan, however, we need to define what we mean by "understanding a work." A great work of literature under continued and intensive investigation would probably yield endless riches of understanding. We are not suggesting that your investigation will reveal the one "true meaning" of a work. Our goal is to help you to understand the work well enough to be able to see its overall principle of organization; well enough to be able to write about it in a way that brings a clearer perception of it to your reader; well enough to discover a theme or meaning that both satisfies you and is logically accounted for by the means of shaping you discover in it. Your satisfaction is an important consideration, for if you yourself are not content with your interpretation, neither will your reader be. Consequently, if you feel a vague discontent with your results at the end of your first investigation, you will need to continue your critical examination until you reach that great good place of satisfaction. On the other hand, you should not be so completely satisfied with the meaning you discover that you cannot see that other meanings might be as good as —or better than—your own. Remember that a great work of literature contains enough wealth for many interpretations. Nevertheless, our belief remains firm that if you can learn to comprehend the totality of a work, you will be able to formulate a succinct expression of the *theme* of that work.

Here, then, is our plan for understanding literature. It has three parts, progressing from the concrete to the abstract, from the simple to the complex.

The first step is to *discover the dramatic experience.*

The second step is to *discover the author's presentation of that experience.*

The third step is to *synthesize Steps One and Two to discover the subject and meaning of the work.*

As you will discover, the plan requires you to read the works more than once. Your first reading will help you obtain an overall view of the entire work. In subsequent readings you will find yourself stopping to analyze details; to study words, phrases, and sentences; to note patterns and allusions. All of these are part of the method by which the author shapes his work.

THE PROCESS OF DISCOVERY

1. DISCOVERING THE DRAMATIC EXPERIENCE

You can discover the dramatic experience of a work of literature by answering the basic questions: what happens and to whom? Most novels, short stories, and plays unfold their dramatic experiences in a fairly obvious way. Discovering them involves merely following the narration. Some works, however, do not have a narrative to follow, and the experience concerns only what someone saw and his resultant musings. There are some works in which the entire dramatic experience may be someone's thoughts or feelings about a subject. Some dramatic experiences, then, are overt, and one can follow them by noting human action and speech. Other dramatic experiences are covert, comprehended by noting expression of thought or feeling. In some works there is a combination of both outward action and inner reflection. An example of this last kind of experience is found in the following poem, "Billiards," by Walker Gibson, which sets before us both a narrative and an internal experience.[1]

> Late of the jungle, wild and dim,
> Sliced from the elephant's ivory limb,
> Painted, polished, here these spheres
> Rehearse their civilized careers—
> Trapped in geometric toil,
> Exhibit impact and recoil
> Politely in a farce of force.
> And let's have no absurd remorse,
> But praise the complicated plan

[1] Walker Gibson, "Billiards," from *The Reckless Spenders* (Bloomington: Indiana University Press, 1954). Reprinted by permission.

That organizes beast and man
In patterns so superbly styled,
Late of the jungle, dim and wild.

Quite simply, the narrative experience of Gibson's poem is this: the writer speaks to another person (perhaps to you, the reader) about thoughts he has while either watching a game of billiards or participating in it. We know that he speaks to someone because of his use of direct address ("let's have no absurd remorse"). Obviously, however, the speaker reflects upon an internal experience. On our first level of understanding we comprehend the internal experience: the speaker of the poem sees that a "civilized" game, like billiards, is not far removed from the jungle life of the elephant from whose tusks the billiard balls are fashioned.

Equally simple to discover is the dramatic experience of the following story by Ernest Hemingway, with its clear narrative line.

OLD MAN AT THE BRIDGE [2]

An old man with steel-rimmed spectacles and very dusty clothes sat by the side of the road. There was a pontoon bridge across the river and carts, trucks, and men, women and children were crossing it. The mule-drawn carts staggered up the steep bank from the bridge with soldiers helping push against the spokes of the wheels. The trucks ground up and away heading out of it all and the peasants plodded along in the ankle-deep dust. But the old man sat there without moving. He was too tired to go any farther.

It was my business to cross the bridge, explore the bridge-head beyond and find out to what point the enemy had advanced. I did this and returned over the bridge. There were not so many carts now and very few people on foot, but the old man was still there.

"Where do you come from?" I asked him.

"From San Carlos," he said, and smiled.

That was his native town and so it gave him pleasure to mention it and he smiled.

"I was taking care of animals," he explained.

"Oh," I said, not quite understanding.

"Yes," he said, "I stayed, you see, taking care of animals. I was the last one to leave the town of San Carlos."

He did not look like a shepherd nor a herdsman and I looked at his black dusty clothes and his gray dusty face and his steel-rimmed spectacles and said, "What animals were they?"

"Various animals," he said, and shook his head. "I had to leave them."

I was watching the bridge and the African looking country of the Ebro Delta and wondering how long now it would be before we would see the enemy, and listening all the while for the first noises that would signal that ever-mysterious event called contact, and the old man still sat there.

"What animals were they?" I asked.

"There were three animals altogether," he explained. "There were two goats and a cat and then there were four pairs of pigeons."

"And you had to leave them?" I asked.

"Yes. Because of the artillery. The captain told me to go because of the artillery."

"And you have no family?" I asked, watching the far end of the bridge where a few last carts were hurrying down the slope of the bank.

"No," he said, "only the animals I stated. The cat, of course, will be all right. A cat can look out for itself, but I cannot think what will become of the others."

"What politics have you?" I asked.

"I am without politics," he said. "I am seventy-six years old. I have come twelve kilometers now and I think now I can go no further."

"This is not a good place to stop," I said. "If you can make it, there are trucks up the road where it forks for Tortosa."

"I will wait a while," he said, "and then I will go. Where do the trucks go?"

"Toward Barcelona," I told him.

"I know no one in that direction," he said, "but thank you very much. Thank you again very much."

He looked at me very blankly and tiredly, then said, having to share his worry with someone, "The cat will be all right, I am sure. There is no need to be unquiet about the cat. But the others. Now what do you think about the others?"

"Why, they'll probably come through it all right."

"You think so?"

"Why not?" I said, watching the far bank where now there were no carts.

"But what will they do under the artillery when I was told to leave because of the artillery?"

"Did you leave the dove cage unlocked?" I asked.

"Yes."

"Then they'll fly."

"Yes, certainly they'll fly. But the others. It's better not to think about the others," he said.

"If you are rested I would go," I urged. "Get up and try to walk now."

"Thank you," he said and got to his feet, swayed from side to side and then sat down backwards in the dust.

"I was taking care of animals," he said dully, but no longer to me. "I was only taking care of animals."

There was nothing to do about him. It was Easter Sunday and the Fascists were advancing toward the Ebro. It was a gray overcast day with a low ceiling so their planes were not up. That and the fact that cats know how to look after themselves was all the good luck that old man would ever have.

Even though "Old Man at the Bridge" is of considerably greater length than Gibson's poem, its paraphrased experience does not take much longer to tell than did the summary of the experience of the poem: a soldier in the Spanish Civil War encounters an aged man at a bridge where the soldier expects the Fascist enemy soon to arrive. The old man has been evacuated from his home in San Carlos, and as the soldier keeps a watchful eye out for the advancing army, he hears of the animals the old man has had to leave behind under enemy artillery. He learns, too, that the old man can go no farther than the bridge where they are.

Discovering the dramatic experience of Gibson's poem or of Hemingway's story—or of any work of literature—represents only a first step toward understanding. The next step is to discover the means by which the author shaped his work.

2. DISCOVERING THE AUTHOR'S PRESENTATION

To see what a writer does with his raw material is to understand the finished product. An author starts with a dramatic experience. He makes this human experience significant—makes it say something about the human condition—by enriching the raw material with his own particular technique. Many literary critics agree with Mark Schorer that technique is the only means a writer has of "discovering, exploring, developing his subject, of conveying its meaning, and finally, of evaluating it." Mr. Schorer's theory implies that without the enrichment of technique a work of literature has no meaning for a reader.

Although "technique" sounds like an artistic term, its elements are easily identified once you become aware of how authors convey meaning in their works. By paying close attention to words, phrases, and sentences (and to their implied meanings), you will be able to interpret what you read.

Words

Since words are the smallest units of writing, you should first direct attention to them. Obviously, you must discover the denotative meaning of all words you do not already know. The **denotative** meaning of a word refers to its simple dictionary definition, independent of emotive or associational implications. You must also discover the connotative meaning of words. The **connotative** meaning of a word adds to the dictionary meaning all the emotions, prejudices, or associations called to mind by the word. You must also note the context in which words appear. Noting the denotation and connotation of words and the context in which they appear is the only way you can discover the meaning and implications of words as they form parts of phrases, images, and figures of speech. For example, the speaker of Gibson's poem, quoted above, says, let us "praise the complicated plan / That organizes beast and man." What does he mean? What "plan" does he speak about, and how are man and beast "organized?" In the Hemingway story the simple words "enemy," used by the soldier, and "artillery," used by the old man, denotatively refer to the same "contact" with the approaching army. In the context of the story, however, these words connotatively convey two very separate views of war. And what are the connotations of the phrase "cats can take care of themselves"?

The denotative meanings of all the words in both the poem and the story are obvious. It is equally obvious that to understand what Gibson and Hemingway are saying with their seemingly simple words necessitates a study of the techniques they employ. It is necessary to study the artistry of any author to understand his work; consequently, you will find it helpful to discover those elements of technique most frequently used to charge a work with meaning. They include point of view, imagery, metaphor, symbol, allusion, myth, voice or tone, structure, characterization, statement, and irony. Naturally, there is overlapping of these elements, and often one element leads into another, making it necessary to study and use more than one element at a time as you attempt to discover the meaning of a work of literature.

The discussions that follow are by no means definitive, but they should serve as an introduction to the various elements of technique.

Point of View

Point of view refers to the identity of the person who records the events of the short story, novel, or drama, or who speaks the words of the poem. Authors seldom tell their stories or speak their poems as themselves —as authors. Instead, they assume an identity. The soldier who tells the story of "Old Man at the Bridge" is not Hemingway; instead he is a narrator (or **persona**), whom Hemingway chooses because a soldier's point of view gives authority to this story of war. Similarly, the person who speaks in "Billiards" is not necessarily Gibson, but rather a person whose identity Gibson assumes to make the point of his poem.

Basically, there are two points of view: first person ("I") and third person ("he," "she," "they"), each of which can be used in many ways. In the first person point of view, the narrator (usually the chief character) can take part in the action, as does the soldier narrator of "Old Man at the Bridge." A first person narrator can also be an observer of the action, relating the story but taking no active part in it (the narrator in Fielding's *Tom Jones*). In poetry, the first person narrator may speak directly to you, as the persona in Gibson's poem does, or he may speak to another person who does not appear in the poem (the case in Shakespeare's "Sonnet LXXIII," when the persona speaks to someone he loves: "That time of year *thou* mayst in me behold").

In third person narration, the author frequently narrates the work omnisciently. God-like, he sees into the minds of all the characters, moves about observing the actions of all characters, and tells us what "he" or "she" or "they" think and do. Many novels are told in this way; Tolstoi's *War and Peace* is an example. In another style of third person narration, the author tells the story or records the poem through a third person narrator, but he limits his point of view to that one character, as Faulkner does in his story, "Barn Burning." A large percentage of short stories and novels employ this third person limited viewpoint, because it gives the reader a sense of participation. Skillfully used, third person limited lets the reader identify with the principal character almost as closely as he does with a first person narrator, yet it allows the author more freedom for descriptive and evaluative comment. All drama may be said to have a third person omniscient point of view, because we can see the actions of all characters and can hear the spoken thoughts of all.

On the surface, it seems reasonable to ask why all novels, short stories, poems, and plays are not written from the same viewpoint. What value lies in choosing one point of view over another? In "Old Man at the Bridge," for example, what do we gain by hearing the old man's story from the soldier instead of from the old man himself? Among other things, the soldier's viewpoint gives us an objective look at the plight of the old man. The soldier sees the old man's desperate situation and is concerned about it, yet he knows that his first duty must be to fight the fight, whatever happens to the old man. Oddly, this objectivity on the soldier's part heightens rather than lessens our awareness of the tragedy of the old man and of all helpless civilians who, like him, are caught in places where battles will rage. Further, the soldier's knowledge of what will happen to the old man—and his inability to move the old man from the area—make us aware of the multiplicity of horrors a soldier encounters in war.

From a technical standpoint, the greatest gain in using the first person soldier narrator is that it enables Hemingway to give us two views of war: since the story is the old man's story, we give our interest and sympathy to the helpless civilians caught as the old man is caught; and, since we hear the story from the soldier who tries (however unsuccessfully) to help the old man, we also give our interest and sympathy to the soldier. Point of view in "Old Man at the Bridge" controls our interest.

Imagery and Metaphor

Imagery in a work of literature consists of any sensory impression brought to the mind by words. Often students tend to think of images as primarily visual, but the term now refers to impressions of sound, heat, pressure, or any other effect produced on the mind by words. Consider Wordsworth's lines "And custom lie upon thee with a weight,/ Heavy as frost, and deep almost as life!" Here in two lines of poetry we have both a visual and a pressure effect—we "see" and we "feel."

In literature imagery occurs either in descriptive details or in metaphor. The term **metaphor** is used in two senses: as a particular kind of **figure of speech** in which two dissimilar things are compared, and as an inclusive term to indicate any figure of speech (see Glossary). We respond to imagery by the associations our minds make, linking impressions to past experience. Because of this association, your response will be peculiarly your own, and can prove a significant step toward grasping the meaning a work has for you.

Sometimes you will find authors using related images, which form patterns or "clusters." Such clusters will give you a clue to the meaning of the work. Also, you will sometimes discover that a metaphor appears repeatedly in a work—and this, too, will point to meaning. In Shakespeare's *Macbeth,* for example, there are a great many images of darkness and light: ". . . dark night strangles the travelling light"; "Let not light see my black and deep desires"; "Nor heaven peep through the blanket of the dark." Taken together, these references become a dominant metaphor, pointing always to tragedy, to the truth that the forces of darkness are winning over the forces of light.

If you re-examine "Old Man at the Bridge," you will find that it is pervaded by images of dust and grayness. The old man has "very dusty clothes"; the peasants plod along in "ankle-deep dust"; the soldier looks at the old man's "dusty clothes and his gray dusty face"; at the end, the old man sits "down backwards in the dust," and the soldier notes that it is a "gray overcast day." Since "gray" traditionally has a connotative meaning of dreariness, one obvious meaning of the imagery is that the outlook for the old man and for the peasants is dismal. Paradoxically, however, the last "gray" image—the overcast sky—is somehow cheerful. Because the skies are gray, the old man will survive a while longer. The paradox is deliberate, a preparation for the ironic comment about the old man's "luck," which is constituted of two factors: (1) that "cats can take care of themselves," and (2) that the overcast skies prevent the planes from coming. To understand the irony of the final statement and its relation to the meaning of the story, you must think of the image both in terms of what it says (its statement) and what it stands for (its symbolism).

Symbolism

A **symbol** is something that stands for or represents something else. Familiar symbols are doves and hawks, the flag, the cross, a green light.

In literature, the simplest symbols to understand are the ones found in an **allegory** (see Glossary), where both persons and objects are clearly labeled by terms that identify the abstract concepts they represent. In the morality play, *Mary Maudlyn,* for example, the characters named Sloth, Gluttony, and Lechery represent the precise qualities for which they are named.

Normally, however, the symbolic words, signs, and objects used in literature exist in their own right and, in addition, evoke images, which in turn suggest further meanings, usually abstract ones. In Nathaniel Hawthorne's novel, *The Scarlet Letter,* for example, the heroine, Hester Prynne, is forced to wear an embroidered scarlet "A" on her bosom. Abstractly, the letter and its attendant color stand for the concept of sin; specifically, the letter stands for the sin of adultery.

Symbolic meaning can often be found in imagery and metaphor. When Macbeth says, "Out, out, brief candle!" he is uttering a metaphor symbolically expressing the snuffing out of an all-too-brief life. In one of his short stories, "Cat in the Rain," Hemingway uses rain symbolically. The rain is quite real, and we at first accept it as merely rain. However, continued references to it give us a picture of dreariness, and finally, as Hemingway insists upon the unceasing rain, it becomes a symbol of the dreariness and hopelessness of the lives of the husband and wife in the story.

All authors, either consciously or unconsciously, use symbolism in their works. Some use more than others; some stay with more or less widely recognized symbolic representations, like the use of black to symbolize evil and white to symbolize purity; some use unusual symbols; and some, like Blake, Yeats, and Joyce, use a system of carefully worked out "private symbols," which make their work almost impossible to understand without a study of their systems.

Your response to symbolism, like your response to imagery, will at first be personal, reflecting your own experiences and associations. In analyzing the symbolic elements of literature, the objective is to broaden your understanding—to move from the strictly personal to the more universal or representative meanings.

Remember, however, that the symbol must be interpreted in context, and the interpretation must include all elements present in the work, not merely those that seem to corroborate your personal interpretation. For example, a personal interpretation of the "spheres" in the poem "Billiards" might be that they stand for animals, the helpless victims of man's plans, forced into a "trapped" condition. This interpretation, however, ignores the author's metaphorical images of the billiard balls, which he describes as possessing "civilized careers," as being "polite," and as being engaged in "toil." These last images might be said to fit man better than the animals who furnished the ivory from which the billiard balls were formed.

Most students say that their greatest difficulty in reading analytically comes from an inability to recognize symbolic relationships. How, they ask, do you know when an object or an image stands for something other than the object or image? Fortunately, there are clues in most works of literature that should alert you to the relationships between images, metaphors, words, and *ideas*. In Hemingway's *A Farewell to Arms,* for example, a disaster occurs whenever it rains. Through repetition, the image of rain becomes symbolically linked to the idea of disaster.

Another way to discover this kind of relationship is to note emphasis. If the work emphasizes over and over some aspect of nature or climate, that aspect probably has symbolic significance. In an earlier discussion, we noted that the imagery of "dust" and "grayness" occurs again and again in "Old Man at the Bridge." We also noted earlier that the usual response to dust and grayness is a sense of hopelessness. In a symbolic translation of this response, you could say that the plight of the old man is hopeless. Further, since the entire scene and all the people in it are covered with gray dust (and even the sky is gray), you could also say that the outlook is dim for all, including the soldier.

Still another method for finding symbolic relationships lies in the recognition of the complexity or the ambiguity of certain images, objects, or metaphors. The very fact that you can find no obvious meaning for these factors should alert you to search for possible symbolic relationships between images and ideas. Unusual applications of metaphors, phrases, or imagery should also be examined for possible symbolic meanings. As Shelley said, metaphorical language "marks the before unapprehended relations of things."

As an exercise in searching for symbolic content, look in detail at the poem "Billiards." Alerted by the unusual metaphorical phrases used to describe them, we have already granted the billiard balls a symbolic meaning. Rereading the poem shows that the origin and present use of the balls form the subject matter of the entire poem, and further that both are spoken of in symbolic terms. The balls are described as being "late" of a "wild, dim jungle," and it follows quite naturally that man is a creature not long removed from his primitive origins. The game being played also seems to represent something other than a literal game of billiards. Here again, note the unusual images of the balls in use; they are all connotative of man's civilized activities. Further, these activities are described as "geometric," an image suggesting that the activities are performed according to regulations that do not allow individual variation. This image, then, could be said to show a relationship to an idea: the idea that man's civilized activities are too rigid, too patterned. In another image we see man "rehearsing" for his career. This metaphor imparts a sense of pretense, and suggests that civilized man is only "acting," not operating from a sense of moral honesty. This interpretation supports the connotative meaning of the word "farce" applied to man's activities, both as an absurd and exaggerated mode of behavior and as a kind of drama based on improbable situations. The elephant, too, can be viewed symbolically. You could say that he represents a creature of the primitive habitat from which man has only lately come—a creature "dim" and untutored, but also "wild" and unfettered (the way man once was).

To summarize our symbolism thus far, we could say that man is of primitive origins, and that his civilized state is "painted and polished," and therefore false. If we stopped here, our interpretation would be incomplete, since it would not have dealt with the idea contained in the lines: "have no absurd remorse,/But praise the complicated plan . . ."

What about the "plan"? Whose plan is it? Several valid interpretations are possible: you might say that the "plan" stands for civilization itself; or that it represents the "plan" of a supreme power; or even that it represents man's own design—what he has made of himself. Whatever you decide is the symbolic meaning of the plan, that meaning is central to both states of man, his civilized state and his "wild, dim" state. It is also central to what you finally decide the poem has to say to you about the human condition.

As we mentioned earlier, the elements of analysis both overlap and interlock. Because they do, they provide still another way to discover symbolic relationships. A central symbol of "Old Man at the Bridge" illustrates this method of discovery. As you recall, the story has a two-part viewpoint; it is concerned with war and with victims of war. The use of individuals to illustrate the two views is a clue that the individuals actually stand for abstract concepts. In short, you could say that man is used in this story as a symbol. The soldier represents war (not the terror nor the violence of war, but the "business" of war). He makes no statement that either indicts or affirms the war; he simply represents it. The peasants, especially the old man, can be seen as representative, the helpless victims of this particular war. Further, the impersonality of the soldier's observations suggest that this war symbolizes all wars. The animals, too, gain symbolic meaning from their relationship to other analytical elements in the story. In speaking of what he has lost as a result of war, the old man mentions nothing but his animals, which, in a way, makes them symbolic of all things that may be lost by victims of war. Ironically, the animals include four pairs of "doves"—themselves symbols of peace. Irony is part of another element of analysis to be discussed later, but the meaning of the author's allusion to doves should be clearer after you read the next section.

Allusion

In a work of literature an **allusion** to persons, events, or objects outside the story can reveal additional levels of meaning. Keats, for example, expands his frame of reference and enriches the meaning of his poem "Ode to a Nightingale" when he tells us that the nightingale's song is

> Perhaps the self-same song that found a path
> Through the sad heart of Ruth, when, sick for home,
> She stood in tears amid the alien corn.

The allusion to the Biblical story of Ruth adds to the already nostalgic quality of the song of the bird.

Allusions you recognize will alert you to added meanings in a work. The reference to Easter Sunday in the last paragraph of "Old Man at the Bridge," for example, is totally ironic (see page 17), because the hope and rebirth associated with Easter Sunday contrasts sharply with the despair and probable death of the old man. Thus, irony serves to shape our attitude toward the entire story. Some allusions, however, are not so simple to recognize. Often you will discover hidden allusions in a work as you discover the meanings of all the words with which you are unfamiliar.

At times even deceptively simple words are allusions, as is the case when authors borrow lines or phrases from other works and place them in the context of their own. Eliot's "The Love Song of J. Alfred Prufrock" [3] has many such allusions. Three lines will illustrate:

> There will be time to murder and create,
> And time for all the works and days of hands
> That lift and drop a question on your plate.

In this passage, the words "works and days of hands" are deceptively simple. For those who recognize their source (they come from the title of the earliest poem of the Greek poet Hesiod), the words evoke a chain of memories and give the reader the key to the meaning of this passage. Hesiod's poem has an ethical enforcement of honest labor. Eliot used the al-

[3] T. S. Eliot, "The Love Song of J. Alfred Prufrock," *Collected Poems 1909–1962* (New York: Harcourt, Brace and World, Inc.). Reprinted by permission.

lusion as an ironic contrast to Prufrock's idleness. In addition, the passage evokes memories of pronouncements concerning "a time for . . ." in Ecclesiastes 3:1–8. Learning to recognize allusions such as these comes only with a broad background in literature, however, and in the beginning, your instructor will probably have to point out the less readily recognizable allusions in the works you read for your classes.

Myth and Archetype

Myth has been defined in various ways: as "any story or legend"; as "any conviction held by a people to explain the origins of nature and of human existence"; and as "any imaginary person or thing." However we choose to look upon myth, we must, above all (as Richard Chase emphasizes), realize that a myth is a *story*. No pejorative meaning is intended when we call the deepest convictions of a people a *story,* for what we mean is that the convictions of a people are always built into a body of narratives (stories) to explain to succeeding generations the beliefs of the people.

In literature, myths are sometimes simply alluded to; at other times, myth becomes a structural part of a fiction. Sometimes authors use myth to evoke a stronger response from us, for a myth effectively used expands our consciousness of the realities that lie beneath the imaginative experience. James Joyce's story, "Araby" (see page 91), illustrates this kind of enrichment. The ending of "Old Man at the Bridge" is also enriched by myth. When the soldier tells us that "it was Easter Sunday," our minds are suddenly flooded with the meanings of Easter in the Christian myth. Some of you may even see in this reference to Easter a ray of hope in the "gray overcast sky." On the other hand, some of you may see a negation of hope by linking the dust imagery to words of the burial rite: "dust to dust. . . ."

There exists today a belief that myths exhibit basic cultural patterns —"archetypal" patterns, they are called. This belief originated with Carl Jung, a Swiss psychologist, whose work with the human mind led him to formulate two ideas that have profoundly affected literary creation and literary criticism. These theories concern the ideas of the collective unconscious and the **archetype.** Jung held that there is a collective unconscious in each of us: an aspect of our mind that goes beyond our own personal experience and draws upon the experiences of the entire human race. This collective unconscious, Jung believed, is not consciously perceived, but is expressed in an archetype, which he defined as a "figure . . . that repeats itself in the course of history whenever creative fantasy is fully manifested." Jung makes it clear that archetypes are not "inherited patterns of thought," but are instead instinctual in nature and represent "inherited forms of psychic behavior." Archeological research supports Jung's theories, for it has shown that people in widely separated geographical areas at widely differing periods of time have developed amazingly similar myths to account for such basic questions as the creation of the earth and of man.

Archetypes are concerned with basic problems of the human race. When a work of literature concerns itself with some universal phase of human existence, we perceive the universality of the presentation and respond strongly. If we accept the archetypal theory, we can say that artists create from primordial memories, and that readers respond from evocation of primordial memories. Archetypal patterns seen over and over in literature of all ages are the death and rebirth theme, the quest hero, the maturation of the young, the sufferings of human beings in war, and the restriction of personal freedom. The plight of man and beast in "Old Man at the Bridge" causes something in us, in critic Maud Bodkin's words, "to leap in response to the ancient theme." We are similarly stirred by the plight of man and beast in "Billiards."

Voice and Tone

The term **voice** has come to mean the unseen but clearly heard person speaking in any work. Since the voice we hear comes from the persona (or narrator) who records the fiction for us, or who speaks the words of a poem, voice is obviously allied to point of view. An example of a clearly heard voice, which we can tell does not come from the author himself but from a persona, occurs in Robert Burns' poem "John Anderson, My Jo":

> John Anderson, my jo, John,
>   When we were first acquent,
> Your locks were like the raven,
>   Your bonie brow was brent;
> But now your brow is beld, John,
>   Your locks are like the snaw,
> But blessings on your frosty pow,
>   John Anderson, my jo!

The voice we hear is that of the aged wife of John Anderson. Identifying the voice proves extremely helpful in understanding a work of literature.

Tone, too, is closely allied to point of view and to voice, because it is from the voice that the reader infers the tone. Tone reveals the attitude of the speaker or narrator to the subject matter of a work. The tone of the soldier narrator of "Old Man at the Bridge" is extremely impersonal. Not once do you "hear" in his voice a hint of the difficulties under which he fights. Nor do we hear sympathy in his tone for the old man and his animals, nor for the other civilians. As we mentioned in the discussion of point of view, the impersonality of his tone heightens our awareness of the tragedy for the victims. Conversely, the person speaking in "Billiards" speaks with the voice of irony. We can detect the sardonic tone he adopts toward his subject matter. The next section on statement will make clear why we label the voice or tone in these two works as we do.

Statement

When attempting to discover the meaning of a work of literature, never make the mistake of overlooking the obvious. Authors often comment, or make a **statement,** on the meaning of their works, but these comments may go unnoticed because they are so skillfully integrated into the events and issues of the work that they seem to be part of the imaginative whole. The fact remains, however, that when an author makes comments (directly, indirectly, or in **irony**), he communicates with you in a way that possesses significance. When the artist makes an evaluative comment upon an issue present in his work, or when he makes a candid comment on the behavior or the thinking of one of his characters, he is telling you precisely how he would like you to view the issue or the character. If comments come from a character or from a narrator or persona shown in a favorable light, they form significant clues as to how you should view issues. On the other hand, if comments from any of these sources are ironic, they suggest that you should believe something other than what is said (as you want someone who has done you a disfavor to know that you express the opposite of gratitude when you respond with an ironic "Thanks!").

The illustration above, of course, represents a use of **verbal irony** at its simplest. In the hands of an artist irony becomes much more varied and complex. Irony does not necessarily express the opposite of what is said. Sometimes the literal statement can suggest subtle implications of attitude. For example, one can see the attitude implicit in this passage from Melville's *Billy Budd:*

> Who in the rainbow can show the line where the violet tint ends and the orange tint begins? Distinctly we see the difference of the colors, but when exactly does the one first blindingly enter into the other? So with sanity and insanity. In pronounced cases there is no question about them. But in some supposed cases . . . to draw the exact line of demarcation few will undertake, though for a fee some professional experts will.

Irony is present also in this statement from Gibson's poem "Billiards": "Let's have no absurd remorse,/But praise the complicated plan. . . ." If the speaker of this poem has presented a plan in which man is trapped, like a billiard ball upon a table, in "geometric toil," the force of which is a "farce," he cannot seriously be suggesting that we praise such a plan. Considering, then, the connotations of imagery, we must see the statement as irony.

The use of ambiguous statements, too, should not be taken literally. **Ambiguity** formerly carried only the pejorative connotation; it designated a statement that could be understood in more than one way because the speaker failed to make himself clear. Now, however (particularly after William Empson's book *Seven Types of Ambiguity*), scholars and critics use the term to refer to poets and fiction writers' deliberate use of ambiguity to give statements more than one meaning. Skillfully used, passages that contain multiple implications of meaning bring subtle enrichment to a work.

Statement, the author's comment upon his work, can be either direct or indirect. In older styles of writing, authors often spoke directly to their readers. Here is an explicitly evaluative statement made by Hawthorne, in his own voice, in his novel *The Scarlet Letter.* Concerning the misery and final destruction of the Puritan minister, Arthur Dimmesdale, who concealed for so long from his adoring congregation that he had fathered Hester Prynne's illegitimate child, Hawthorne says:

> Among many morals which press upon us from the poor minister's miserable experience, we put only this into a sentence: "Be true! Be true! Be true! Show freely to the world, if not your worst, yet some trait whereby the worst may be inferred!"

The reader must realize that even in direct statement authors often use ambiguity. However, noting statement will provide your first convenient clue to understanding meaning.

An example from poetry of explicit comment occurs in one of Wordsworth's sonnets. Protesting materialism, Wordsworth has the speaker of his poem say directly that

> The world is too much with us: late and soon,
> Getting and spending, we lay waste our powers.

As literature moved closer to what we recognize as the modern form (in which the author is more or less effaced), writers became more circumspect about their comments. In contrast to the candidly evaluative comments quoted above, here is an example of oblique comment from Flaubert's novel *Madame Bovary.* The author does not directly criticize the adultery of his heroine, but he manages, with a figure of speech in the mind of his heroine, to make clear in what light we are to view the adultery. In the following passage, Madame Bovary reflects upon her lost illusions.

What happiness there had been in those days! What freedom! What hope! What an abundance of illusions! She had none left now. Each new venture had cost her some of them, each of her successive conditions: as virgin, wife and mistress; she had lost them all along the course of her life, like a traveler who leaves some of his wealth at every inn along the road.

With this oblique comment Flaubert shows Emma Bovary's despair and prepares the reader for her subsequent suicide: he compares her succession of adulteries to losses experienced on a trip. The comparison makes clear to the reader Emma's gradual loss of the sense of worth and hope that had been her "wealth."

Neither obliquity nor explicitness belong exclusively to any age of writing. Authors of all times have used both methods and will continue to use both; and one is, perhaps, as good a way of making statements as the other. The point is that regardless of how the author chooses to make his comments, those comments form important clues to what he wishes to say to you with his work. Note them well.

Only one example of significant statement appears in "Old Man at the Bridge." At the end of the story, the narrator observes, "It was a gray overcast day with a low ceiling so their [the Fascist] planes were not up." Then he makes his statement: "That and the fact that cats know how to take care of themselves was all the good luck that old man would ever have." Like many modern writers, Hemingway makes few direct comments in his works, and often those comments are cryptic, as this one is. However, the statement does bring some understanding: it allows us to know that the soldier feels fairly certain that the old man will be killed by the advancing army's artillery. We can see, though, that the statement contains ambiguity, because the old man's "good luck" is merely that his death will be deferred for a short time because the planes are not up, and further that the cat may (not necessarily will) be spared. The ambiguity of the final statement leaves its interpretation to the reader. If you choose, you can conclude that perhaps animals fare better in war than human beings—or you might wish to think that even though the old man will not survive, something he loves will live on.

There is also comment in the poem "Billiards," and it, too, occurs at the end of the poem when the persona states with great ambiguity that we should "have no absurd remorse,/But praise the complicated plan/That organizes beast and man." Based on these lines alone, it would appear that the persona accepts the plan. However, in the last line of the poem, he refers to the plan as "Late of the jungle, dim and wild." Obviously the statement is ambiguous, because the phrase "a jungle, dim and wild" is to be understood in two ways: one in praise of innocence and naturalness in its original state, the other in criticism of that unenlightened and corrupt disorder that characterizes modern life. Considering the words of criticism ("farce," "trapped," "recoil") in the progression of the poem, we realize that the speaker makes his statement in irony. The phrase as used in the opening lines carries a far different meaning from that of the last line. Thus we discover that instead of actually praising the intricacies of modern society, the persona is criticising them.

We can reach satisfactory understanding of "Old Man at the Bridge" and "Billiards," along with many other modern works, only if we go beyond the surface expression of statement and see statement in the light of other elements we have discovered.

3. DISCOVERING SUBJECT AND THEME

We talked earlier about your final discovery of true subject and theme, but before we discuss the method by which you accomplish these final discoveries, we need to define the sense in which we use the terms *subject* and *theme*.

Subject

First, we must recognize that the ostensible subject of a work does not always represent the true subject. For example, on the surface, E. M. Forster's story "The Celestial Omnibus" seems to be a fantasy about a boy's dream-like ride on an omnibus to a sort of celestial realm. A synthesis of the shaping elements of this unusual dramatic experience, however, leads to the discovery that the true subject of the story is concerned with the ability of certain individuals to transport themselves beyond earthly confines by projecting themselves into good literature.

The poem "Billiards" is another good example of this variance between the apparent and the true subject. Because of the title and the dominant image, one might suppose that the game of billiards is the subject matter of Gibson's poem. However, you have noted enough of the developing techniques of the poem to see that the true subject is man and what he has made of himself in his process of becoming civilized.

The true subject of a work, then, is the one you discover when you delve beneath the surface subject and bring to light the deeper concerns of the work.

Theme

As you have probably already discovered, most literary terms have more than one definition. This holds especially true for **theme.** Some very noted literary critics even deny that imaginative works have a theme. They prefer to designate "theme" as a term more suitably applied to the thesis or doctrine of a didactic work. Other critics prefer to think that imaginative works do not have a single theme, but they do acknowledge that such works may contain one or more motifs. The term **motif** (which also has more than one meaning: see Glossary) is used in this connection to mean an idea that appears and reappears in an imaginative work. Other critics use the word "theme" to refer to the over-all unifying action of a work—that is, the action shown in the work both as overt physical action and as an inner condition.

We believe, however, that both imaginative and didactic works possess identifiable themes, and that the theme (or the abstract concept each author is attempting to make clear in his work) can be identified and stated once the true subject is discovered.

This belief does not suppose that the abstract concepts (or themes) of literary works can be neatly tied into little messages as they are in most detective and schoolboy stories, which are built on the respective themes that "crime does not pay," and that "honesty is always the best policy."

Such apt phraseology oversimplifies the concept of a rich imaginative work. With a literary work, you will have to experiment with your expressions of the theme until you find words that clearly express what you think the work has to say about its true subject.

Synthesis

Thus far, we have stressed that when you have grasped the dramatic experience of a work (which can be either explicit or implicit), and when you have discovered how an author develops or shapes that experience, you possess all the information necessary to apprehend the true subject and theme of a work. Your final task is to synthesize your separate pieces of information—to put them together into a unified whole.

A mere listing of the elements you discover in a work would serve little purpose. To understand the work, you need to bring all the elements together around what Reuben Arthur Brower calls a "key design." Unfortunately, there are no methods or handy rules that will help you determine what the key design is—what it is that holds all the elements together. We can only say again that you must apply logical thought processes to your information. Ask yourself if the work has *unity*. Ask whether any element of technique is *needed* to complete the whole. Ask if any sort of *principle* relates all the elements to one another. To clarify this process, let us apply these abstract ideas to the story we have been analyzing in this chapter.

We need first to ask if any point of unity exists in "Old Man at the Bridge." War is obviously with us throughout the story. However, it does not seem to matter particularly between what factions the war is being waged. Therefore, we may say that ideologies for which people fight do not seem to figure as a unifying factor.

The next question is, What then does matter about the war? The answer depends upon human response. Our earlier consideration of point of view and of tone revealed that there are two separate responses in the story: the soldier's impersonal, businesslike response, and the old man's helpless resignation. We may say, then, that in this story, war unifies two different kinds of human experience. However, as we looked at imagery and symbolism, we saw that the soldier's situation in this story is as hopeless as that of the civilians. Statement and imagery showed us that the animals will all fare better than the human beings: "cats can take care of themselves," the narrator tells us, and the doves will "fly away" to safety. As a simple fact, we can even assume that the advancing army will probably care for the goat. The story also makes it clear that the old man suffers in war, not because of personal fear of danger, but because of his concern for the animals he loves; and that the soldier suffers in war, not because of personal fear of danger, but because of his concern for the old man.

At this point, it seems safe to conclude that the principle that relates all the elements in the story is human response to war: human beings suffer in ways that are subtly different from the ways of other creatures. The two separate views of war we noted in the story are now unified. The true subject of "Old Man at the Bridge" concerns itself with human response to war.

Having discovered the subject matter of the story, let us try to state the theme, keeping in mind that the themes of great works of literature usually give readers some view of the human condition. To discover that view in the Hemingway story, let us recapitulate the factors of the subject of the story by reviewing the reaction of these particular human beings to the reality of war. The soldier remains impersonal. The old man retains a simple dignity. Both reveal compassion for their fellow creatures. War is shown as neither good nor evil, but rather as an inevitable force that hovers over the dust-covered scene of the story.

Two possible themes emerge from this summation. The first is that fighting wars is part of human nature; the second is that compassion for fellow sufferers is a part of human nature. Thus, the story may be said to show the human condition as essentially tragic because of basic conflicts in the nature of man. Some readers, however, may see the theme as an affirmation of the nature of man, capable of dignity and compassion in the face of inevitable disaster.

Studying literature, analyzing it, hunting for its meaning will deepen your understanding of the works you read. And you need have no fear of losing that first pleasure of enjoying a poem simply because you like its sound or its emotional effect upon you, or the pleasure of enjoying a novel because you become lost in its world. These pleasures will remain, and other, more profound, pleasures will be added. To discover the *source* of your emotional reaction, to know the *essence* of the world you experience, and to learn the *elements* that make up the pleasurable sounds serve to increase rather than to diminish the pleasures of reading literature. In addition, a more complete understanding of literature expands your view of life, deepens your understanding of others and of yourself, and sharpens your powers of understanding. The greater the understanding, the greater the pleasure.

SECTION TWO
CRITICAL WRITING ABOUT LITERATURE

When we read critically, we discover a work of literature. When we write critically, we record our discoveries. In the last chapter, we used the analogy of a town both to demonstrate the broad traditional approaches to understanding literature and to illustrate that there are a great many short essays that can be written about almost any work of merit.

As we face the problem of writing about literature, let us reiterate that beginning students are seldom given writing projects that stress considerations *extrinsic* to the story (considerations like biography, history, sociology, psychology). Considerable research and study are required to understand these extrinsic factors, and, even understood, they are too comprehensive to be dealt with in a short essay.

Your best approach to writing creatively about literature (and your best approach to meeting the deadlines for your class assignments) lies in making a close study of the *intrinsic* nature of an individual work. In short, you must consider each work as a complete aesthetic experience, which you can discover through a close textual study of the work itself.

Let us assume that you have been asked to write a short essay about a work of literature. Following the procedure outlined in the preceding chapter, you have already

1. discovered the paraphrasable narrative
2. analyzed the techniques the writer uses to present his insights, experiences, philosophical points, or observations about man

3. synthesized the first two steps to deduce the meaning or meanings of the work.

Now the problem is what to write, how much to write, and how to organize and present your observations in an appropriate essay. To draw another analogy, assume for a moment that a work of literature is like a pond. Any bystander can see its surface, but it is the world below the surface (the depth, the texture, the fish, the plants, and the contours) that really makes up the pond. As a critical reader, your job was to investigate the depths to the bottom. Your job now, as a critical writer, is to tell the bystander what he has missed by looking only at the surface.

You can guide your reader toward an understanding of a work in several ways, depending on the nature of the work itself. Your problem centers on finding the approach and presentation that will most effectively express your discoveries and your conclusions. As you begin to consider your essay, there are some rules, methods, observations, and suppositions to keep in mind.

1. Your essay should be addressed to an intermediate reader—one who has read the work and perceived the dramatic experience, but who has discovered little or none of its rich, metaphorical meaning. Consider your reader to be a fellow student who has read the work, but who has not made a study of it.
2. Remember that each work has its own unique texture and composition, and thus requires its own analysis. Just as no two towns are ever the same, so no two works and no two critical essays are ever the same.
3. You are writing a short essay; therefore, your subject must be restricted. If a work is very short you can discuss much (but not all) of it in a short essay. If the work is long, you can write about only a small (but significant) part of that work.
4. Finally, two reminders. Your purpose in writing a short essay of literary criticism is (1) to explain to a reader what you have discovered in a critical reading of a particular work, and (2) to interpret the meaning of the work by subjecting its technique either to *explication* or to *analysis*.

EXPLICATION

Explication is a method of literary criticism involving a close and systematic examination of specific elements in a poem (or a passage from a longer work). It usually follows a sequential development, beginning with the first line and ending with the last. In short works you can examine key aspects of the whole work. In longer works you can examine only a key passage, selected to demonstrate a particular use of technique and containing important elements of the form or meaning of the entire work.

The goal of explication is to explain to a reader the deeper relationships and meanings of each individual part of a work, and subsequently, of the work as a whole. By making a close examination of the texture of the work (explication is sometimes called the "textural approach"), you can call attention to the connotations of words, to the imagery, to the point of view, and to other patterns of development discussed in the preceding section on critical reading. If the work contains unfamiliar words or words used in an unusual manner, you should explain their meaning or use. If the work refers to terms or names having symbolic, historical, or mythological significance, explain the reference and its use in the passage. Always call attention, as the work unfolds, to its development—to its form and structure.

Explication is not to be confused with paraphrase. Paraphrase (a summary of action or situation) is the surface or literal dramatic experience any reader can give after his first reading. Although some use of paraphrase may be necessary as transitional material, use only as much as is needed.

Explication of a Short Work

To illustrate explication, here is a student essay about "Billiards," the poem you studied in the preceding section.

A CLOSE READING OF WALKER GIBSON'S "BILLIARDS":
MEANING THROUGH STRUCTURE AND IMAGERY

Late of the jungle, wild and dim,	1
Sliced from the elephant's ivory limb,	2
Painted, polished, here these spheres	3
Rehearse their civilized careers—	4
Trapped in a geometric toil,	5
Exhibit impact and recoil	6
Politely, in a farce of force.	7
And let's have no absurd remorse,	8
But praise the complicated plan	9
That organizes beast and man	10
In patterns so superbly styled	11
Late of the jungle, dim and wild.	12

Walker Gibson's "Billiards" is structured upon the dominant image of modern man as a billiard ball, a comparison that results in a sardonic picture of modern civilization. Divided into two parts, with images formed by words in groups of twos, the poem itself structurally becomes an image. The first half (lines 1 through 7) establishes the central image. The last half (lines 8 through 12) continues the image, but, in addition, provides an ironic stricture in an implied comment upon that imagery. Throughout the poem the subtle intertwining of images forms an effective yet subtle argument.

Lines 1 and 2 describe the origin of the balls. Made of ivory, they come from a wild and dimly lit jungle where an elephant was slain to procure the ivory for their making. "Here" (modern society) the ivory is processed into one of the highly refined products of modern technology: the balls are "painted and polished" for use in the civilized game of billiards (3). In the four lines that follow, phrases like "rehearse," "civilized careers," "trapped in geometric toil," and "exhibit impact and recoil" make clear the symbolic meaning of the balls. These phrases describe the daily activities of civilized men.

The first seven lines serve also to set the critical intent of the imagery. Here, when the balls—or men—are said to be "late of the jungle," the use of the word *late* calls forth a picture of civilized man as not far removed from his primitive origins. The image further shows society as a place of tangled growth and confused paths, but, symbolically, as a place where mental and spiritual freedom is impaired. Man is lost, trapped. He is forced to conform to the rigid monotony of his life much as the billiard balls helplessly follow their patterns of "impact and recoil" across the table.

There is an additional adverse view in the poem's dominant image. The polished, painted falseness of the balls is placed in sharp contrast to the creamy beauty of ivory in its natural state. The balls have been shaped into the figures society chooses for them. There is the further growth of the idea of "primitivism," which suggests that man, far removed from his original state of naturalness and freedom, has lost his individuality and self-determination and has become merely a decorative plaything. As a result, the image mocks modern man and his activities. All that he accomplishes with his "impact and recoil" (6) remains only a "farce of force" (7). Implications of his activities as a farce are present also in the use of the word "rehearse" (3): man merely play-acts with his activities.

In the second half of the poem, the speaker's indictment of modern civilization continues. In lines 8 through 12, the poem expresses disdain for society, which the speaker pictures as a busy, ultimately artificial game. Sardonically the speaker says we are to praise the plan (9). Obviously he speaks in irony, because he cannot suggest that a plan which traps man into "geometric toil" (5)—a computed pattern of life—is truly "superbly styled" (11). Further, he returns in line 12 to the image of line 1 to call the patterns themselves "late of the jungle"—that is, man is still primitive, as are his modern technology and sophistication, but now he is primitive in another way—this time in the sense of having lost, in the process of his upward climb, his mental and spiritual vision and his ability to make choices. The civilizing cycle has come, ironically, to full circle.

The sounds of the stylized phrases ("wild and dim," "civilized careers," "farce of force," and the many others) form auditory images that suggest the sound of billiard balls in motion. Further, these sound images, with their strict, rhythmical beat, augment that sense of farcical activity which was begun in the visual imagery of the first lines. Thus, the poem conveys its message by means of imagery. This method of both structuring the argument and evoking the reader's sensory perceptions by imagery results in a forceful criticism of modern civilized society.

This essay contains several features of good critical writing. First, notice that the writer has limited his subject, even though he is explicating a very short poem. "Billiards" contains only twelve lines, yet it is impossible in a few hundred words to explicate all the features of the work. In this essay the writer has chosen to explicate only in terms of structure and imagery. Other essays are certainly possible: essays that closely examine the use of rhyme, of rhythm, or of assonance or alliteration as they convey to the reader the sense of colliding, rolling balls.

Second, notice that the intention throughout the essay is to *explain* the meaning of the poem. The writer's interpretation (or "reading") is based on an objective analysis of material found in the poem itself. The writer does not evaluate the worth of the poem by reacting subjectively ("I don't like 'Billiards' because I'm not interested in table games"). Neither does he judge the work in the manner of the reviewer, who rates a new work as good or bad depending on how closely his intellectual position, his prejudices, and his aesthetic sensibilities happen to coincide with those of the author. Throughout the essay, the tone (the writer's attitude toward his material) is serious and informative rather than facetious or personal. In other words, the essay is *objective*.

Objectivity is especially important for the beginning writer of essays. People read criticism to gain understanding of a work of literature, and they do not appreciate a writer's interjecting irrelevant, personal reaction. Here, we need to draw a distinction. It is irrelevant to criticism for you, as a human being, to say: "I like this poem because it reminds me of the many happy hours I spent in a pool hall as a child." On the other hand, it is not irrelevant for you, as a critic, to say: "This poem falls short of its stated goals." In both cases you are stating personal reactions. But your nostalgia for the good old days is fit subject only for a personal essay, and the personal essay should never be confused with criticism. Your second comment is a critical one, a comment on the effectiveness of the poem. As such, it is perfectly acceptable.

A certain amount of judgment is always permissible. We assume that art, like everything else, has standards of excellence by which we can both evaluate and study individual works. Comparing a work against these standards of unity, of wholeness, of the truths of universal experience (and, of course, in part against personal taste) is the job of the critic. For example, objective as it is, the use of the word "effectively" in the introduction and conclusion of the student essay printed above clearly expresses the writer's appreciation of the work.

Most of the works you read for your classes will be literary classics —novels, poems, short stories, and plays that have already been accorded continuing attention from writers and critics because they examine the human condition in meaningful and profound ways. Generally speaking, these works are distinguished by richness of subject matter and technique, and by language dense with connotations and metaphorical meaning. They are not sacrosanct, however. Even the classics have flaws, and if you note a failure or a limitation (something promised or implied that the author never develops), you are certainly free to comment upon that specific failure and upon its overall effect on the work.

Criticism is a creative process. Obviously impressions and appreciation form part of our response to a work of literature. But just as we found it unwise to judge a town on first impression (see pages 1–2), so we urge caution in finding fault with the works you will study in this course. Unless your understanding is comprehensive, any judgment you make concerning the artistic merit of a work may reflect an inadequate or incomplete reading on your part rather than any real shortcoming in the work itself. (For a discussion of the process of writing an essay of evaluation, see page 172.)

John Dryden once said that "The last verse is not yet sufficiently explicated." By that he meant, in part, that any work of artistic value merits several readings—and further, that each reading, by each person, will likely yield a new and slightly different interpretation. For this reason, we can often agree on what a work contains, but not on what it means. This is natural, because a work rich in connotative meanings, like a metaphor, is subject to multiple interpretation. We can strive for agreement, but fortunately we will rarely attain it.

If, in your own reading of "Billiards," you arrived at an interpretation different from that expressed in the student essay, your interpretation is perfectly legitimate if you can substantiate it with material from the poem itself. Look at Shakespeare's *Hamlet,* for example. Some critics say that the character Hamlet is sane; others that he is insane. Some say he is weak and indecisive; others that he has great strength of character. Hamlet has been analyzed through Freudian, existential, and Christian interpretations, and each analysis produces a slightly different Hamlet. Yet each interpretation, rather than confusing the issue, expands and rounds out the possibilites of character.

Consider this interpretation of "Billiards," which is quite different from the preceding one:

> A man who questions the real value of the complexities of our world addresses his fellow man in the poem, "Billiards." The game of billiards is used as an analogy to show how similar man's struggle is to the senseless interaction of billiard balls colliding and recoiling on a closed table. There is the implication in the poem that the billiards game provides amusement for men—and further, that man's ceaseless activities provide amusement for a greater power. Man's game is to watch the impact of billiard balls; God's game is to watch the struggles of men. The narrator clearly believes in a Supreme Being who designed this world and who uses men as toys in a game he plays for his own amusement. The theme of the poem lies in the narrator's criticism of man, who praises rather than condemns the maker of this confusing jungle, the world.

If the writer of this introductory statement can explicate the poem, omitting no key lines or words that would contradict his interpretation, he can justify this rather extreme reading. The point is that there is no single "right" reading of any work. Many works are purposefully ambiguous, and it also follows that the richer the work, the greater the possibilities for multiple interpretation.

ORGANIZING THE ESSAY.   When explicating a short work, you will find the organization of your essay a relatively simple process. For easy reference, you will either include a copy of the text or quote extensively from it. In the body of your paper you will make comments that refer, in sequence, to the original text. There are three methods for organizing the essay that explicates a short work: you can quote the full text before opening your essay; you can divide the text into sections and explicate each section in the body of the essay; or, if the text is familiar, you can omit the text and quote lines only when you specifically refer to them.

Method One: Quoting the Full Text   The student essay on page 26 illustrates the first method of organization. The full text of the poem appears immediately beneath the title, and the lines of the poem are numbered consecutively along the right margin of the text. Had a prose passage been used, the lines would have been numbered in the same way.

In the body of the paper, notice that the lines of the poem are referred to by number. Notice, too, that the title indicates the subject of the paper and includes the name of the poem and the author. The main title, "A Close Reading of Walker Gibson's 'Billiards'," clearly indicates the purpose and subject of the paper. Since the writer has chosen to explicate only two aspects of the poem, he indicates this restriction in the subtitle: "Meaning Through Structure and Imagery."

In this first method of organization the introduction appears immediately after the quoted text. The opening lines of all essays should contain background information calculated to capture your reader's interest and aid his understanding. In the introduction you can place the author (or his work) in context by commenting on the author's works in general, or on how they have been received and interpreted by other critics. You can offer information about the original publication of the work. You can state whether the work is representative or atypical. In addition, your introduction must contain a brief *thesis* statement in which you define as concisely as possible what you want to say about the work. The thesis usually is placed at or near the end of your introductory paragraph.

Once you have committed yourself in the introduction to a specific interpretation, the body of the essay must explain and amplify this interpretation, usually by examining the poetry or prose line by line. There are several ways of organizing the paragraphs in the body of the essay. You can group your material by line references, by clusters of images, or by author statement. As you explicate, look for units of development in the work itself. Make sure that your topic sentences directly support the thesis, and that they also state the subject of the paragraph. This continuous, clear reference will give your essay unity.

Your conclusion should be quite short. A formal concluding paragraph usually circles back to the introduction and summarizes your interpretation or main statement. At their best, these last lines will expand and round out the vision you bring to your interpretation.

Sometimes you need not have a concluding paragraph. The general rule for concluding paragraphs is this: If the content in the body of the essay has been complex and filled with details, a concluding paragraph is probably needed to restate the main idea or thesis. However, if you feel that you have kept the thesis in clear focus during the discussion, you need not restate it in a formal, separate conclusion. Merely add a concluding sentence to the last paragraph of the body of your essay in the manner of the final sentence in the student essay on "Billiards" (see page 26).

Method Two: Dividing the Text   In the second method of organizing the essay of explication, the introduction (in which you discuss the overall features of the work) comes first. Then, in a separate paragraph in the body of the essay, the first few lines are quoted. Study the following arrangement of material. It is identical in wording to but different in form from the previously cited essay. If you use this style, you will alternate paragraphs of quotation with paragraphs of comment.

A CLOSE READING OF WALKER GIBSON'S "BILLIARDS":
MEANING THROUGH STRUCTURE AND IMAGERY

Walker Gibson's "Billiards" is structured upon the dominant image of modern man as a billiard ball, a comparison that results in a sardonic picture of modern civilization. Divided into two parts, with images formed by words in groups of twos, the poem itself structurally becomes an image. The first half (lines 1 through 7) establishes the central image. The last half (lines 8 through 12) continues the image, but in addition provides an ironic structure in an implied comment upon that imagery. Throughout the poem the subtle intertwining of images forms an effective yet subtle argument.

Gibson opens his poem with the following lines:

> Late of the jungle, wild and dim,
> Sliced from the elephant's ivory limb,
> Painted, polished, here these spheres
> Rehearse their civilized careers—

Lines 1 and 2 describe the origin of the balls. Made of ivory, they come from a wild and dimly lit jungle where an elephant was slain to procure the ivory for their making. "Here" (modern society) the ivory is processed into one of the highly refined products of. . . .

Method Three: Text Omitted   In the third method of explicating a short work, you delete the text on the assumption that your reader is already familiar with the work. When you use this method you must make your references to specific lines in the work perfectly clear. Quoting lines from the poem in the order of their occurrence will eliminate confusion on the part of the reader. Using this method, the first paragraph of the body of the student essay on page 26 might be arranged like this:

> By opening his poem with the lines, "Late of the jungle, wild and dim,/ Sliced from the elephant's ivory limb,/" Gibson introduces the dominant metaphor upon which his poem, "Billiards," is structured. He compares civilized man to a billiard ball, and in the lines that follow the comparison results in a sardonic picture of modern civilization.

This third method is more difficult to write because references and quoted lines and phrases within the essay must be orderly and grammatical. This method, however, will prove advantageous when you are explicating a work that is well known to your reader.

Explication of a Representative Passage

A line by line explication is a satisfactory method of discovering and organizing your subject if the work is very short. However, if you are dealing with a long poem, a short story, a play, or a novel, you must find some way of restricting your subject, because a line by line explication of an extended work would result in a piece of writing as long as or longer than the original. Were you to set out to explicate *War and Peace,* for example, you would have years of work ahead of you, and you would be dealing with so many ideas your essay would have no focus.

Recall that in a very short essay the central idea must be particularly restricted; yet to be worthwhile, it must make an important statement about a work. One way to accomplish both goals when dealing with a long work of literature is to explicate a brief passage. Explicating a brief passage not only permits you to restrict your discussion to those points contained in the passage, but also provides a specific point of reference from which to get at essential truths about the work as a whole. The passage becomes the hub of a wheel, and the spokes are the ideas and the observations you make that radiate out to those aspects of the whole work that are in some way related to the passage.

When you use this approach to discover and develop your subject, you must select a passage dense with meaning, one that contains key elements that shed light on the entire work. To find such a passage, you must first determine which of the author's techniques carry one or more of the important meanings of the work. In the preceding section on technique, you learned that the keys to the meaning of a work may lie in the author's use of such devices as imagery, characterization, symbol, or myth. Therefore, the passage you select should dramatically contain or reflect one of these techniques. The passage may consist of a description typical of the author's style, or it may consist of dialogue that reflects a basic truth about one of the characters in the work (and thus about the meaning of the work as a whole).

Hemingway's story, "Old Man at the Bridge," is a good example of a work one could interpret by explicating a representational passage. The story is short, but it is still too long for a line by line explication. Further, many of the lines in the story do not warrant explication because the prose is simple and literal in meaning. However, some passages in the story are complex and filled with connotations that contain keys to the story's meaning. The last paragraph, for example, could be explicated to show that the theme of the story is contained in the concept of the innocent caught in forces beyond their control. You could point out the relevance of its being Easter; you could discuss the motif of the gray dust that symbolically settles over the world of the story; you could discuss the obvious importance of the cat's ability to take care of itself; you could discuss the irony and pathos in the idea that the old man's only luck consists of a distant, independent cat and a benign, dust-colored sky that keeps the enemy's planes on the ground.

The following student essay uses a line of dialogue from Homer's *The Odyssey* to explain a basic and profound change in the character of Odysseus, the epic hero. Note how the representative passage gives the essay a frame of reference from which the writer makes broader statements concerning the meaning of the work as a whole. By giving us a visual, specific reference we can understand, the writer—in a sense—lets us begin where he begins. As he correlates and explains, he helps us discover additional meaning in this great poem.

NONE FRAILER THAN MANKIND

The Odyssey contains many eloquent and memorable passages, not the least of which is Odysseus's profound statement in Book XVIII to Amphinomos. Disguised as a beggar and preparing his revenge on the suitors who have usurped his palace, Odysseus proclaims: "Of all the creatures that breathe and move upon this earth, none is so frail as man." This passage serves not only as a warning to gentle Amphinomos to leave the palace and go home while there is still time, but it also reflects three important aspects of Homer's epic. First, this passage illustrates a certain superhumanly concentrated element in Odysseus's character which, in turn, represents one of the virtues in living. Second, the quotation reveals the epic hero's courageous acceptance of life and his attitude of resignation toward the irresistible hand of destiny. Third, it serves a didactic purpose and hence, represents several of the ideals held by Homer and much of early Greek civilization.

Odysseus's statement to Amphinomos first expresses a major virtue in the hero's character. In contrast to the dreaded *hubris* or false pride, which is represented as the greatest evil in much of Greek literature, Odysseus evidences a surprising amount of humility—surprising, indeed, when the hero's social and economic position is taken into account. The picture is clear. One need only compare the young Odysseus, mighty in battle and filled with pride, with the sage, humble figure seated before Amphinomos. Odysseus's proclamation of righteous humility is a far cry from his haughty earlier boastings to Polyphemos, the one-eyed cyclops. From this contrast we can see that the hero's long journey provided him with more than just a few lessons in Mediterranean geography. Most certainly, Odysseus's trials led him to believe that a patient heart, a righteous mind, and a contented soul are to be desired. This realization allowed Odysseus, a great king and warrior, to assume the humble form of a beggar and suffer humiliation and persecution without complaint. Thus, in his statement to Amphinomos, Odysseus reveals the humility which has developed in his heart during his long journey away from home.

The quotation is also significant in that it is indicative of the hero's courageous acceptance of life and of his equally courageous acceptance of death. Here again is a significant contrast, a change of character. Odysseus is first introduced in Book V, not as a warrior slaying scores of the enemy, but as a sad and weary man, weeping on the beach of Ogygia. Undoubtedly Odysseus asked himself many questions while he sat staring at the sea. He must surely have pondered over numerous problems concerning the meaning of his life and the possibility of death. Subsequently, near the end of his trials, we can deduce from his statement to Amphinomos that he apparently formulated the following conclusion: Man is basically weak and, thinking that he has free will, he takes his life for granted instead of seeing that it is controlled by the hand of destiny. But the gods teach man through pain and trials and when he reaches maturity, he can see the importance of fate and accept what comes to him, including death, in an attitude of quiet resignation. It is this courageous and healthy attitude that Odysseus brings out in his statement to Amphinomos.

Finally, this passage represents certain of the ideals held by the Greek people. Throughout *The Odyssey,* Homer, as a representative of Greek society, occasionally becomes more teacher than storyteller. Through the words of Odysseus, Homer emphasizes the fact that false pride is evil and that humility and resignation to one's fate are to be desired. The didactic nature of this quotation can be more readily seen when one considers it in the context of much of the book. Throughout, humility leads to honor (as it did when Odysseus's self-abasement in the palace of Alkinoos leads him to a seat of distinction). Conversely, false pride is rewarded with punishment and death (as the last chapters concerning the suitors and their unhappy fate so amply illustrate). Therefore, we can conclude that Homer, the teacher, is speaking for the ideals of the whole Greek society when he utters this eloquent speech through Odysseus.

When Odysseus says, "Of all the creatures that breathe and move upon this earth, none is so frail as man," he actually illustrates three major points in Homer's *Odyssey:* the superhumanly concentrated virtue of humility, the courageous acceptance of life and destiny, and—by the didactic nature of the statement—Homer himself reveals that the passage represents an articulation of one of the ideals of the Greek people. Viewed in this way, the passage represents a high point in the dynamic nature of the book.

ORGANIZING THE ESSAY.   When explicating a passage, or using it as a frame of reference to analyze various aspects of the work as a whole, you must identify the passage in the introductory paragraph by author, title, edition, and page number. You must describe the circumstances of the passage (who is talking, and to whom) and the situation that surrounds the passage, and tell how the passage is key to the dramatic situation. You must also state why you have selected the passage, and tell why it is important and what it reflects upon the work as a whole. This statement becomes your thesis or purpose. Your introduction tells your reader the specific subject of your essay, and it must also tell him what you are going to say *about* your subject.

In the body of the paper, you must discuss and show point by point and in detail what the passage means and what it represents in terms of the remainder of the work. In each case you will be enriching the reader's understanding. Each paragraph in the body of your essay should develop a new point of understanding for your reader.

In the essay on Odysseus, the writer makes three key points about the passage he selected. He states these points in his introduction and then devotes a paragraph in the body of his essay to each point. He concludes his essay with a summary paragraph in which he briefly restates his basic three points. The writer never deviates from his purpose, which is to show how the passage reflects three important aspects of Homer's epic as a whole.

If you will reread the essay on Odysseus, you will notice that it deals almost exclusively with ideas and has little or nothing to say about technique. Though it is possible in one essay to consider both the theme of a work and the technique the author uses to develop the theme, it is more common in the short essay of explication to emphasize—as a major objective—either technique *or* theme. Let us consider both approaches.

Emphasizing Theme   In a preceding section, we discussed the meaning of that most elusive term, theme. We stated that in most cases you would be unable in an imaginative work of literature to find or to accurately formulate a single theme or meaning, which could be stated as a moral or maxim. For example, to propose that the theme of "Old Man at the Bridge" is contained in the statement, "Avoid war because it is evil," would be both to oversimplify the meaning of the story, and to overstate the case. Similarly, to express the theme of "Billiards" in the statement, "Man traps himself in his own web," is to limit the poem to only a fraction of its meaning.

Nonfiction prose, however, differs in this respect from imaginative literature. In a prose essay, for example, a reader can discern the theme or thesis because it is either directly stated or strongly implied. Such writing is *didactic,* because the whole substance of the work is assembled solely to illustrate or prove a specific idea. Essays, including the ones you write, should be didactic. You should formulate a central idea or thesis and support it in the body of your paper.

There are some works of fiction, of course, which are considered didactic. The author begins with a doctrine (moral, social, aesthetic, religious, political) and illustrates that doctrine in narrative or dramatic terms. *Paradise Lost* is said by some to be built around an argument in which Milton attempts to "justify the ways of God to man." Harriet Beecher Stowe's *Uncle Tom's Cabin* is not only didactic but propagandistic. It consists of a thinly veiled plea to abolish slavery.

Most imaginative works, particularly modern ones, will be neither didactic nor propagandistic. These works are written as ends in themselves —that is, to present an experience, an emotion, or a situation. The "meaning" of these works is the experience. Often such *aesthetic* works contain an abstract concept. In such cases, the experience you perceive as you read, an experience that broadens and expands your understanding of life, constitutes the theme of the work. "What happens" is not the theme; the *meaning* of what happens is the theme. Often, to deduce the theme, you will ask: based on the totality of the experience of the work, what does the work finally say about life; what is its overall view of human existence?

We can say, for example, that the story, "Old Man at the Bridge," deals with the abstract concept of the innocent (the old man, the animals, and to an extent the young soldier) faced with adversity. Although the story contains other themes, the abstract concept of the innocent and helpless facing the unknown and the menacing certainly lies at the heart of the story.

Long works of literature will contain several truths embodied in their texture, and your best essays will state and support one or more of them. (By truths, we mean merely valid observations about one or more of the abstract ideas presented in the development of the work.) In the essay on Odysseus, the writer makes several valid observations about some of the "truths" contained in *The Odyssey,* but he by no means states all the possible meanings, for *The Odyssey* is too vast in scope to be so contained. For this reason, when you write an essay of explication that examines theme or meaning, you must restrict yourself to basing your paper either on how the theme affects the outcome or lends a particular effect to the work; on how the theme is contained in character or symbol or myth; or on how the passage reflects larger meanings in the work as a whole. To discover the author's theme, you must study his technique, for as we explained in the preceding section, the author depends upon some facet of his craft to reveal his theme. The passage in which you discover the theme is the passage you quote for explication.

As a final word, remember that the theme does not equal the story. The theme merely allows you and your reader to return to the story with a better understanding of the total experience of the work.

Emphasizing Technique   When you explicate a passage through an examination of some particular technique employed by the author, you select a passage that demonstrates, for example, point of view, structure, diction, characterization, action, or dialogue. In a practical sense, a line of dialogue or a description of one of the characters can become the reference for a character analysis; a specific use of point of view can hold the key to either the author's or one of his character's manner of viewing a situation or condition; a passage that contains a key symbol can open the way to discussing the use of broad metaphorical meanings in the work; a reference to myth, when you explain its use and meaning, can lead to another, deeper level of meaning in the work. In using a passage to explicate technique, you can also quote a representative passage and analyze the author's style: his diction, his sentence rhythms, his manner of writing dialogue or description. You can examine the structure of the work by referring to a stylistic device (the use of time, point of view, the flashback) that reflects that structure. For example, *The Odyssey* is filled with extended similes and figures of speech based upon mythology and early Greek customs. Consider the following passage, which opens Book V of the epic:

> Dawn, out of her bed, from beside the noble Tithonos,
> Rose up to bring light to immortals and to mortals.[1]

Using this quotation as the basis for an essay, you could relate the mythological story of Dawn, or Eos. You could show how the figure of speech reflects the Greeks' desire to present natural phenomena in supernatural, but human form. You could show how this passage foreshadows Odysseus' safe return home, and his successful conquest of evil through the combined powers of fate and the gods. You could also point out, by means of this passage, how Dawn is used as a motif to tie together many of the books of *The Odyssey* and how, as a figure of speech, Dawn serves as a poetic transitional device. An essay that explicates only these few lines from the thousands that make up the entire work could prove valuable and informative to a reader if it showed him the interrelated workings of the texture and style of the Greek epic.

[1] Reprinted from Homer, *The Odyssey*, A New Verse Translation by Albert Cook. By permission of W. W. Norton & Company, Inc. Copyright ©.1967 by Albert Cook.

ANALYSIS

The second major method of finding and developing a subject for your essays uses analysis, which literally means to loosen or break into parts. As we mentioned in Section One, when one analyzes a subject, he separates the whole into its component parts for the purpose of examining each part and discerning its relationship to other parts and to the whole.

Finding and Narrowing the Subject

If you recall the analogy we drew of the town, you can better understand the basic principle of division, which characterizes analysis. The town consists of people, of streets and stores, parks and homes, factories, gardens, public buildings, and all of the many activities concentrated in each. These component parts—people, things, and actions—make up the whole of the town. If you wrote an essay discussing the general features of the town, you would divide your subject into these parts, each as a major division in your paper. By dividing the whole into its parts and discussing each part, you would have fulfilled one of the major requirements of analysis, which is completeness. In analysis, regardless of how restricted, your subject must always represent the whole. You cannot discuss various parts at random. Completeness consists of discussing all points relative to the main subject.

There are practical limitations, however. If you set out to write an essay about all aspects of the town, you would not progress far in your outlining before you realized that you were dealing with book-length material. You would soon see that the people alone would be a vast subject. (*The Odyssey* is primarily about one man in the city-state of Ithaca, and "Old Man at the Bridge" is concerned with only one incident and two people in a long, highly complex war involving millions of people.) Given a word limit, it is impossible to write a complete essay about all aspects of an entire town. If you tried, your essay would be very general and therefore very incomplete, even though the divisions were logical.

The alternative to the generalities and incompleteness that result when your subject is too large lies in taking a single part of the whole, one of the divisions (for example, the physical features of the town), and considering it as a whole—as your main subject. But before you progressed far here (you would be involved in everything from sewage plants to sunsets) you would see that your essay was still too broad.

To avoid an endless repetition of outlining and re-outlining, you can save time and effort in selecting and developing your subject matter by first determining your *interest*. Ask yourself what, specifically, commands and holds your attention? And for what reason? The *what* becomes your subject; the *why* becomes your purpose. When you know why you want to write about your subject, you will already have defined the points you will use as main divisions in the body of your paper.

Let us suppose, as you begin to look for the key feature, which is specific and limited and which represents some truth about the town, that you become interested in the architecture of the homes. You write, "One of the most memorable features about this quite unusual midwestern town is the southern Colonial homes that line the quiet, shady side streets." You have made a specific and sound beginning. If you know precisely what causes the homes' uniqueness, these causes become the major divisions in the body of your essay. If you do not know, you will not have a clearly established purpose. You will not have answered the *why*. Therefore, you may need to add to your thesis. "As symbols of the past, the old Colonial homes best characterize the principles of peace and integration." Now you have limited your subject and you have established purpose, or direction. Your thesis and the basic outline of your paper become easy.

THESIS: One of the unique and most memorable features about this quite unusual town is the southern Colonial homes. Lining the quiet, shady side streets, they symbolize the past and characterize the principles of peace and integration.

A. (Topic sentence) The homes were originally built and owned by freed slaves and were dedicated to the memory of a Southland they loved but which had rejected them.
B. (Topic sentence) From such rejection, the town's citizens, both black and white, agreed to dedicate their homes as symbols of the concept of peace among all men.
C. (Topic sentence) Today the old homes represent not only a memory and an original dream but a continuing and successful freedom from racial persecution.

Analyzing a work of literature is identical to analyzing a town. Your interest narrows and focuses the subject; it also determines the content of the essay. The following diagram illustrates the many techniques that an author uses to construct a work of literature. In all but very short poems, each of the terms contained in the circle (there are, of course, many others) constitutes ample subject matter for a short, critical essay.

If you can view a work of literature in this manner—as composed of all the elements of the author's technique—a method quite naturally emerges for finding and developing a subject. Rather than using a passage

THE WORK

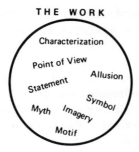

to explain theme or technique as we did in explication, you can examine the author's use of a particular technique and show how that technique functions in the work. As in the explication of a passage, your purpose will lie either in revealing theme, or in showing the resultant effects of using such technique, or both. In either case, you will be explaining how the author controls his reader to achieve a specific response.

ANALYZING TECHNIQUE.   Analysis is sometimes called the structural approach, because its goal is to separate and study a significant thread that runs through the texture of a work. Often this thread (sometimes reflecting a major thematic development) will be found in the recurrent use of a specific technique. Consider the following student essay, which effectively analyzes the author's use of symbol to reveal the meaning of the story.

THEME THROUGH SYMBOL:
WATER AND ITS EFFECT UPON GEORGE DANE

Henry James's short story "The Great Good Place" can be compared to the facets of a fine stone. Regardless of the angle from which it is viewed, the story casts subtle lights and shadows, which both reflect and emanate from the same source of meaning. Upon close examination the story shifts and changes, like light moving upon water. This effect is accomplished through the use of a variety of literary symbols such as bells, slow footsteps, closed eyes, the concept of payment, and a picture. However, the meaning of the story slowly emerges primarily through a major symbol, which is that of water, and the theme is found in its effect upon the main character, George Dane, as he stands on the brink of a nervous collapse.

The first suggestion of water and its effect appears at the end of the first paragraph as Mr. James writes, "It was the old rising tide, and it rose and rose even under a minute's watching. It had been up to his shoulders last night—it was up to his chin now." In this first reference, water as a rising tide is used to symbolize the pressures in

George Dane's life. As the pressures increase, Dane feels he is drowning. This image is further dramatized and strengthened in a flashback in Part III as Dane says, "The wild waters would close over me and I would drop straight to the dark depths where the vanquished dead lie." Dane feels that the world of success is engulfing him, and that he is dropping straight to the dark depths with those who have not been able to withstand the incessant demands of material success in the modern world. It becomes perfectly clear that he is on the verge of a breakdown.

In the opening of the story, as Dane approaches the time to face the morning's duties, the reader is confonted with still another development in the use of water and its effect. Mr. James states, "Washing the window in a steady flood, it had seemed the right thing, the retarding interrupting thing, the thing, that if it would only last might clear the ground by floating out to a boundless sea the innumerable objects among which his feet stumbled and strayed." In this use of imagery, Dane longs desperately for his duties and responsibilities to vanish suddenly. He is indulging in the fantasy and wishful thinking of a physically and emotionally exhausted man. He dreams of a wild rampaging flood that would sweep away his problems: his unfinished work, and an endless parade of visitors, appointments, and telephone calls. Dane has driven himself to success and now he cannot withstand the pressures that accompany too much success. The spiritual and creative forces that once enabled him to write have been crushed in the business of success. As a result, the image of a flood also serves as a transition in the story, blurring the world as Dane begins to lose touch with reality. Part fantasy, part dream, part sleep, part nightmare, the rain becomes a transition and the story and Dane move to "The Great Good Place."

In Part II of the story, Dane finds himself in "The Great Good Place." The author accomplishes this transitioning through the use of water: "He didn't want, for the time, anything but just to be there, to steep in the bath. He was in the bath yet, the broad deep bath of stillness." Through the comparison of the Place to a bath, the reader understands that the bath, or Place, is healing Dane. In fact, James refers to the bath as the "water-cure." Dane is steeping there, in perfect stillness, no longer drowning in the pressures of his world. Dane has found "the great good place" which is the world of pure art, that state of mind where perfect peace can be found. Dane continues to steep in the bath of stillness in perfect ease through Parts II, III, and IV of the story, progressing from a peaceful, almost prenatal state to one in which he is healed and his need for unthinking peace changes, with his recovery, to a need for rational logic.

At the beginning of Part V, his peace of mind, his creativity and faculties restored, Dane states, "Why it's raining!" Simultaneously he makes a slow transition back into the world of everyday reality. Changing, as a good symbol should, the image of water shifts into gentle "summer sprinkles that bring out sweet smells." During this transitioning process from his enchanted fantasies, Dane realizes that life must contain the anxieties of the wild rampaging floods if he is to appreciate or find the world of pure art with all its connotations. And so, in the latter portion of Part V as "the patter on the glass that showed him how the rain—the great rain of the night—had come back," life has returned for George Dane.

Henry James's mastery of the changing image that assumes the proportion of a major symbol enables him to portray George Dane as a man escaping from the wild overwhelming waters of too much success, to the deep still bath of inner peace where Dane crawls into the womb of pure and timeless art as the true means of recovering his sense of self and his perspective. Then, using the gentle patter of summer rains, James pulls Dane back into the world of reality. Through his major symbol, James has developed his theme—that mankind is denying and neglecting the value and peace of the inner mind for the surface tensions of material success. The imperative is clear: the only "great good place" in today's chaotic society is to be found in one's own mind, and we can enjoy the wild waters of success only when they are tempered by the calm and beauty of deeper, lasting values.

The preceding essay typifies the method of critical analysis. The student chose *one* of the many techniques that Henry James used to convey the meaning of his work, and by explaining the meaning and use of a major symbol, discovered a theme in the story. The symbol of the water is divided into parts as it is used to convey different meanings, and each meaning is analyzed in a separate paragraph in the body of the paper.

Essays can be written to analyze character, point of view, structure, or, in short, any of the techniques employed in the telling of the story. If you have read "A Great Good Place" you already know that you could write an essay analyzing the point of view. Your purpose could be to explain how James' use of limited omniscience permitted him both to describe objectively Dane and his motives and at the same time to enter Dane's mind to achieve dramatic authority and immediacy. You could also write an essay in which you analyzed the character of the young ambitious guest as he functions as a counterpoint or balance, or you could analyze the dull efficiency of the servant Brown. You could even analyze James' use of transitions to achieve the effect both of fantasy and of philosophy.

But in each case the approach would be the same. The method in analysis is first to determine the theme and how it is dramatically rendered, then to justify and explain your interpretation by calling the reader's attention to one of the vehicles or techniques that the artist uses to convey that theme and to achieve a particular artistic effect. A good work, of course, is an integrated unit. In analysis you break the work into its parts and examine one of those parts or "threads" if the part runs through the story in the manner of the symbol in James' story.

The essay you have just read is structured much like the preceding essays of explication: the writer opens with an introductory paragraph, which identifies the story and the author. The first lines of the introduction discuss the story as a whole; then, more narrowly, the general use of symbols. The writer finally states his thesis and purpose, which is to explain George Dane's condition by means of a major symbol.

The body of the essay is developed in the order of the story's presentation. The writer moves through the short story, page by page, explaining the use and function of water as the symbol occurs in the story. The final paragraph summarizes the use and meaning of the symbol, and in the conclusion, the writer states the theme of the story (which has been implied but never succinctly defined). By this method, the conclusion becomes the culminating point in the essay rather than a paragraph that merely summarizes and adds nothing new or informative.

The student essay not only fulfills the requirements of analysis by its use of division, but by its *completeness*. The writer has considered *all* the evidence. Had there been a use of water in the story that did not function symbolically, the writer would have had to account for the exception. Similarly, if you should choose to analyze the dust motif in "Old Man at the Bridge," your essay of analysis would be incomplete if you omitted any use of dust that contradicted your interpretation. When you divide the whole into its parts, you must account for every part.

Note that the essay above is written in the present tense. This is because all literary works are considered to exist in the present. We say "Hamlet *is*" not "Hamlet *was*" because Hamlet exists, as a figure in literature, in the eternal present. When you write about a work of literature, you always consider the work as a present experience. You write "The old man is" (not "was"); "The narrator in the opening lines of the story states that" (not "stated that").

There are, of course, instances when you will use the past tense. When referring to a past action *within* the story, you will refer to that action in the past tense, as, "The old man had abandoned his animals in San Carlos. Now he looks blankly at the young soldier." Also, when referring to biographical data on an artist's life, you will say, "Hemingway lived for some time in Spain." But when referring to Hemingway or any other writer in a general sense, we say, "Hemingway is a great writer," not "Hemingway was a great writer." To use the past tense in this case would imply not that Hemingway is dead but that his writings are no longer great.

Most fiction is written in the past tense, but we understand it as a present experience as we read. In criticism, we use the present tense to denote the same sense of the present, which is that great works *are*. They are as much a part of the present as when they were first written. As a story, "Old Man at the Bridge" *is;* as a character in the story, the old man *is*.

ANALYZING THEME.   You can write an analysis of the theme of a work without explaining it through the use of a specific technique. When the theme is complex and difficult to discern, a critical essay is helpful if it focuses primarily on meaning or interpretation alone. You may need to refer to parts of the work to make your essay specific and clear for your reader, but you should place your emphasis on explaining theme and any of its relevant implications. To make this clear, consider the following student essay. The student uses Oedipus' tragic act of blinding himself as a focal point, but his paper is concerned with exploring the philosophical and thematic significance of the play as a whole.

APOLLONIAN AND DIONYSIAN ASPECTS
OF THE SELF-BLINDING OF OEDIPUS

The eternal Apollonian-Dionysian conflict tragically controls and governs Oedipus' motivations and actions throughout Sophocles' play *Oedipus the King*. An act which fully illustrates such unresolved conflict occurs when Oedipus fully realizes the truth concerning his relationship to his family and blinds himself. In this final and dramatic action, the precepts of Apollo—the oracle of fate and supporter of law and order—and Dionysus—the unchained god of wine, of creativity and excess—are shown in Oedipus' hot-tempered yet noble desire for truth at any cost. Through this action, which is preceded by a long series of unsuccessful attempts to divert the hand of fate and yet to do the right and just thing, the theme of guilt through innocence is clearly illustrated.

For years, prior to and during his kingship, Oedipus has been engaged in a search for truth. This quest is Apollonian in nature because it consists of an attempt to set his life in order both in his own eyes and in the eyes of the world. Oedipus has abandoned his home in Corinth in the hope of averting two terrible crimes—one against his mother, and one against his father. On one level, the Apollonian level, he has striven to be an honest and just son, king, father, and husband. He wants to conform to the rules set by society. It is natural, then, that in the fifth episode of the play blinding also conforms to the fate set by the oracle of Apollo. Intended by the gods to endure suffering, his self-inflicted loss of sight becomes both a discipline and a punishment he has to carry out himself. Closely related to the Apollonian principle is the restriction Oedipus imposes on himself in deciding to leave Thebes forever. Blind, he will not have to look upon the people of Thebes whom he has unwittingly harmed; but to remove the curse he has placed on his home and the plague he is responsible for, he has to leave the town to restore Apollonian order and unity. Oedipus therefore always submits to the higher order of good for the many as opposed to the convenience of, or even justice for, the few.

The other aspects of Oedipus' actions, however, are Dionysian in character. In his search for truth, Oedipus also tries to avoid the fate assigned him by the oracle. In this, he pits himself against the gods. Further, his tempestuous, unthinking drive to find the truth (even if justice is tilted in the process) is a Dionysian trademark. He uses his temper to force the facts from such Apollonian individuals as his wife and the herdsman and in the process, through insult and misunderstanding, does damage to all.

Finally, the action of self-blinding is a Dionysian measure. Such an act of rage, passion, and despair entirely fits the personality of Oedipus; however, this venture of the tragic king to uplift himself after discovering the terrible truth is an expression of the principles of Dionysus. Oedipus chooses only to torture himself and to live in enlightened despair rather than to take the easy Apollonian way out by killing himself. The wisdom he receives after his blinding is Oedipus' reward for standing firm in his search of the truth in the Dionysian manner.

Oedipus' tragic defect of looking for the truth with his temper is apparent throughout the play. From his search for facts to his subsequent life in darkness, the theme of guilt through innocence is demonstrated. In looking for the truth, he found himself guilty of two great sins against his family. Yet by blinding himself, he excluded from view the outward misery caused by his deeds, and symbolically, remained in the dark as he had been before finding out that he was at fault. Through his tragic flaw both Apollonian and Dionysian precepts trace a journey from ignorance into knowledge.

The following is a very brief analysis of the theme of Walker Gibson's "Billiards." Notice the difference between this essay and the previous essay in which the same poem was explicated (page 26). Both discuss theme, but the essay of explication is concerned with a line by line explanation; this essay centers on a discussion of the overall thematic interpretation.

THEME IN WALKER GIBSON'S "BILLIARDS"

Walker Gibson, in his poem "Billiards," uses the game of billiards to illustrate his conception of the complexity and limitations of the society that man has made for himself. At the beginning of the poem he conveys the image of the jungle, "wild and dim." Yet contained within this image of the primitive is the highly organized game of billiards. The balls in the game symbolize modern man. The balls appear to Gibson to have once been a crude part of the "elephants' ivory limb." Now they are painted, polished spheres. Here an analogy supports the theme of the poem, for the billiard balls are analogous to man himself. Once a part of uncivilized nature, man has refined himself and adapted to his new society. His life now has a plan, a "geometric toil."

Gibson implies that man no longer has the freedom or the power he once had as an uncivilized being. The laws and mores of society have limited and diminished man until now he possesses only a "farce of force." He is unable to act truly according to his desires. Like billiard balls rolling and rebounding across a table, free to move only until they hit a bank and bounce back, so men are free to move only within the bounds laid down by society. He "exhibits impact and recoil" but is unable to cross the *banks* of society.

Man's forcefulness, again the "farce of force," has become impotent and ineffective in a too highly organized and complex society. Yet Gibson says sardonically in the last five lines of his poem that we should feel no pity for man. Though he is trapped in his own "complicated plan" and perhaps pleased with it, we should give him credit for his "so superbly styled" though vacuous existence.

In the last line of his poem, Gibson presents the same image with which he opened the poem: "Late of the jungle, dim and wild." With this line he is implying that man still lives in a "jungle," yet not in the untamed environment he once had to combat. Now he is faced with a highly organized pattern of living that threatens him in a different way as an individual. It is this "geometric" maze-like jungle of patterned life that he is caught in now. Man originated in the primitive jungle; now he lives in a mechanical jungle.

If you chose to write an essay in which you analyzed the theme in "Old Man at the Bridge," your purpose would be to state and justify your

interpretation. If you contended that the theme lies in the concept of innocence, and you decided to use the old man as your main subject, you could
mention the innocent animals and the young soldier in the introduction,
then structure your essay on a discussion of the "parts" of the old man's
innocence in the following manner.

> INTRODUCTION. (Thesis) "Old Man at the Bridge," like many good stories,
> is both a specific and a general statement about the condition of man.
> The old man represents the idea of the innocent caught up in forces be-
> yond their control. As a sacrifice, the old man is a victim of a war he
> does not understand and which he did not cause; he is faced with the prob-
> ability of death.

> BODY.   A. (Topic sentence) The old man, feeble and unarmed and
>   unpartisan, is helpless.
>   B. (Topic sentence) He is ignorant of the causes of his condi-
>   tion.
>   C. (Topic sentence) He is ignorant of the effect of his situa-
>   tion, which may be his death.
>   D. (Topic sentence) His attitude is one of exhaustion, and
>   childlike, he yields to those nameless forces beyond his
>   experience or understanding.

> CONCLUSION. As a sacrifice on Easter Sunday, the old man represents the
> innocent victims in a world of overpowering adversity.

WRITING YOUR ESSAY

In the preceding pages we have discussed the broadest yet most specific approaches to finding and organizing your essay. The following is a
review and further guide to the process of selecting a subject, arranging the
material, and writing the finished essay.

Finding the Subject

Never attempt to write generally about any work. Never make random statements, however pertinent they may be. A list of observations,
without a central idea, will not make a good essay. If you are assigned a
subject, write on it. But if you are permitted to find your own subject, remember that many essays can be written about each work. You will not
fully understand *all* aspects of any work, particularly in a survey course
that moves rapidly through the field of literature. Search for a subject,
therefore, which you are equipped to handle. Begin your search, as you

read, by looking for the theme. Then study the keys in the work that seem to reveal that theme best. Select a key you understand and about which you feel you may have something to say. The key may lie in a particular passage, a statement, a line of dialogue, a symbol; you may have discovered meaning in the plot, or structure, or in the representation of a character, his realization or failure, or in the search for a specific meaning or goal. Unless otherwise instructed, find your subject *within* the work.

As you search, look for your subject in terms either of explication or of analysis. Remember these approaches:

1. If the work is very short, you can make a line by line explication of the whole work.
2. If the work is long, you can find and explicate a brief, but key passage.
3. If you become interested in a "thread" running through the work, you can analyze that thread, whether the work be long or short. You can analyze the theme; you can also analyze a technique that furthers or heightens the effect of the work.

Finding the subject involves a search for a method of "getting into" the parts or components of a work and selecting an area of interest.

Narrowing the Subject

After you determine your approach and general subject, your next task is to narrow or restrict your subject to the point that it becomes appropriate to the short essay. For example, if you choose to write about characterization in "Old Man at the Bridge" you will have a general subject. Your task still remains to make your subject specific and purposeful.

The more you limit your subject, the more specific it becomes. Further, the more specific the subject, the clearer it becomes what you need to say about the subject. You cannot write about characterization in "Old Man at the Bridge" as a general, single subject, because the old man, the young soldier, the unseen army, the animals, and the other people fleeing across the bridge are each appropriate subjects for an essay on characterization. To make your subject specific, narrow your interest to one aspect of your subject. The role of the cat, for example, is specific. The rule for specificity is this: narrow from a general classification (such as characterization) to a specific example. Imagery in "Billiards" becomes the billiard balls; characterization in "Old Man at the Bridge" becomes the role of the cat, or the integrity of the old man, or the professional attitudes of the young soldier, or the fleeing population and the approaching army as background. Use one, but not all.

Helpful steps in narrowing are (1) select a technique from the many present in the work; (2) select a specific example of that technique; (3)

state the function in the story of that specific example. In "Billiards," if you selected imagery as your technique (1), the specific example (2) might be "billiard balls" and their function (3) might be stated as "a symbol of mankind."

Establishing Purpose

What you say *about* your subject becomes the reason for writing your paper and the guiding principle that helps you select your supporting material. Therefore, establishing purpose becomes one of your most important jobs, because a clearly defined purpose determines the success of your essay.

To establish purpose, it is helpful to ask the following questions about a work:

Why is this part included in the work? For example, why is the cat in the story? What is there in the nature of a cat that brings such a response?

Why is this part presented in the way that it is? For example, why does the cat not appear in the present action of the story? Why do the old man and the soldier dwell on the cat?

These two questions, when answered, will help you establish purpose. Remember that in a good essay, purpose is usually found in or near your thesis statement, and it consists of a specific indication of what you intend to say about your subject. Study this thesis statement: "The cat serves three important functions in 'Old Man at the Bridge': as an object of the old man's love; as a contrast to the old man; and as a symbol of independence and instinctive survival."

It is not necessary in your thesis to state your reasons for believing as you do. You can state, "The role of the cat is functional to the basic symbolism and characterization presented in the story." The body of your essay will contain your reasons for believing as you do. But you must have a purpose or thesis to insure direction in your essay. Stating your purpose will provide a specific series of comments or insights into the nature of your subject; it will cause your essay to become informative; it will also serve to organize your essay.

Organizing the Essay

When you know what you want to say about a specific subject, organizing your essay becomes a reasonably simple process. First, consider each essay to consist of three parts: the introduction, the body, and the conclusion. Each part has its function, and in the integrated essay, each part makes up one division or aspect of a single statement. This statement is your thesis or central idea.

THE INTRODUCTION.   The introduction literally introduces your unin-
formed reader to your subject, to any background material you feel may
aid his understanding or heighten his interest, and finally, to your central
idea or thesis. Remember that your thesis consists of two parts: (1) your
specific subject, and (2) what you intend to say about your subject. The introduction also indicates how you intend to approach your subject—by explication or analysis—and further, how you intend to organize and present
your material. Look briefly at the following introductory paragraphs and
study how they fulfill the requirements suggested above.

ART AS OPPOSED TO EMPTY FORM IN "THE GREAT GOOD PLACE"

Like any truly excellent piece of art, Henry James' short story "The
Great Good Place" is subject to a wide variety of interpretations. However, one obvious aspect of the work is the striking contrast between the
beautiful, symmetrical quality of 'The Great Good Place' and the stagnant, tedious, law-and-order existence of George Dane's servant, Brown.
Both represent conscious approaches to an orderly life, yet the former is
desirable in its quiet moderation while the latter seems terrible in its
extremism. This contrast can be seen in three ways. First, one can see the
difference in the dimensional qualities of these two subjects. Second, one
can see the contrast in the various aspects of the two subjects within their
dimensional framework. Finally, George Dane's reaction to both approaches to an orderly life can be studied and compared.

This opening paragraph introduces the writer's subject and states his
central idea. We can see that he intends to analyze moderation versus
extremism by comparing Brown's way of life with the Place. Further, the
student writer enumerates specifically the points he intends to discuss to
accomplish his comparison. Obviously each point will become a paragraph
in the body of the essay. (For a detailed comment about structuring an
essay by comparison and contrast, see page 169.) Here is another introductory paragraph:

CENSORSHIP

In Thomas Mann's short story "Gladius Dei" Mann examines various concepts and approaches to art, religion, and indirectly, to politics
and aesthetics through a painting of a Madonna. Censorship of art, in this
case the censorship of a Madonna, is one of the main themes of the story.
Censorship manifests itself in many ways, one of which is found in the
conflict between a clerk in an art gallery and the main character, Hieronymus. When Hieronymus asks the assistant to remove the picture and
burn it because it is blasphemous, the assistant replies: "But should we
not be allowed to exhibit any Madonnas—or paint any?" This question

leads us to more penetrating issues. For instance, what is art? And who determines the moral worth of a work of art, or of any of man's work? Finally, it leads us to the question: what kind of values should society use in determining how to balance the evils of moral excess with the evils of censorship?

In this introduction, the student identifies the work and the author, lists several thematic considerations present in the work, and narrows to his main subject, which is censorship in art. He further restricts his attention or focus to a specific incident. He relates the incident that elicits the clerk's question to Hieronymus and then lists several issues central to the question and to the story as a whole. Based upon this introduction, if his essay is to succeed the student must discuss each question in the body of his essay and must answer each question in terms of the *story,* not his personal opinions. Finally, note the use of narrative summary by which the writer makes a real attempt to gain his reader's interest.

THE BODY.   If your introduction concludes with either a stated or a strongly implied thesis statement, you will be able quite easily to relate your supporting points or topic sentences to your central idea. Each paragraph in the body of your essay will usually open with a topic sentence, which is the subject of the paragraph. The content of each paragraph must support its topic sentence, just as each topic sentence must support the thesis. This arrangement insures unity in your essay, because all material presented either directly or indirectly supports your central idea. At its simplest, such an arrangement resembles the diagram on page 53.

Presenting your supporting ideas (your topic sentences) as paragraphs in the body of your essay is a matter of choosing the most effective order. You can arrange your paragraphs by order of occurrence, by logical order, or by enumeration. If you choose to use logical order or enumeration, you will often want to present your paragraphs in order of ascending importance.

Order of Occurrence   Order of occurrence is equivalent to following a work of literature from the first page to the last, or from the real rather than the presented order in a work. It is the method most natural to line by line explication. When ordering your paragraphs in this manner, you follow the work, generally, from its opening to its conclusion. Order of occurrence has the advantage of following the natural development of the work. It gives your reader a sense of continuity, and it provides him with an easy method of page by page reference and identification with the work itself. The student essay, "Theme Through Symbol: Water and Its Effect upon George Dane" is arranged by order of occurrence; the images of water are presented as they occur in the development of the story.

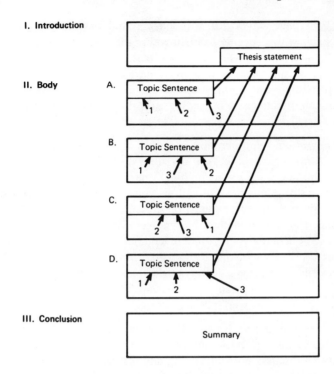

I. Introduction

II. Body

III. Conclusion

Logical Order   Logical order is a general term, but applied to the critical essay it is closely related to the spatial arrangement most often found in analysis. It involves the method you choose as the most desirable arrangement for your paragraphs. You have many choices, depending upon the effect you want to achieve.

1. You can order your paragraphs by subject matter, *from the general to the specific,* or *from the large to the small.* For example, in analyzing the use of the dust motif, you can move in your discussion from the use of dust on the whole landscape to the dust on the old man's face. This arrangement will focus on the human and specific element in the story. Such arrangement places the emphasis of your paper on intricacy and detail.

2. You can develop your paragraphs from the *specific to the general.* Again using the dust motif, you can begin with the dust on the old man's face, move to the dust on the roadway, and end with the gray dust-colored hills and sky to emphasize, in your essay, a sense of pervading hopelessness, desolation, and death.

3. You can order your material from the *outside to the inside.* The student essay, "Apollonian and Dionysian Aspects of the Self-Blinding of

Oedipus" on page 45 begins with background outside the play proper and concludes with a specific incident within the play.

4. Finally, you can arrange your paragraphs in *order of ascending importance*. By this method your essay develops from the least important to the most important point you want to make about the subject. Your essay gains in effectiveness by ending with the strongest point you have to make.

Enumeration   Enumeration is not an examination of the parts of a whole by some logical process of division; it is a simple list. This list can consist of the reasons for your holding a particular position, or it can consist of a series of points or observations you want to make about a work of literature. Since your reasons must be presented one by one in the body of your paper, choosing a method of arrangement is always necessary. Most often you will arrange your points or enumerations by order of ascending importance. The essay "None Frailer than Mankind" is organized by enumeration. The writer subsequently arranges his points, or paragraphs, in order of ascending importance. He first discusses Odysseus; he concludes with a discussion of the whole Greek nation.

Relating Content to Thesis   One of the most difficult tasks you may face in organizing your basic outline is to avoid digressing from your true subject into a discussion of interesting and informative aspects of the work not directly related to your thesis. Several rules will help you avoid including essentially irrelevant points. First, to insure that your points are directly related to your main subject, and further, that they are parallel in importance and subject, decide whether you will structure your essay by enumeration, by analysis, or by explication. If you are using enumeration ("There are three reasons why the old man is unable to take effective action to avoid the oncoming artillery and enemy planes") be sure that each point is formulated to follow directly the word "because" (*because* life in a strange place and without his animals seems pointless; *because* he is old and totally exhausted; *because* he does not fully understand the peril of being so close to the bridge).

If you are analyzing a work by dividing a subject into its parts, be sure that each part is a necessary and valid component. (Imagery in "Billiards" divides into three parts: the jungle as society, man as a billiard ball, society as a game.) Each part must be equal and necessary to the whole.

If you are explicating a work be sure that each section in the body of your paper supports your thesis. If your thesis consists of a statement of the theme, be sure each paragraph of your explication reinforces your interpretation of that theme. If it does not, you will either have to revise your interpretation or cut that point from your essay.

Study the diagram on page 53 and use it as a guide to ensure that each point supports your main idea.

THE CONCLUSION. We have stressed in earlier pages that there are three basic methods of writing your conclusion:

1. You can summarize the basic points of your essay and restate your thesis. This method is effective if your essay is long and complex.

2. You can make your final and most important point in your conclusion. Often this will entail giving a full definition of the theme or making a final summation of the author's use of technique—material that you have led up to but have not previously given.

3. If your essay is short and the points you have made are explicitly clear, you can often effectively omit a formal concluding paragraph. Merely add a final summary sentence to the end of the last paragraph in the body of your paper. (See page 31.) You will have to exercise your own judgment here. The only rules are to be clear, to avoid needless repetition, and to end your paper on a last meaningful statement.

For more detailed methods of organizing your essay, see Comparison and Contrast, page 169, and Illustration, page 217.

Developing the Essay

A well-developed essay consists of a detailed discussion of one specific idea or observation about a work of literature. The keys to achieving full development lie in a sound and logical outline of your main ideas (your thesis and topic sentences), and in complete explanation and proof of each of these ideas. Each major subordinate idea or point that supports your thesis becomes a paragraph in your essay, and each paragraph consists of an essay in miniature.

A paragraph in the body of an essay usually opens with a topic sentence. Following the topic sentence, you will need to offer a series of supporting remarks, which amplify and make clear your topic sentence. In addition, you will often need to provide your reader with appropriate quotations from the work of literature you are discussing. Explanations and quotations will make up the bulk of the content of your essay. Both are often thought of as your *proof,* and without adequate proof, your essay will not be convincing.

A general rule for the development of paragraphs is this: Never make a statement without explaining it. For example, if you contend that the dust motif exists as an important thematic element in "Old Man at the Bridge," you must prove it. You must show that your contention is true and you must demonstrate *how* it is true. Look at the essay, "Apollonian and Dionysian Aspects of the Self-Blinding of Oedipus," on page 45. Each paragraph in the body of the paper opens with a topic sentence. Within each paragraph the writer fully explains his topic sentence. As a result, each paragraph is a fully organized unit. For a good example of the use of quotations as proof, look at the essay, "Theme through Symbol: Water and Its Effect upon George Dane," on page 41. Each paragraph in the body of the paper contains quoted sentences and phrases that offer concrete proof of the presence in the story of water as a major symbol. Each quotation is highly relevant to the student's thesis, and each directly focuses upon the central idea.

In both essays the use of supporting material—as explanation and as quotations or as paraphrase—is responsible, accurate, and fully developed. If you discover in the writing process that you have a very long introduction followed by a series of short, choppy paragraphs in the body of your paper, your organization is out of proportion. To correct this error, rewrite your introduction to include only background and thesis; rework your topic sentences until they are clear and parallel in importance; write each paragraph as a full discussion of each topic sentence. In this manner you can achieve full development of each subordinate idea (your topic sentences) and can insure rounded paragraphs that focus on your major subject.

MODES OF EXPRESSION

After you have chosen a topic, narrowed it, and organized it, you must put your ideas into words. The words you choose and the way you put them together determines the style of your essay, for style is nothing more nor less than your way of thinking and expressing yourself. In expository writing, the idea is everything. Your entire essay—paragraphs and sentences—must have a clear, natural order, free from ambiguity and confusion.

Use the Plain Style

There are five modes of expression: the *substandard,* the *flat,* the *experimental,* the *ornate,* and the *plain.*

Substandard writing is characterized by lapses from standard usage, a heavy reliance upon slang, and a limited vocabulary. Such lapses are unsuitable for your essays, though at times you will see them used for a particular effect—as they are in *Huckleberry Finn,* in which Mark Twain writes from the first person viewpoint of the delightful but semiliterate Huck.

Flat writing is characterized by short, simply constructed sentences, a simple vocabulary, and few figures of speech. Most often, flat writing is used by literate but untrained writers. Skillful fiction writers like Ernest Hemingway sometimes assume this style with great success, but flat writing can limit expression, and it can also become tedious.

Experimental writing is difficult to characterize, because it attempts new modes of expression. Experimental writers may deviate from conventional spelling, punctuation, and syntax. They sometimes arrange words on the page in unusual ways. Their goal is to produce effects that are impossible in conventional writing, so literally any method is potentially acceptable. Experimental writing has its place, but beginning writers will do well to state their ideas succinctly and with clarity. Master conventional ways of writing before you experiment.

Ornate writing is seldom used today. Its complex syntax, studied metaphors, polysyllabic vocabulary, and calculated rhetorical effects call attention to themselves, to the detriment of ideas. Modern writers avoid ornate writing as pretentious.

Most modern poets, playwrights, essayists, and fiction writers use *plain* writing. They use standard English, conventional spelling and punctuation, and, except in the personal or informal essay, avoid abbreviations, contractions, and slang. Plain writing does not strive for form for form's sake. Instead, it strives to express thought in the clearest manner possible. In the plain style, sentences are of mixed length—short sentences alternating with long as rhythm, ideas, and variation demand it. Metaphors are used when they will clarify what is being said, and the vocabulary is selected for its precision rather than for its impressiveness. Simplicity, however, does not rule out beauty:

> Man that is born of woman is of few days, and full of trouble (*Book of Job*).

> And what rough beast, its hour come round at last,
> Slouches toward Bethlehem to be born? (Yeats' "The Second Coming").

> What a piece of work is man! (Shakespeare's *Hamlet*).

The plain style is firm, vital, and mature. It derives its firmness from orderly progress and sustained structure, its vitality from the elimination of the superfluous; it emphasizes the important; it achieves maturity through discrimination and qualification. Here are some suggestions to help you achieve the plain style in writing, the mode of expression most useful to you as a beginning writer.

CONTROL YOUR TONE. Tone reveals your attitude toward your subject and your audience. To write well, you must believe in your thesis and in the material you use to support that thesis. Write honestly. Be prompted by a sincere desire to communicate your convictions to your reader. Be serious.

Sincerity does not necessarily eliminate humor from your essay; humor serves both to relieve and to underscore the seriousness of a subject. But never mistake flippancy or breeziness for humor. Humor in the serious essay comes from the unexpected turn of thought, the wit in a surprising comparison, the irony in an original way of looking at a subject. If you use humor, use it with discrimination.

As a reader, you already know how sensitive you can become if a writer adopts a tone of condescension. As you write, let your reader know that you respect his intelligence. Never write down to your audience, and remember that a reader sufficiently interested in a serious subject to bother reading about it at all can be offended by overexplanation and oversimplification. Let your material speak for itself, and lead (do not push) your reader to the conclusion you want him to reach. Overpersuasiveness causes a reader to suspect insecurity in the writer. Finally, do not call attention to yourself as the writer. An essay about a work of literature should present your idea about some aspect of the work, not your personality and disposition.

In summary, use a tone that shows respect for both your subject and your audience and consistently maintain that tone.

VARY YOUR SENTENCE PATTERNS.   Immature writing tends to follow a typical pattern: there is an excessive use of coordination and the sentences too often follow the subject-verb-object pattern. Any sentence structure can become monotonous, but a string of coordinate clauses joined by *and* is particularly tedious: "We went to the store, and we bought a pound of hamburger, and we came home, and Mother barbecued it for us."

Although coordination is both natural and necessary, its excessive use reveals a lack of writing experience. To relieve the tedium of coordination and (more importantly) to clarify ideas, subordinate the subsidiary and qualifying elements of your sentences and save your main clauses for your main ideas. Make sure, though, that you subordinate properly. Note the ludicrous effect of "upside-down subordination," which places the important idea in the dependent clause: "When the escaped convict burst into our house, we were in the kitchen cleaning out the hamster cages." Note also the weakness of the sentence that gives equal emphasis to two ideas unequal in importance: "The temperature was below freezing, and he took his daily swim in the lake." When the subservient idea is put into a subordinate clause, the sentence takes on the strength its author intended: "Although the temperature was below freezing, he took his daily swim in the lake."

The simple sentence is emphatic. It is effective. Use it often, but remember that even the good, simple sentence becomes monotonous if it always appears with the subject-verb-object pattern. Here are some ways to vary the pattern:

1. *Invert the natural order of your words:* "Three times I read the poem before I understood it."
2. *Insert phrases that modify the subject:* "His essay, rich with meaning, firm with economy of expression, strong with concrete words, evoked a favorable response from his instructor."
3. *Qualify the object:* "Walker Gibson criticizes modern society, that rigid, geometrical, farcical activity of man."
4. *Qualify the verb:* "Pope writes, sometimes caustically, sometimes bitterly, about the nature of man."
5. *Use appositives:* "Gray's 'Elegy Written in a Country Churchyard,' the best-known poem in the English language, glorifies the common people."
6. *Begin with a participial phrase:* "Striving to perfect his art, Yeats worked out a brilliantly integrated system of symbols."
7. *Begin with an infinitive phrase:* "To judge from his first paper, you would have thought him incapable of writing such an excellent exam."

Like any other stylistic device, variation can be overdone. Never vary simply for the sake of variation. Let what you have to say guide your choice of sentence structure. Choose the sentence forms that logically fit your thoughts.

USE THE PRESENT TENSE. Customarily the essay about literature uses the present tense, because in this type of essay we are not telling what a writer did at the time he wrote a work, we are telling what is now observable in the work: what he *does* in it. Instead of saying, "In 'Ode on Melancholy,' Keats *gave* a rationale for melancholy," essayists say, "In 'Ode on Melancholy,' Keats *gives* a rationale for melancholy." Literature —as we stated on page 44—belongs to the eternal present.

PREFER THE ACTIVE VOICE. The active voice has more vitality than the passive: "Mary *despised* the book" is stronger and more forceful than "The book *was despised* by Mary." Here is another example: "For my topic the symbolism of Blake's poetry was chosen." Changed to the active voice, the expression of this idea takes on strength and precision: "For my topic I *chose* the symbolism of Blake's poetry."

At times, however, you will need to use the passive voice to place emphasis where you want it. This sentence has misplaced emphasis: "I *can see* a rich use of symbolism in Blake's poetry." The verb is in the active voice, but it should be changed to the passive voice to place the emphasis on the subject rather than on the essayist: "A rich use of symbolism *can be seen* in Blake's poetry." In general, prefer the active voice; use the passive voice only when the idea you wish to express demands it.

MAKE POSITIVE STATEMENTS. Positive statements have more life than negative ones. When you begin a sentence by saying, "I think that . . ." you give it a much firmer sense of direction than when you say, "I do not think that . . ." The same applies to positive and negative words. Whenever possible use a positive word rather than a negative phrase. Say "dishonest," for example, rather than "not entirely honest."

Remember also that a phrase in negative form forces the reader to make a positive rearrangement. If you say "a not inconsiderable wealth of imagery," you force your reader to erase the negative words to see that you mean "a wealth of imagery." Negative statements are halting, tentative, weak. If you find them in your own writing, recast your sentences to achieve firm, positive statements.

USE EFFECTIVE TRANSITIONS. Transitions are one of the writer's most valuable tools. Used effectively, they help the reader follow the smooth development of your ideas. Without transitions, there is no smooth development; you have only separate statements, and your reader may not be able to make an association between the parts. There are several types of transitions, each serving specific needs, but all are used to link sentences and paragraphs into a cohesive whole. Each time you shift from one thought to another, from one idea to another, you must provide your reader with a transition.

1. *Use conjunctions* (*like, and, or, but*): "Oedipus discovered his relationship with his mother, *and* in so doing, he discovered himself."
2. *Use pronouns:* "Oedipus, in blinding himself, proved his tragic vision. *He* left the city of Thebes without sight, but with understanding."
3. *Repeat key phrases:* "Oedipus, in blinding himself, proved his tragic vision. His *self-blinding* indicated his final understanding of his condition."
4. *Use parallel structure:* "Oedipus, blind to his true condition, insulted Teiresius, charged Creon with disloyalty, threatened the poor herdsman, and questioned the loyalty of Jocasta."

Another common method of transition is to use words and phrases at or near the beginning or end of new sentences and paragraphs that will provide your reader with a clue to the relationship between a new block of information and that which preceded it. At their best, transitions not only indicate the relationship between elements in an essay, but also make the divisions between these elements clear and distinct.

The following list of transitions may prove helpful in thinking and emphasizing your ideas:

1. *If you want to add new information to the development of a key idea, use transitional words like these:* similarly, in addition, finally, in conclusion, again, also, in the first place, furthermore, secondly, another, one reason.
2. *If you want to introduce supporting material, use words like the following:* and so again, similarly, another good illustration of this, at the same time, in like manner, one of the best examples, for instance, to illustrate, for example, thus.
3. *If you want to point out a contrast or a qualification, say:* in spite of this, still, to the contrary, despite this, nevertheless, conversely, however, in opposition to this, in contrast to this, though this is so, on the other hand.
4. *If you want to point to a conclusion or result say:* finally, after all, in conclusion, therefore, to sum up, consequently, as a result, it is apparent, accordingly.

AVOID JARGON.   In its simplest form, jargon consists of words or expressions peculiar to a single profession or occupation. Beginning writers, trying to appear well-informed, often use technical words. Such attempts to parade a knowledge of legal, scientific, psychological, or other specialized terms confuse rather than clarify your ideas. Here is an example from a student essay:

> When in Chapter Twenty she forgets that she had ever been to London, she exhibits a clear case of functional forgetting. The traumatic experience of the earlier visit to the city had, through additional experiences, become affectively conditioned to such an extent that the initial experience had been inhibited by her other dominant mental processes.

Chapter Twenty is not illuminated; the only thing made clear in the passage is that the student had access to a textbook of psychology.

Jargon represents a real danger to the vitality of our language. Through long usage, jargon becomes accepted. When you use weak and ineffective words and phrases like "finalize," "update," and "get in contact with," you are simply proliferating jargon, not communicating with precision. Unfortunately, literary criticism is burdened with its own jargon. Once you learn it you will have to struggle to avoid using it in your essays.

AVOID WORDINESS.   Sentences sluggish with verbiage, like rivers thick with mud, are not inviting. Entice your readers with sentences that are clean, clear, and swift moving. Cut out unnecessary words. Do not write "there is no doubt but that." Say "doubtless." Use "heats" instead of "used for purposes of heating." Say "receive" instead of "be the recipient of." If you pay close attention, you will find hundreds of loose phrases in our language that can be shortened to a single, precise word.

Another way to write crisper sentences is to cut out meaningless tags. Phrases like "the fact that," "in the case of," and "is a subject which" can be snipped off and never missed. Here is a wordy sentence: "It is seldom the case that students write clear sentences, owing to the fact that, in my opinion, they use unnecessary words." Here is the same sentence with the deadwood cut away: "Students seldom write clear sentences, because they use unnecessary words."

Beware of modifiers. Adjectives and adverbs, although colorful and necessary, often weaken rather than help the words they modify. Look critically at those you use. Do you need that "very," that "rather," that "somewhat"?

To avoid wordiness make sure that every word works for you. Never leave out words necessary to clarify your thought, but use only as many as you need for adequate expression. Delete any word that does not serve a purpose.

AVOID FINE WRITING.   "Fine writing" is anything but fine. It uses showy words and expressions, and the result is fuzzy and roundabout. Good writing aims at clarity and directness, and to achieve good writing, you should use the most straightforward way you can find to express your idea. Often the short, concrete word has more force than the big word: *fat* is stronger than *adipose; drunk* is stronger than *inebriated.* Use phrases you are comfortable with, and resist the temptation to search for a high-sounding phrase. The beginning writer, stretching for an expression, usually comes up with a trite one. Even if he comes up with an original one, it usually sounds stuffy or pretentious, because the expression is out of character with the rest of his writing. As a result, he repels rather than attracts his reader.

WRITE AND REWRITE.   Never be discouraged if your first try at a paragraph or sentence or word is unsatisfactory. Even the best writers say they throw away more pages than they keep. Good writing never just happened to anyone; it is the result of rewriting and revising. Usually you will be wise to move ahead rapidly on the first draft, focusing attention on the ideas you wish to express. If you become bogged down in a sentence, stop and recast it in several ways. Sometimes you need to make two sentences of one; sometimes a sentence before the troublesome one needs changing.

As you write, always keep a definite purpose in mind and work toward that purpose. Never leap about or backtrack, but move in orderly fashion, using transitions as you go. Keep to one subject for several sentences, changing paragraphs when you move to another subject. In this way, the elements that form the divisions of your thesis will move with firm orderly progress from the beginning to the end of your essay.

Notes on Documentation

You assume several responsibilities when you begin to write. The first involves ethical rules, which, if followed with integrity, will distinguish your writing as honest and authoritative. Ethically, you must give other writers full credit for their thoughts and hard work. Acknowledging the ideas of other writers not only rescues you from the dangers of plagiarism; you benefit by automatically receiving the respect of your readers and full credit for your own thoughts.

You must always give credit to the original writer for any direct quotations you use in your text, any scattered phrases you incorporate into your sentences, or even any ideas gleaned from the work of another that you paraphrase. It is not necessary to footnote all these borrowings. For example, you can incorporate scattered phrases simply by mentioning the author and, as in the following, by placing quotation marks around the phrase: "In this connection Coleridge speaks of 'the just distinction.' " You can give credit for ideas indirectly: "Myth," as Richard Chase reminds us, "is always concerned with a *story.*"

It is not necessary to mention the source of universally recognized quotations ("To be or not to be"; "In the beginning God created the heaven and the earth"); be sure, however, to place them within quotation marks. It is not necessary to footnote all direct quotations; footnote only if you have reason to believe your reader may wish to be able to check you or may wish to read more on your subject. (An exception is the research paper; in it you should footnote all references.)

Your essays will make a better impression if you prepare your pages and document your sources according to the generally accepted form for manuscripts. The following brief guides will help you in these matters. *The MLA Style Sheet,* compiled by William Riley Parker, and *Preparing the Research Paper,* by Robert Morell Schmitz offer detailed instructions. Your instructor may prefer a particular style; you should learn his preferences and follow them.

PREPARING YOUR MANUSCRIPT.   Type your paper on one side only, with double spacing, leaving margins of at least one inch at the top, bottom, and sides. Number the pages consecutively (including notes and bibliography if you have them).

Always have a *title.* Center the title two or three inches from the top of the first page. Capitalize the initial letter of major words in your title or capitalize all the letters of the title, but do not underline it or place it within quotation marks.

In your text indicate italics by a single underline.

Do not use abbreviations (exceptions are A.M. and P.M. if used with figures, A.D. and B.C.; Mr., Mrs., Dr., and academic degrees, like Ph.D.). Spell out numbers, except dates and references to page and line numbers.

Avoid formal divisions of short essays. If some division is required, separate groups of paragraphs by leaving four lines between them.

USING QUOTATIONS.   Usually you should reproduce quoted material exactly, including spelling (even archaic spelling) and all *internal punctuation* (for rules regarding *end punctuation* see "Punctuation" below).

Titles   The titles of published material used in your essay should be underlined if they are titles of long works (books, periodicals, operas, plays, very long poems) and placed within quotation marks if they are titles of short works (short poems, short stories, essays).

Indicating Omissions   If you omit words within a sentence or a line of poetry use three spaced periods (. . .) to indicate the omission. If you omit words at the end of a sentence use the three spaced periods and the additional sentence period (. . . .). If you omit whole sentences or paragraphs from a prose quotation or whole lines or stanzas from poetry quotations, type a line of periods to indicate that an extensive omission exists.

Do not use periods at the beginning or end of a few quoted words, which obviously are not the complete work ("Keats speaks of 'droop-headed flowers' to create a mood").

Punctuation   The first word of a quotation should begin with a capital letter (regardless of whether it was capitalized in the original) if it is the first word of your sentence. You may change to lower case a capital of the original if it is grammatically part of a sentence in your text ("Hamlet soliloquizes that 'to be or not to be' is the question").

When a quotation ends a sentence in your text, use a period, even though the original had another kind of punctuation.

Periods and commas always belong inside the quotation marks. Semicolons and colons belong outside the quotation marks. Question marks and exclamation points belong inside the quotation marks if they are a part of the quotation; they belong outside if they are not a part of the quotation.

Interpolations   You may insert words of your own in quoted material if you put them within square brackets ([]). If your typewriter does not have brackets put them in your typed manuscript by hand.

Quoting Poetry   There are two ways to quote verse in your text: they may be run on as part of your text or they may be indented. A general rule to follow is that quotations of two lines or less should be run on and quotations of over two lines should be separated from your text by dropping down two or three spaces, and centering on the page. When run on, the quotation should be placed within quotation marks and the lines separated by a slash mark, like this: Students often agree with these lines from Wordsworth: "Up! Up! my friend, and quit your books;/Or surely you'll grow double." When dropping down and centering the lines, do not use quotation marks. Your quoted lines should look like these, from Emily Dickinson's "A Bird Came Down the Walk" [2] :

A bird came down the walk:
He did not know I saw;
He bit an angle-worm in halves
And ate the fellow raw.

Quoting Prose   To quote prose you may run on up to ten lines. Longer prose quotations should be dropped down two or three spaces from your text and indented three to five spaces from the margin of your text. As with verse quotations, place quotation marks around run on quotations; do not place quotation marks around indented, centered quotations.

FOOTNOTES.   The sample essay on pages 113–116 documents quotations from both books and periodicals. Study the incorporation of citations in a student essay as you read the following rules, to fix the forms in your mind.

Keep your citations concise. Put brief references in parentheses in your text; put long references in a footnote. Place in a footnote your first, long reference to a work that you quote more than once. You may place subsequent references to it in your text.

Footnotes should be numbered consecutively, beginning with 1. Type the footnote numbers slightly above the line, after the punctuation, if there is punctuation, and immediately following the quotation.[1]

Footnotes may be placed at the bottom of the page on which the quotation occurs or they may be placed on a separate sheet at the end of your essay. Indent the first line of the footnote, and type the number slightly above the line (as you did the corresponding number in the text). Always end a footnote with a period.

If you wish to use a footnote for a quotation from a source you have quoted before, you need not use a complete footnote. Instead, simply use the author's last name and the page number (Brown, p. 12).

If you have given the name of the author and the title of his work in

[2] Emily Dickinson, "A Bird Came Down the Walk," *The Complete Poems of Emily Dickinson* edited by Thomas H. Johnson (Boston: Little, Brown and Company, 1960).

your text along with the quotation, you do not need to footnote; instead you may place the page number or numbers in parentheses, like this: "In *The Rhetoric of Fiction* Wayne C. Booth says that 'some realists are not interested in whether the subject matter does justice to reality outside the book' (p. 55)." Note that the period is placed after the parentheses.

Form for References to Published Books

1. the author's name in normal order, followed by a comma
2. the title of the book, underlined, and followed by a comma, unless the next item will be enclosed in parentheses
3. the edition, if one is named
4. the editor's and translator's names (if they are shown), in normal order, preceded by the abbreviation "ed." or "trans."
5. the city and the date of publication, the two separated by a comma, placed within parentheses, and followed by a comma
6. the page number or numbers, preceded by "p." or "pp."

Sample Footnotes for Books

[1] James R. Kreuzer, Lee Cogan, *Literature for Composition* (New York, 1965), p. 78.
[2] Maurice B. McNamee, *Reading for Understanding,* Third Edition (New York, 1968), pp. 1–28.
[3] Edward D. Mackland, *Three Plays of Samuel Beckett,* trans. F. L. Villon (London, 1948), pp. 450–501.

Form for References to Articles in Periodicals

1. the author's name in normal order, followed by a comma
2. the title of the article, enclosed in quotation marks, followed by a comma. Place the comma within the last quotation marks.
3. the name of the periodical, underlined, and followed by a comma. If the name of the periodical is long, you may abbreviate it.
4. the volume number, in Roman numerals, followed by a comma, unless the next item will be enclosed in parentheses
5. the issue number
6. the year of publication, placed within parentheses
7. page numbers, not preceded by "p." or "pp."

Sample Footnotes for Articles in Periodicals

[1] Eugene R. August, "Tennyson and Teilhard: The Faith of *In Memoriam,*" *PMLA,* LXXXIV (March 1969), 217–226.
[2] Hardin Craig, "The Shackling of Accidents: A Study of Elizabethan Tragedy," *Philological Quarterly.* XIX (1940), 1–19.
[3] Northrop Frye, "Blake After Two Centuries," *Univ. of Toronto Quarterly,* XXVII (October 1957), 10–21.

FICTION

Compared to the ancient forms of poetry and drama, fiction is a recent arrival on the literary scene. It was foreshadowed in ancient tales and romances and in the world's epics, yet it was not until the eighteenth century that fiction became a distinct literary **form** (see Glossary). Because it abandoned the classic and traditional form (its style was the vernacular, its subject matter rooted in the social conditions of its time), the new genre was rejected by many who saw it as neither art nor respectable. Today, however, the short story and novel represent by far the most popular of the literary forms. Fiction not only entertains, but at its best dramatically illuminates life, broadening and deepening our understanding of the human condition.

Today's fiction writer draws freely from both poetry and drama as he seeks new ways to express his vision of the world. Descriptive passages often border on pure poetry, and dialogue now leans heavily on the conventions of the stage. Further, modern writers have so vastly refined and expanded the technique of expository narration that fiction becomes increasingly difficult to define. Its forms are no longer restricted by length, language, or subject matter. A brief anecdote is fiction; at the other extreme, the volumes of Proust's *Remembrance of Things Past,* written as one continuous, interrelated story, are also fiction.

Short stories and novels can be structured on the formula plot line as pure entertainment, or they can become deeply involved in experimental language and technique as do stream of consciousness novels like Faulkner's *The Sound and the Fury* or James Joyce's *Ulysses* or *Finnegans Wake*. Vladimir Nabokov wrote much of his novel *Pale Fire* in verse. Recent French experimentalists like Robbe-Grillet are concerned with the non-novel, in which they seek to reverse the standard conventions of fiction. Yet one factor remains constant: whether told in the comic or the tragic mold, serious prose works portray the artist's vision of the world. Sometimes this vision is unique and private; more often it is representative, portraying a recognizable facet of or truth about the human experience to which we as readers respond with our emotions and intellect. Although fiction evades a precise definition, at least three factors characterize this form of writing.

First, fiction is dramatic. The artist creates a world and presents it primarily through action, dialogue, and images. When we read fiction we are not looking for an essay about life, but for dramatically re-created experience. Modern fiction is usually *objective*—that is, the artist does not tell us what to think about the characters or the situation in which the characters are involved. When the artist makes his presence obvious in his fiction by openly describing his personal experiences or attitudes, his method is considered to be *subjective*. When he employs explanation rather than action to convey his meaning, we say he uses the expository technique. In most of the fiction you will study, the artist will be objective. He will not tell you about a story; he will render it through action. Your job will be to study the artist's presentation of that action and the involvement and reaction of the characters within it and, as you do in life, try to discern its meaning.

The second distinguishing characteristic of fiction is that it is centered in the narrative—a recounting or presentation of an event, an experience, or, abstractly, sometimes an emotion or situation. You will most often read fictional narratives in the form of a *short story, novella,* or *novel.* Critics debate the fundamental differences between these forms, because there are no essential requirements that truly distinguish the short story from the novel; and certainly the novella, which is either a long story or a short novel, sits squarely in the middle of the controversy.

The novel, however, is clearly an extended narrative and it can be differentiated from the short story by its longer length and its potential for more elaboration and complexity. The short story seldom exceeds fifteen thousand words; the novel traditionally exceeds one hundred pages. Works that seem too long for a short story and too brief for a novel are often called novellas or novelettes. Though the novel must be ordered through some unity of time, place, character development, or series of related events, the novelist is free to introduce and leisurely explore as many characters as he sees fit over an indefinite period time and in a limitless number of settings. His plot can also operate on an extended, multiple level.

On the other hand, the restrictions imposed by length force the short story writer to introduce limited action and settings, and he cannot engage in extensive character evolution. For these reasons, the short story writer will often begin his story at or near the climax of the main situation or conflict, and limit his complication or action to a single but crucial episode. There are many exceptions to this pattern, but such differentiation will serve as a general guide.

In your study of the three narrative forms—the novel, the short story, and the novella—it will prove helpful to determine whether the artist has placed his emphasis on *incident* or on *character*. In a work of incident, the writer will emphasize the action, the adventure, or "what happens." In a story or novel of character, the artist will concentrate his narrative on his characters' behavior, motives, and reactions, and the reader will be most interested in the outcome of the work in terms of the inner experience.

In addition to the broad framework of character and incident, critics further classify works of fiction according to type or **genre** (see Glossary): **picaresque** or **episodic** if the characters go from one adventure to another (Cervantes' *Don Quixote* or Twain's *Adventures of Huckleberry Finn*); **sociological** if the social or economic influences of a period are emphasized (Stowe's *Uncle Tom's Cabin,* Steinbeck's *Grapes of Wrath*); **historical** if the author takes his setting, events or characters from history (Dickens' *Tale of Two Cities,* Tolstoi's *War and Peace*); **psychological** if the emphasis is on the complicated mental state of its characters (Dostoevski's *Crime and Punishment,* Thomas Mann's *Death in Venice*); **autobiographical** if the author draws heavily from his own life experiences (Lawrence's *Sons and Lovers* and Joyce's *Portrait of the Artist as a Young Man*).

The third characteristic of fiction is that it is basically a work of the artist's imagination. If a work deals only with fact it becomes history; if it purports to recount the artist's actual life experiences, it becomes an autobiography or a memoir; if it is restricted to a factual record of the life of some real person other than the writer, it becomes biography. But fiction is both fantasy and truth, held together and made real by its similarity to, or reflection of, real life. In a work of fiction the artist must form from the chaos, the irrelevancies, and the realities of everyday life a work that is ordered and aesthetically satisfying. To do this, he distorts time and compresses or omits many details from ordinary experience. He dramatically emphasizes those actions and characteristics of people that will best demonstrate his observations. He orders and selects scenes and events and people to illustrate what he believes to be truths.

In the first chapter of this text you read about several of the elements of fiction, particularly those dealing with language and literary references. There are others. Fiction can be loosely defined as an imaginative prose narrative, conceived and ordered by the artist to dramatically illuminate some truth about the human condition. As such, fiction will have a *setting;* it will contain a *mood* or *atmosphere;* it will involve a *story*—a plot or action. Finally, fiction will concern itself with people (*characterization*).

Setting

As you read a work of fiction you will become aware of the time and location in which the action of the story is taking place. These spatial and temporal surroundings are referred to as the **setting.** The artist may choose any time and any place for his narrative, including the future and the remote past. He may place his characters on another planet, in hell, or in heaven. He may choose to set his action in a timeless void. In some cases, you may be able to discern the time and place of a work of fiction from the author's description in the opening lines; in other cases, you may simply be told. James Joyce's *Ulysses,* for example, is unusually explicit: Dublin, June 16, 1904. Conversely, Franz Kafka sets his long story "In the Penal Colony" somewhere in the "tropics" in a timeless but realistically portrayed place called the "colony." Kafka's story belongs to the eternal present, to the nightmare, to oppression; and its lack of a specifically recognizable time and place frees the action to become allegorical (see page 224).

In some works you may only gradually discover the setting. This method of revealing the setting will become, in itself, a subtle dramatic device, carefully calculated by the writer. Henry James' "A Great Good Place" and E. M. Forster's "The Celestial Omnibus" are examples of works in which setting carries a heavy thematic load. You must recognize the relevancy of the setting to understand the meaning or theme of the story.

In a good narrative the relationship between the setting and the other fictional elements is crucial. **Verisimilitude,** the appearance of truth, is essential if the artist is to achieve and maintain the convention of dramatic illusion. Coleridge described our acceptance of the artist's fictional world as "that willing suspension of disbelief for the moment which constitutes poetic faith." By this he meant, quite accurately, that a reader will go to any place and to any point in time without raising the question of whether the action and characters are representations of actual experiences, so long as the artist portrays his world in a convincing manner.

To achieve verisimilitude, or the belief on the reader's part that the action is possible, the artist may place his work in a realistic or actual geographical setting. Erich Maria Remarque concentrated his work *Arch of Triumph* in a Paris we know and recognize. Virginia Woolf set the action of her impressionistic novel *Mrs. Dalloway* in London. William Faulkner restricted fifteen of his nineteen novels to Yoknapatawpha County, a fictitious world that closely resembles the Oxford, Mississippi area where he was born. If a writer chooses a historical period for the action of his work, he usually takes great care to describe the setting as it actually was. Walter Van Tilburg Clark in his novel *The Oxbow Incident* and John Guthrie in *The Way West* realistically re-create the American frontier. This use of real places, realistically described, is the most common method used in fiction to achieve verisimilitude.

If the artist chooses a place devised totally from his own imagination, he will usually describe so many small, physical details that we acknowledge the reality of the place even though we know it does not actually exist. In his novel *1984,* George Orwell used such concrete and reasonable details in his description of a London in the future that such a world seems not only possible but probable. Another example can be found in Shirley Jackson's story "The Lottery." Like Kafka's "In the Penal Colony," the narrative lacks a specifically recognizable time and place. The setting consists of an imaginary small village where, every summer on June 27, the villagers draw names from a black box to determine who will be stoned to death. Though the reader has no idea where the action occurs geographically, Shirley Jackson's minute and detailed description of the village makes plausible and chillingly believable the bizarre actions of the town.

Setting sometimes also serves a dramatic function, substantially influencing both the events and the characters in a work of fiction. Writers know that environment shapes and influences people and their actions. By placing fictional characters in isolation, under the hardship of natural surroundings, or even in untoward luxury, an artist can use setting to actively advance his narrative. An African safari in Hemingway's "The Short Happy Life of Francis Macomber" distills and reveals in an accelerated manner the character weaknesses and strengths of the three characters in the story. In Katherine Anne Porter's "Flowering Judas," the pervading sense of Mexico subtly points up the sense of alienation of the American girl, Laura. The landscape becomes an enigmatic symbol of all that is foreign, and yet in its details—the Catholic Church, the Mexican men, the revolution itself—the setting ironically helps to reveal that the protagonist's main conflict is her own inability to love or to be genuinely committed on any level.

In some works, setting not only influences behavior but becomes an active protagonist or antagonist. It is the geography of Russia itself, vast and ultimately even more indestructible than the Russian spirit, that finally defeats and destroys Napoleon's armies in Tolstoy's *War and Peace.* In Thomas Hardy's *The Return of the Native,* the moor, Egdon Heath, becomes a brooding presence that overshadows and dooms all the characters' hopes for human happiness.

If a particular setting or locale is emphasized because of its unique-ness, its inherent interest, or its effect on the customs and behavior of the characters, the work is said to be **regional.** If a regional setting is stressed —with dialect and attendant customs and attitudes—the author is said to use **local color.** Many works by southern writers (Carson McCullers' *The Heart Is a Lonely Hunter,* William Faulkner's *As I Lay Dying,* Eudora Welty's "Powerhouse") are regional, and much of the reader's interest de-pends on the author's use of local color. Rudyard Kipling's novels and sto-ries about India and Alan Paton's novels about South Africa are regional. In a regional work that emphasizes local color, setting not only provides dramatic background, but plays a major role in explaining character moti-vation and attitudes. Bernard Malamud, in his novel *The Fixer,* depends heavily on the customs of the people and the conditions prevalent in czar-ist Russia to dramatize and make real the suffering of his protagonist. Set-ting is not limited to the physical background against which the characters and actions of a narrative evolve. Setting also includes the psychological, religious, moral, social, and emotional milieu in which the characters exist and by which they are influenced and, in varying degrees, controlled.

The scope or magnitude of setting the author selects has a direct in-fluence on the resulting work of fiction. Every writer chooses the time-space relationship he feels will best demonstrate his theme. He uses time and space simultaneously, but in varying proportions. He determines the length of time he wishes his narrative to encompass, and he selects the limits of the space he intends his time-events to occupy. A work may, for example, cover no more than an hour in the lives of various people. The characters may be widely separated geographically. Such works, which move in space rather than in time, are referred to as **spatial.** At the other extreme, a work may relate the evolution of generations of people, who live out their lives within a single household. Such a work is linear in structure, or **chronological.**

A setting increasingly characteristic of modern fiction is the **micro-cosm** ("little world"), in which the writer confines his characters and their actions to a very limited space. Stephen Crane's "The Open Boat" con-cerns four shipwrecked men, isolated in a small dinghy, and their struggle against the sea to reach land. The boat, the world of the story, a micro-cosm, becomes a symbol of the fragility of life in the midst of a vast, indif-ferent sea. The sea represents the forces of nature, the universe, or the **ma-crocosm.** Katherine Anne Porter creates a microcosm by confining the characters of her novel, *Ship of Fools,* to a larger boat, a transport making an Atlantic voyage. Spatially confined during the long voyage, her charac-ters act out the prejudices, the failures, and some of the nobility of man-kind. By isolating representative groups of people, an artist is able to por-tray certain aspects of (or truths about) human nature with concentrated precision. William Golding, in his novel *Lord of the Flies,* isolates civilized schoolboys on a deserted island to illustrate the basic animality that lurks just below the surface of our civilized behavior, which, he contends, will emerge with savage lack of restraint when the restrictions imposed by society are stripped away. The microcosmic world enables the writer to probe deeply into a particular facet of human motivation. Conversely, works of epic proportion tend toward universal inclusiveness and may encompass years and much of both the known and the imaginative worlds. The setting of Tolstoi's *War and Peace* approaches *The Odyssey* in its long time span and its inclusion of vast space.

Setting, then, can be used not only to establish the credibility of place, but to further the artist's theme. Setting can symbolically reflect states of mind, as it does in Conrad's *Heart of Darkness,* in which the dark jungle mirrors Marlow's miasmic confusion, or philosophical dilemmas, as it does in Kafka's "The Country Doctor," in which the nightmare setting dramatizes the nightmarish quality of man's insoluble conflicts between duty to self and to the world. When you read a work of literature, your understanding will be greatly aided if you determine the role that setting assumes in the narrative. Essays that illuminate the dramatic function of setting will be of value to your reader.

Atmosphere and Mood

Atmosphere is a general term used to denote the pervasive emotion, feeling, or belief one senses within the world of a work of literature. It is the prevailing tone or mood of the work and is established in part by setting. Used successfully, atmosphere builds in the reader expectations and attitudes about the action or outcome to follow.

The following is a descriptive passage that opens Thomas Hardy's novel *The Return of the Native.*[1] Both atmosphere and mood are established through setting:

> A Saturday afternoon in November was approaching the time of twilight, and the vast tract of unenclosed wild known as Egdon Heath embrowned itself moment by moment. Overhead the hollow stretch of whitish cloud shutting out the sky was as a tent which had the whole heath for its floor.
>
> The heaven being spread with this pallid screen and the earth with the darkest vegetation, their meeting-line at the horizon was clearly marked. In such contrast the heath wore the appearance of an instalment of night which had taken up its place before its astronomical hour was come: darkness had to a great extent arrived hereon, while day stood dis-

[1] From Thomas Hardy, *The Return of the Native,* Rinehart Edition, edited by Albert J. Guerard (New York: Holt, Rinehart and Winston, Inc. . , 1969), p. 1. Reprinted by permission.

tinct in the sky. Looking upwards, a furze-cutter would have been inclined to continue work; looking down, he would have decided to finish his faggot and go home. The distant rims of the world and of the firmament seemed to be a division in time no less than a division in matter. The face of the heath . . . could . . . retard the dawn, sadden noon, anticipate the frowning of storms scarcely generated, and intensify the opacity of a moonless midnight to a cause of shaking and dread.

We analyze or understand atmosphere intellectually. We perceive its existence. In the passage above, for example, we can understand, by studying the methods used by Hardy to describe Egdon Heath, that here is a world of oppressive vastness, which confuses, overwhelms, and diminishes the efforts of men who pass into or under its influence.

If we were to make a distinction between atmosphere and mood, we would say that **mood,** as a part of atmosphere, consists of the emotional quality of a work—of sadness, excitement, tedium, mystery, elation—and that mood, like atmosphere, is created by the artist through a combination of tone (his attitude toward his readers and subject), and his use of setting, action, and characterization. More subtly, such literary devices as imagery, metaphor, alliteration, and the rhythm of sentences and dialogue will, when effectively employed, set up in the reader a sense of a particular "felt life" or "felt reality."

The mood in the passage above is emotional; we sense the coming darkness, and like the furze-cutter, we are bewildered and perhaps a little frightened by a sense of mystery and foreboding. We breathe the same air that pervades the heath, and we become involved with the work's "felt presence" as we watch the actions of the narrative unfold. Atmosphere and mood, like setting, aid verisimilitude; they cause us to believe, by appealing to both our intellect and our emotions, in the truth of the world presented.

I. A. Richards, a noted literary critic, maintains that art uses "emotive language" to produce an emotion or attitude in the reader. The artist appeals, through language, to our emotional being. In the passage above, Hardy uses imagery to produce mood and atmosphere. To evoke a sense of the brooding presence of the heath, which approaches the supernatural, Hardy uses **personification.** Personification is a figure of speech in which inanimate objects are given human form, character, or sensibilities. Egdon Health "embrowns itself"; the "face" of the heath can "retard the dawn, sadden noon, anticipate the frowning of storms. . . ." Through personification, the heath subtly assumes a life of its own; it becomes a presence with both the power and the will to somehow alter the natural and commonplace events of men and nature.

Hardy further intensifies the somber mood of the passage through metaphor. The sky is "a tent" with "the whole heath for its floor." The sky becomes the tent's "pallid screen" while the heath below darkens prematurely, wearing "an instalment of night." Finally, the line between the sky and earth becomes not only a physical division but "a division in time."

Metaphor and personification stand as central figures in Hardy's description, but for full understanding of precisely how Hardy achieves his emotive effects, note also his sentence rhythms, and his more obvious use of verbs and adjectives. Hardy's sentences are long and complex. Rhythmically his sentences are slow, and a heaviness in the phrasing both accentuates and dramatizes the effect of oppressiveness and foreboding. His verbs ("shutting out," "retard," "sadden," "intensify") and his adjectives ("vast," "pallid," "darkest," "distant," "moonless") add to and evoke the emotional quality of the passage and give the reader a sense of the eerie quiet that sometimes precedes an oncoming storm. Such tense, oppressive quiet, with the attendant expectation that it must erupt in violence, functions dramatically and thematically as metaphor, because *The Return of the Native* is a story about the frailties of human love and the storm and cruelty of passion.

Note also Hardy's use of voice and psychic distance. As readers, we view the heath in a detached manner, yet we become participants. Hardy gives us angles of vision both above and within the heath. We look down, as if distantly, on the small, insignificant furze-cutter. At the same time we are told what the furze-cutter thinks, and so we identify with and participate in his confusion. Yet with our larger view of the sky and the heath, we also perceive the causes for his confusion. We are guided in this view by Hardy's omniscient voice, as it echoes, detached and bodiless, a part of the heath itself.

Sometimes our inability to understand the full impact of what we read results from failure to correctly analyze a work's atmosphere. Sensing the mood (a part of atmosphere) is a matter of being emotionally receptive. It is difficult, however, to objectify a writer's technique in order to ascertain what the atmosphere means. In *Gulliver's Travels,* for example, failure to distinguish Swift's tone from the words and thoughts of his protagonist reduces the book to a children's adventure story; differentiating the author's tone (which reflects, in this case, his beliefs) from the thoughts and words of the work's protagonist reveals a highly complex and satirical commentary about the period in which Swift lived.

In some works the reader may miss the irony, and thus the full meaning of a work or passage, because the atmosphere may seem so singularly inappropriate. For example, if you have read Remarque's *All Quiet on the Western Front,* you will recall that the young German soldier, the story's protagonist, dies from a stray bullet on a quiet, peaceful, sunny day. It is spring, and the truce has begun. The exhausted young soldier has miraculously lived through the terrors and horrors of war on the German front, and now, finally ready to go home, he is killed pointlessly. To find his death pointless is, in fact, the point. The irony and absurdity of his death at such a time intensifies rather than diminishes Remarque's strong and passionate argument against war. To dramatize his theme, Remarque reverses what we traditionally expect from spring and sunny fields (rebirth and hope). The setting, the action, and the voice of the writer with its measured, objective tone dramatize the theme of the novel through irony in atmosphere and setting.

In one very important sense the success of the work depends upon the degree to which we as readers are immersed in the artist's created world. Often we feel an intensity of truth seldom experienced in real life. We can best understand the nature of this "reality" by comprehending the elements that contribute to the work's atmosphere. Like setting, atmosphere may not actively promote the theme of a work. However, if mood and atmosphere function dramatically—if they provide a key to the meaning of the work —an explication of a representative passage or an analysis explaining the function of mood and atmosphere will significantly aid your reader's understanding of the work as a whole.

Story: Plot and Structure

At the heart of all fiction lies the story. For centuries, accounts of people and what they do have been of deep and lasting interest to readers and listeners. The story that endures always expresses through the actions of people some fear or hope that man holds to be true and that explains and gives meaning to his life. For this reason stories are always concerned with the actions of characters. We say, this story is about a man who loved his wife inordinately, and, suspecting her of unfaithfulness, is driven by his jealousy to kill her; then, in despair, he kills himself. Or we say, this is a story about a group of soldiers and how those who survive emerge as heroes or traitors as a result of their experiences in war.

Story is an inclusive term. It consists of the totality of what happens and its subsequent meaning. Story includes characters and their actions in a particular setting. It includes atmosphere and all the other elements that contribute to some meaning and, logically arranged, gives the audience a sense of an aesthetic whole. As such, action *in fiction* differs from the actions of people in everyday life.

The first difference between life in the everyday world and life in fiction is that actual life is chaotic and, taken as a whole, unstructured. Truth in life lies buried in detail and the endless jumbled continuum of human experience. Life in fiction, though it may be chaotic for its characters, is nevertheless presented to the reader as an ordered experience. The writer consciously simplifies life by extracting some segment from the flux of experience and giving it order and unity. He introduces thought; he distorts time; he creates a unified experience by imposing on the action some logically related sequence. In the story about the jealous husband, for example, the action is consciously restricted. It centers upon a single misunderstanding and its tragic results. Similarly, though the second story line about the soldiers is more inclusive, it too will involve the conscious selection of characters and actions in some limited time sequence. The artist will necessarily select only those events that explain or show development and change in attitudes of each of the soldiers.

In terms of the flux of life, the conscious omission of certain details and the focus on others is an artificial device. But the fiction writer does not attempt to imitate life. He clarifies and reveals what is otherwise obscure, and he does this by omitting certain details and selecting only those that fit his needs. Story, therefore, can further be defined as a *structured* presentation of specific actions that particular characters perform.

In both life and fiction it is difficult to separate character from action, to visualize events in a story separate from the people who perform them; but we make such a distinction and separation in our study of fiction in order to understand the nature of action and its role in story. We think of the arrangement of the action in a story as *plot;* we think of the overall design or movement in a story, of which plot is a part, as *structure.*

PLOT. At its simplest, **plot** consists of what happens in a story, and nowhere is the imaginative quality of fiction more evident than in plot. Plot is action consciously arranged by the writer in an effort to compel us to read on; developed in a cycle of beginning, middle, and end, plot gives us a sense of aesthetic completeness.

We think of the story line or **action** as a series of events occurring naturally in a chronological sequence. By action we do not mean a single event (the jealous husband shoots his wife; one of the soldiers eats his K ration in a water-filled trench). By action we mean the total sequence of events presented as a movement through time (the husband begins to suspect his wife of infidelity; day by day his suspicion and torment grow as he discovers or imagines actions on her part to further his suspicions. Finally, believing proof of her guilt to be incontestable, he shoots her as she is getting dressed, disregarding her explanation that she is going out to a friend's house for the evening.)

This action, and all that follows to the conclusion, is a chronological presentation of the story line. It is unlikely, however, that the writer will tell his story in exactly this order. He will rearrange the scenes to heighten his opening presentation, or to better dramatize the ensuing violent confrontation, or to preclude the necessity for dramatizing *all* the plot action. He may, for example, open his story in the middle of the complication or action (*in medias res*) to engage his reader's interest. He may open immediately before the jealous husband shoots his wife, or with the wife just dead, or before the husband shoots himself. The writer may subsequently re-create prior actions in one major flashback, or he may weave back and forth in time. The conscious arrangement of scene order in plot structure can be clearly understood when one realizes that in life several events can occur simultaneously, but in fiction the writer must present those events one at a time. The order he chooses makes up his plot.

The opening or beginning of a plot structure will usually introduce the **situation** or, as it is sometimes called, the **exposition.** We are introduced to the characters; we learn something of the setting. The opening situation will also introduce an unresolved and present **conflict.** Conflict consists of the struggle that grows out of two or more opposing forces. The struggle may be overt (the confrontation between the jealous husband and his wife). In such case, the conflict is said to be *external*. The conflict may also be one of inner emotional stress (the husband's torment). Conflict in the mind of one of the characters is said to be *internal*. Very often—as it is in the story of the jealous husband—conflict will be both external and internal.

Conflict constitutes the basic and essential element of plot. Conflict holds the plot together and provides the story with its interest and suspense. If there is no conflict, there is no story. In fiction, conflict usually involves one (or a combination) of four basic kinds of struggle: a struggle against another person (the husband against his wife; two fighters locked in deadly combat; one character trying to outwit another); a struggle against nature (climbing the highest mountain; surviving a hurricane; shipwrecked men on a raft struggling toward land); a struggle against society (the revolutionary; the outcast fighting for acceptance; men and women trying to change or maintain some existing order); an internal struggle (two forces within a character fighting for mastery: honesty versus the desire for material profit; pride versus humility; acceptance versus rejection).

From the opening situation and initial conflict, the action in the body of the plotted story develops into a series of difficulties, or into the **complication.** Each successive difficulty or complication must grow logically out of the initial conflict, and each episode must add to an increasing entanglement of affairs. For example, once his suspicions are aroused (the initial conflict), the jealous husband furtively listens to and watches his wife's every activity, judging all that happens in the light of his suspicion and fear. His emotions and interpretations become increasingly entangled and his wife's actions seem to violate his love and former trust. Such complication, presented scene by scene, comprises the **rising action** of the story.

When the tension has reached its peak and at the point where some act (physical or emotional) turns the conflict toward resolution, the story reaches its **climax.** Here the story can end, or the conflict can be resolved through a series of **falling actions** to a **resolution.** The husband can immediately kill himself in an act of passion and despair, or he can discover that his wife was really innocent; or, discovering further proof of her guilt, he can realize that life is meaningless without her. The movement toward final realization or discovery constitutes the beginning of the resolution.

However the action and realization are plotted by the writer, the action must be terminated, and the causal relationship of one episode to another must be resolved. The reader must be led to the point where final understanding or perspective is possible. In a tightly plotted story the final unraveling of the plot is called the **denouement.** The mystery is solved; all the secrets and misunderstandings are made clear to the characters, to the reader, or to both. The conflict may end in a draw (the characters living to fight another day). The conflict may end in **catastrophe.** The term catastrophe is traditionally reserved for the tragic ending, the term denouement for works that are not tragic. In modern usage, however, some writers use the term denouement to denote the end or resolution to any story, tragic or not. Many writers restore equilibrium or order at the end of their work, even if that end is the grave. Such restoration of order is often termed the denouement.

In terms of overall development, stories generally follow a movement from instability to stability, from conflict to resolution. In the process, a permanent change in the situation or characters occurs: the man and his wife are dead; the war ends. Those soldiers who survive emerge from the war exhausted, but more knowledgeable about life and death than when they began the fight. In this sense, stories at their best expand a specific experience into a general statement about experience as a whole. Reading about specific men and women, we come to understand more about jealousy and passion in general, more about war and its effects in general. Not only are the characters in a piece of good fiction changed at the end of the story, but we as readers are changed, too. We realize more about the human experience than we knew before.

Two movements progress simultaneously through a work of fiction: the story or action line as it would occur if presented chronologically, and plot as the structured arrangement of that action. We understand the story line as the dramatic experience. We look to the plot to see what the artist has emphasized as an aid to our discovery of the story's meaning. In following both movements we as readers are continuously required to exercise our imagination and apply our understanding. We not only study emphasis through plot but learn that omitted scenes that can be understood or supplied by our imagination will often suggest dimensions more inclusive than the presented action.

During your reading you will discover that some stories are highly plotted, and further, that stories which depend on action for much of their interest (like detective and suspense stories) will often contain complicated subplots. Other types of stories, however, will seem to have little or no plot. Virtually nothing happens; the characters do little, and their situation may seem unchanged at the conclusion of the story. Episodes loosely linked together and lacking any discernible plot are referred to as stories of **incident** or **situation.** The interest in such stories lies not in the actions performed, but in understanding the meaning of a way of life, a condition of mind, or a state of being. Hemingway's story "Old Man at the Bridge" is a story of incident. It consists of a portrait or description of a condition. In stories such as this, you will often look not for plot, but for the story's *structure* to discover how the story is put together and what it may mean.

STRUCTURE.   **Structure** is often a major key to understanding the theme or true meaning of a work. Finding the structure may prove difficult, but most modern critics agree that structure, at least in prose, consists of the essential framework or overall interior pattern or organization employed by the author both to express and to contain the content of the story.

To find the structure in a work, we examine the story to see if there is a general plan or organization larger and deeper than the plot. Usually some more meaningful order will shape a work of fiction, and plot will constitute only one of its internal workings. The structure of Henry James' novel *The Ambassadors,* for example, clearly differs from its story line or plot. Lambert Strether goes to Paris to rescue Chad Newsome from sin and a "woman." His initiation to Paris brings about profound changes. As he moves from ignorance to knowledge (the theme of initiation), he comes to a new understanding of freedom and love. He decides to stay in Paris. Conversely, Chad Newsome, who has achieved emotional freedom and worldly understanding in Paris, decides to return home to New England responsibility and convention. During the course of the novel, the two men's positions are reversed, and they actually exchange continents and worlds. This reversal and exchange constitutes the structure of the novel, and if it were diagrammed in a spatial "shape" it would resemble an hourglass on its side, the sand from each end somehow flowing simultaneously to the opposite end until all the sand is exchanged.

The structural movement in fiction is not restricted to geometrical diagrams, however. It may also resemble other art, according to critic and teacher Ray B. West, Jr., who compares the structure of William Faulkner's *The Sound and the Fury* to the traditional development of the four parts of a symphony. Thomas Mann's story "Gladeus Dei" is another example of a work of fiction with an unusual structure. It opens with a visual description of a scene ("Munich was radiant") that becomes a word painting. Mann then moves his main character into that scene to view a real painting in a shop window. By this method a static, visual description is set into narrative motion. We perceive a picture within a picture, and since the subject of the story is in part censorship and the nature of art, the structure takes on significant thematic meaning.

The short story "Old Man at the Bridge," thin in plot line to the point of episode or incident, is structured as a visual (but symbolic) scene. The scene consists of two sides of a river connected by a bridge. On one side lies danger and, ironically, home and the place the old man loves; on the other side lies temporary safety—which for the old man is no safety at all because the other side symbolizes the unknown, the alien land. Essentially spatial, the action of the story involves a young soldier's attempt to induce an old man to cross a bridge. The old man cannot. The action and content involve an explanation of why the old man cannot pass from danger to potential safety, and the bridge itself becomes a visual and psychological structure from which the story takes its basic framework.

Because fiction has no conventionalized structure or form, each work must invent or evolve its own structure; to express its own unique material, each work must achieve its own form. In the best of modern fiction, structure is as varied as the works themselves. Structure is difficult to perceive, and few works will contain neat, identifiable designs in movement and development. However, when you can discover the structure in a work (and thus realize its form), your understanding of the meaning or theme will be greatly increased. Certainly, you will have a valuable tool with which to explain, in an essay of analysis, the essential movement or organization by which the author reveals the meaning of his work. For a discussion about organizing the content of an essay that analyzes structure, see pages 211–212.

Characterization

Characterization is concerned basically with what people do and think, and our understanding of a work's characters leads directly to an understanding of the work itself. Characters move the plot; characterization conveys the theme.

We define characterization, in fiction, as the artist's creation of imaginary persons who seem so credible that we accept them as real. Their reality may be presented on various levels, from an abstraction or stereotype to a highly complex, fully realized representation. Works of fiction will contain characters who are delineated in greater or lesser detail, and by determining both their type and how they are presented, we can better arrive at an understanding of their function and nature.

We look, for our first step in understanding, to the artist's method of presenting his characters. Three techniques are most commonly used. First, in a block of direct exposition, the artist describes his characters and tells you precisely who and even what the characters represent. He can analyze succinctly or at great length, for your immediate understanding, the nature of the character and the workings of his mind. This technique is referred to as the *expository* method and it is particularly useful in presenting (1) minor characters who need to be understood quickly so that the narrative can move on, and (2) the first of a series of comments about a highly unusual main character. The description below, from Junichiro Tanizaki's short story "The Tattooer," [2] uses the expository method.

> Seikichi had formerly earned his living as an ukiyoye painter of the school of Toyokuni and Kunisada, a background which, in spite of his decline to the status of a tattooer, was evident from his artistic conscience and sensitivity. No one whose skin or whose physique failed to interest him could buy his services. The clients he did accept had to leave the design and cost entirely to his discretion—and to endure for one or even two months the excruciating pain of his needles.
>
> Deep in his heart the young tattooer concealed a secret pleasure, and a secret desire. His pleasure lay in the agony men felt as he drove his needles into them, torturing their swollen, blood-red flesh; and the louder they groaned, the keener was Seikichi's strange delight. Shading and vermilioning—these are said to be especially painful—were the techniques he most enjoyed.

By the second method, the *dramatic* technique, the author reveals little or nothing about the character's situation. He refrains from mind reading or character analysis and presents his characters to his readers primarily through what they say and do. From such purely dramatic presentation the reader must deduce the nature of the characters for himself. The following passage, from John Steinbeck's *Of Mice and Men,*[3] demonstrates this technique. Note that Steinbeck does not explain the past or the inner thoughts of either Lennie or George.

> The first man stopped short in the clearing, and the follower nearly ran over him. He took off his hat and wiped the sweat-band with his forefinger and snapped the moisture off. His huge companion dropped his blankets and flung himself down and drank from the surface of the green pool; drank with long gulps, snorting into the water like a horse. The small man stepped nervously beside him.

[2] From "The Tattooer," by Junichiro Tanizaki. Reprinted from *Seven Japanese Tales,* trans. by Howard Hibbett, by permission of Alfred A. Knopf, Inc. © Copyright 1963 by Alfred A. Knopf, Inc.
[3] From *Of Mice and Men* by John Steinbeck. Copyright 1937, copyright © renewed 1965 by John Steinbeck. Reprinted by permission of The Viking Press, Inc.

"Lennie!" he said sharply. "Lennie, for God' sakes don't drink so much." Lennie continued to snort into the pool. The small man leaned over and shook him by the shoulder. "Lennie. You gonna be sick like you was last night."

Lennie dipped his whole head under, hat and all, and then he sat up on the bank and his hat dripped down on his blue coat and ran down his back. "That's good," he said. "You drink some, George. You take a good big drink." He smiled happily.

George unslung his bindle and dropped it gently on the bank. "I ain't sure it's good water," he said. "Looks kinda scummy."

These two methods of presenting characters in fiction necessarily involve the artist's use of point of view. In the first, the narrator openly tells the reader, in as much detail as he deems advisable, all about the individual character: his thoughts, attitudes, dreams, appearance, mannerisms, and habits. This overt knowledge and the subsequent analysis is often called *explicit* characterization. The advantage of this use of point of view is that the writer is able to tell a great deal about his character in few words. For example, if the reader should see only Seikichi's impassive face as he tattoes his customers in a purely dramatic scene, the reader would not realize Seikichi's sexual aberration. Details from the passage that make this clear are the explicit references to Seikichi's "secret pleasure" and "strange delight" in inflicting pain upon people he finds attractive. Exposition enables the writer to explain the meaning of emotions the character himself may not fully realize.

In the passage from Steinbeck's novel, however, the method is one of suggestion and implication. The writer reports the characters' actions; he describes their appearance in the manner of the astute observer, and he refrains from going inside the characters' minds to reveal their thoughts. The writer in this case uses the effaced point of view—telling only what can logically be perceived from outside observation. This method is often described as *implicit* characterization. The writer does not state; he shows the characters in action, and the reader must deduce their essential natures for himself. For example, from the Steinbeck passage the reader can deduce that George is the leader, that he, the smaller man, takes care of Lennie; that Lennie is childish and irresponsible; that the two men are fond of each other, and that they are "on the road." We know nothing else, and this use of point of view effectively arouses our curiosity about the true situation.

In the third method of presenting characters (which also falls into the category of implicit characterization), the author moves inside the consciousness of his characters and presents the workings of their minds and emotions as an immediate experience. The author can use either the first person or the third person, but in either case his method is *subjective;* he restricts himself to the mind and vision of the character whose head he enters and through whose emotions and eyes he views the world. Note the passage below from Shirley Jackson's *We Have Always Lived in the Castle.*[4] We as readers must come to understand the characters and the world of the story by experiencing only what the first person narrator hears and sees, and what she thinks and feels.

> . . . "Here, lazy, take some of these packages. Where's my cat?"
>
> "He went off chasing butterflies because you were late. Did you remember eggs? I forgot to tell you."
>
> "Of course. Let's have lunch on the lawn."
>
> When I was small I thought Constance was a fairy princess. I used to try to draw her picture, with long golden hair and eyes as blue as the crayon could make them, and a bright pink spot on either cheek; the pictures always surprised me, because she *did* look like that; even at the worst time she was pink and white and golden, and nothing had ever seemed to dim the brightness of her. She was the most precious person in my world, always. I followed her across the soft grass, past the flowers she tended, into our house, and Jonas, my cat, came out of the flowers and followed me.

Using the first or third person subjective point of view, the author can move deep into the mind of the character to the level of consciousness where the experience is presented in all the immediacy of its instant occurrence. This method is often described as *impressionistic,* and the author may use the interior monologue or some other stream of consciousness technique. The following, from Brian Moore's *The Lonely Passion of Judith Hearne,*[5] demonstrates a combination of the interior monologue and the writer's guiding description. The viewpoint is, for this moment, double.

> Avoiding me, O, it's shameful of him, running away like that, as if I had the plague or something. You hurt me, James Madden, if you knew how much, you'd come back on your bended knees to apologise. Clutching her handbag to her stomach, she stared down the road. Ran from me. When I ran after him. Humiliated myself for him. He rejected. He turned away. But my own fault, yes, I'm the only one to blame, no I'm not, that horrid sister of his, telling him heaven knows what awful tale. Rejected, she looked at her long pointed shoes with the little shoe-eyes winking up at her. Little shoe-eyes, always there. But the magic didn't work. The shoe-eyes were just buttons. Just shoe buttons.
>
> O, she said, a woman in love can't afford to be proud.

[4] From *We Have Always Lived in the Castle* by Shirley Jackson. Copyright © 1962 by Shirley Jackson. All rights reserved. Reprinted by permission of The Viking Press, Inc.

[5] Brian Moore, *The Lonely Passion of Judith Hearne* (Boston: Little, Brown and Co., 1956). Reprinted by permission.

Determining the author's presentation and use of point of view is essential to full understanding of characterization. The author will provide you with the necessary clues to understanding, but he may be devious. If he uses the expository method, you will usually attend to and believe what the author says; if, however, he uses the point of view of one of his characters you must determine whether the character is trustworthy. In *We Have Always Lived in the Castle,* for example, we come to understand the character and see her story in a new light when we realize that she is insane. We read to experience the wonderfully vivid, unexpected workings of her mind, and in addition we learn that much of the truth of the work is to be found not precisely in what she says, but in the warped, paradoxically accurate view she has of the townspeople. Similarly, in the novel by Brian Moore, we experience, first hand, the anguish of a lonely, aging spinster, and we learn from that breaking anguish why she acts as she does. We participate, as she experiences it, in her destruction.

In the four works cited above, characterization forms the core of the meaning of the work. Each character, though highly individualized, represents some larger truth about the human condition. Recognition of both the uniqueness of the individual character and the truth that the character represents and dramatizes forms the center of understanding. Remember that what is not available to us in real life is made available in fiction by the author. He directs our understanding by stating and showing what he wants us to hear and see, and through his use of viewpoint we can often understand even when the character cannot. Fiction reveals the hidden life —the dreams and anxieties and motivations in men that are never evident in our daily associations. It follows that you and I can never understand each other; but we can understand characters in a work of fiction because the author will expose both the inner and the outer lives of his characters. Thus, whereas history, like life, exposes outward events, fiction reveals what the artist supposes to be the truths of the inner world of the mind.

In studying characterization we must, in addition to examining the author's techniques, determine the role the character plays in the work of fiction. First, determine if the character is the **protagonist** or the **antagonist** or a minor, supporting character. This broad, initial classification will not, in all likelihood, yield more than a basic position from which to begin your analysis, since characters in modern fiction are seldom presented as all good or all bad. The protagonist, traditionally defined as the hero who overcomes the antagonist, or villain, is largely obsolete. Artists today attempt to make their characters more like ordinary human beings. In modern fiction, the protagonist is the main character on whom the author centers his story; the antagonist is some individual who opposes the main character—or some force (such as society, nature, or war) which opposes him. As a person, yesterday's villain, like yesterday's hero, has become a complex human being who is struggling, for better or for worse, with one or more of life's situations. We read to find out how and why he acts and believes as he does. His goodness, if a value judgment is implied, is usually mitigated by some human failure; his "badness" is explained, and if not condoned, at least accepted as understandable.

Main characters—the protagonists and the antagonists—are always central to the conflict and receive the most careful development. Characters who support and sustain the narration but who are not central to the action or outcome are *minor* characters. Minor characters are usually drawn quickly and are often, though not always, immediately understood as types. Like major characters, their place and importance in the narrative depends upon how they are developed: as flat or round, as static or dynamic.

E. M. Forster in his *Aspects of the Novel* defines two major kinds of characters in fiction: *flat* and *round*. Flat characters are usually minor in the story. They play supporting roles. Round characters, on the other hand, are usually main characters; they are differentiated by the detail or development the author gives them.

Flat characters are one-dimensional; they are built around a single idea or character trait and are easily recognized and subsequently easily remembered. Flat characters usually do not undergo any basic change in their attitudes or beliefs, and once introduced in a work of fiction they do not require reintroduction or modification. They represent an idea or an attitude that remains the same throughout the story. Drawn quickly in strong bold strokes, they add texture and contrast to a work. They also contribute to the story's atmosphere in as reliable a manner as setting, and in a work centered upon a main character or characters who do evolve and develop, the flat character provides a safe and reliable point of reference.

In Shirley Jackson's *We Have Always Lived in the Castle,* for example, senile Uncle Julian, dribbling food down his chin, talking only of his unfinished manuscript, provides a sharp, clear portrait—and one we discover will not change. His stability as a character is comforting, because the personality of the main character shifts with bewildering speed. Similarly, in Steinbeck's *Of Mice and Men,* the bored young wife who causes Lennie's final trouble and downfall is presented as a flat character. Her portrayal represents a central idea: "I want attention and love and no one gives it to me." Candy, the old man who comes to share Lenny's and George's dream of a place of their own, represents quite simply the itinerant farm worker's desire for permanence and security. In much the same way, Mrs. Henry Rice, the landlady in Brian Moore's *The Lonely Passion of Judith Hearne,* represents the calm, polite disinterest of a person accustomed to having people come and go in her life. In the novel she functions primarily as a representative of humanity's indifference to the loneliness and need of others.

In good novels all flat characters have a dominant trait ascribed to them, which adds dimension and complexity to the work of fiction. An essay describing the role and function of a flat character as that character contributes to the thematic texture—to plot, atmosphere, setting, or as an aid in understanding the major characters—will be of benefit to your reader. A characteristic line of dialogue or a succinct description of a flat character by the author or narrator will provide a convenient passage for analysis or explication.

Of course, if all the characters in a work of fiction were flat, we would be dissatisfied. We would sense that the writer had failed to grasp the complexities of the human mind and heart. And we would be right. The typical detective or spy story fails as literature precisely here; its protagonists and antagonists (as detective versus criminal, as sympathetic master spy versus opposing evil syndicate or country) are usually as flat as a photograph. Perhaps one distinguishing and vital difference between literature and those works of fiction that never take on the dimensions of literature is found here, in the artist's success or failure to probe the deeper truths about the human condition. If the story succeeds on its own level, if it is purely an action narrative for entertainment alone, we will not be disappointed. But characterization provides a writer with one of his primary tools, and instinctively he turns to the round character to reveal his major themes—his interpretations of the world. The round character, usually the main character as either antagonist or protagonist, mirrors the multiple facets of the human personality.

If we speak of stories as "imitations of truth" we discover that round characters, those drawn to show the complexity of the individual, are fully developed. They are three-dimensional and they may change; they may develop and evolve as the story progresses. If they change and grow they are referred to as *dynamic;* if they are complex but remain essentially the same at the end of the story as they were at the beginning, they are *static.* Flat characters, of course, may be dynamic, but because they are used most often in support of the main story, they will usually be static. The dynamic, round character, in contrast, will change as a result of his experiences, his realizations, and his decisions. To determine the degree of his roundness and the nature of dynamic change he may undergo during the course of the story, we ask how variable and how complex he is in his emotions as he reacts to his situation. How real, as an expanding, many-sided and contradictory personality, is he? What does he realize? What does he learn? How do the forces he meets reshape him?

We must be cautious, however, in our examination of the rounded, multifaceted character. He may be round, as we have said, but he may also be static. He may be highly complex, but he may not change. From the epic we inherit the concept of a hero who undergoes great pressure and hardship but who remains the same virtuous, strong man regardless of his experiences. He may change the world, but if time and adventure have any impact on him, it is only to make him stronger, wiser, and more virtuous. In modern fiction we have round, static characters like Wilson, the hunter in Hemingway's "The Short Happy Life of Francis Macomber." Wilson is complex, but he is basically unchanged at the end of the story. In cases such as his, we read to discover his essential, unchanging nature and philosophy. We also look to see if there may be a developing character who is portrayed in direct contrast. In the same story, for example, Macomber changes from a frightened man who does not understand the rules of manhood to a happy, complete man who achieves, for a brief moment, understanding and acceptance of himself. In this story of initiation, Macomber is a dynamic character, and the theme is to be arrived at through an analysis of the difference between the two characters.

The round, static character is common to the short story, in which lack of space often prohibits extensive character evolution. The round, dynamic character is most often found in the modern novel, in which change and development can be accomplished leisurely, and in which we expect some change in the protagonist, some growth or deterioration in his human relationships and attitudes as a result of his experiences. To determine the nature of the character we must study the evidence the writer gives us, deleting nothing from the character's actions, dialogue, attitudes, or thoughts, or from the other characters' attitudes toward him. We must watch for ironies, inconsistencies, and the character's own bias. Subsequently taking all the author's presented material into account, we try to find some *consistent principle.*

A consistent principle, in characterization, consists of some key provided by the author that will lead us to the essential nature of a character. The key may be a behavioral pattern, a dominant idea, emotion, or goal, or even some outside motivating force that will invariably determine the character's actions and attitudes.

The consistent principle is based on several assumptions. First, we tentatively assume that each man can be identified by some aspect of his character, personality, or behavior, which will help both to classify and to separate him from other men. We assume, secondly, that people are similar to one another in that they are all subject in varying degree to the same hopes, fears, and passions; that they can suffer, and that they are all potentially capable of enjoying life. Third, we assume that the writer is interested in demonstrating, through his characters, some observation about life, some truth as he sees it. Art distills and clarifies, and characters exist to embody some idea, philosophy, or theme. Finally, we know that to make himself understood, the artist will provide us with clues and guidelines to help our understanding. In fiction, he will weave these clues through his narrative in some type of pattern so that we can discover them and attend to their meaning. This pattern is the consistent principle.

To discover this principle, and the manner in which the artist reveals it, we apply several questions and criteria:

1. What is the character confronted by? What are his choices?
2. A character reveals himself by how he chooses to act, and by how he reacts. What is the character's attitude toward the situation that faces him? Does he reveal, through any discernible and repeated pattern of behavior, a consistent attitude or stance?
3. In the narrative, does the character act or is he being acted upon? Does he control his actions, or is he forced to action by some event or situation?
4. What is the character's perception of reality in relation to the world he inhabits? How does he view his situation? How does he see life? In what way is his view of life special or unusual? Does this perception repeatedly determine what happens to him?
5. In relation to the action or the situation in the work itself, what is the character's driving motivation? What does he most want? Does his motivating drive, or lack of it, repeatedly affect his attitudes and actions?
6. Finally: Who is he? What is he? What is his meaning?

By answering the questions that apply in a particular case, we discover the dominating principle by which we are to understand the character. Lennie in *Of Mice and Men* truly wants to do the right thing. But because he is a child in mind and a great, powerful man in body, circumstances beyond his control (his physical strength, his stupidity, and his desire to love warm, live things) converge into an action that finally proves him incapable of living free in society, in spite of George's protection. The consistent principle in Lennie's character is that he cannot understand the rules of survival. This principle or truth guides the entire novel, moves the plot, and points up the story's theme: Man destroys what he loves and what he doesn't understand.

Like Lennie, Mary Katherine Blackwood, the narrator in *We Have Always Lived in the Castle,* is also unfit for society. She is brilliant and neurotic, lacks a sense of guilt, is loyal to those she loves, and is vindictive to the point of murder toward those she thinks do wrong. The consistent principle in her character is shaped by her insanity. She narrates the story, and it is through her particular perspective that we come to understand the action of the novel. The theme, similar to that in *Of Mice and Men,* is contained in twists of irony as we discover that society is also depraved, but knowledgeable, and therefore without the saving grace of the innocence of mental derangement. We wonder, finally, whether it is the girl or the townspeople that bear the guilt for the events in the story.

In Brian Moore's novel, Miss Judith Hearne, unable to cope with her own loneliness, also violates the rules of society and so proves herself unacceptable to a world in which only the strong and less sensitive can adjust and survive. Her consistent principle is, of course, her anguished need to be loved.

Each of these characters displays a consistent principle: Lennie is feeble minded; Mary Katherine is insane; Judith Hearne aches with loneliness. In each of these novels we discover either the reasons for these conditions or their effects. In our analysis, we look at each of these characters in relation to society and we find ourselves finally gazing at the cruelties and injustices of man. All three characters lose in their search for a place in society, yet in each search and subsequent failure (Lennie is executed like an animal; Judith Hearne is left alone in the agony of her final despair; Mary Elizabeth takes her sister into permanent seclusion and isolation) we are led as readers to a deeper understanding of the condition of man in general.

During your study of a work of fiction your attention will be drawn to many elements in the work, but plot and characterization will be central to every story. You need to determine whether the author has emphasized action or character revelation. Some very fine stories like "The Short Happy Life of Francis Macomber" integrate plot equally with character development, but an author usually will emphasize one or the other. If he emphasizes plot, you will want to determine whether he uses his characters as flat types representing some abstract concept, as embodiments of a single idea, or as typical representations of humanity caught in some force or action. Determine always how the author conveys his theme, then discover the part characterization plays.

If the author emphasizes character, try to discern some consistent principle in the character, then determine how the principle conveys theme. Remember, however, that even when you find a consistent principle there will be others as valid and as meaningful. Dynamic, round characters especially are susceptible to multiple interpretation. If you are asked to write an essay using characterization, your main purpose will be to explain or interpret a character as he appears in the work. You can explain the nature of the character if he is complex and not easily understood; you can analyze the problems he faces, particularly if they are insoluble and reflect the theme of the work. You can analyze the change or evolution that occurs during the course of the narrative action; you can state and analyze how the character functions in the story (if a minor character, how he affects the major characters; if a major character, the way the character becomes a dramatic representation of the theme). The author will often use various motifs, or repetitive actions and descriptions, to point up the nature of a character. The color black and the use of fire effectively characterize the boy's father in William Faulkner's "Barn Burning." The meaning of the fires the father lights—the small, niggardly ones when he camps, and the great flames of burning barns as he seeks revenge—not only reveal the nature of the father but lead directly to the theme of the story. *Remember that you will always direct your paper toward the theme.*

DISCOVERING A STORY

James Joyce, one of the twentieth century's greatest writers, wrote complex, experimental, and profound stories, poems, novels, and plays. We have chosen "Araby," an early story from his collection *Dubliners,* to demonstrate the many principles and techniques of fiction. Read the story below and, using the steps suggested in Section One on critical reading, discover first the work's dramatic experience (what happens on the surface or paraphrasable level). Then reread the story slowly, trying to discover the techniques the author uses to dramatize and convey the meanings contained in the work. After you have studied "Araby," read the following detailed analysis to test your interpretation and to better understand how a consideration of the different elements of fiction will reveal levels of interpretation not apparent on first reading.

ARABY [6]

North Richmond Street, being blind, was a quiet street except at the hour when the Christian Brothers' School set the boys free. An uninhabited house of two storeys stood at the blind end, detached from its neighbours in a square ground. The other houses of the street, conscious of decent lives within them, gazed at one another with brown imperturbable faces.

The former tenant of our house, a priest, had died in the back drawing-room. Air, musty from having been long enclosed, hung in all the rooms, and the waste room behind the kitchen was littered with old useless papers. Among these I found a few paper-covered books, the pages of which were curled and damp: *The Abbot,* by Walter Scott, *The Devout Communicant* and *The Memoirs of Vidocq.* I liked the last best because its leaves were yellow. The wild garden behind the house contained a central apple-tree and a few straggling bushes under one of which I found the late tenant's rusty bicycle-pump. He had been a very charitable priest; in his will he had left all his money to institutions and the furniture of his house to his sister.

When the short days of winter came dusk fell before we had well eaten our dinners. When we met in the street the houses had grown sombre. The space of sky above us was the colour of ever-changing violet and towards it the lamps of the street lifted their feeble lanterns. The cold air stung us and we played till our bodies glowed. Our shouts echoed in the silent street. The career of our play brought us through the dark muddy lanes behind the houses where we ran the gauntlet of the rough tribes from the cottages, to the back doors of the dark dripping gardens where odours arose from the ashpits, to the dark odorous stables where a coachman smoothed and combed the horse or shook music from the buckled harness. When we returned to the street light from the kitchen windows had filled the areas. If my uncle was seen turning the corner we hid in the shadow until we had seen him safely housed. Or if Mangan's sister came out on the doorstep to call her brother in to his tea we watched her from our shadow peer up and down the street. We waited to see whether she would remain or go in and, if she remained, we left our shadow and walked up to Mangan's steps resignedly. She was waiting for us, her figure defined by the light from the half-opened door. Her brother always teased her before he obeyed and I stood by the railings looking at her. Her dress swung as she moved her body and the soft rope of her hair tossed from side to side.

Every morning I lay on the floor in the front parlour watching her door. The blind was pulled down to within an inch of the sash so that I could not be seen. When she came out on the doorstep my heart leaped. I ran to the hall, seized my books and followed her. I kept her brown figure always in my eye and, when we came near the point at which our ways diverged, I quickened my pace and passed her. This happened morning after morning. I had never spoken to her, except for a few casual words, and yet her name was like a summons to all my foolish blood.

Her image accompanied me even in places the most hostile to romance. On Saturday evenings when my aunt went marketing I had to go to carry some of the parcels. We walked through the flaring streets, jostled by drunken men and bargaining women, amid the curses of labourers, the shrill litanies of shop-boys who stood on guard by the barrels of pigs' cheeks, the nasal chanting of street-singers, who sang a *come-all-you* about O'Donovan Rossa, or a ballad about the troubles in our native land. These noises converged in a single sensation of life for me: I imagined that I bore my chalice safely through a throng of foes. Her name sprang to my lips at moments in strange prayers and praises which I myself did not understand. My eyes were often full of tears (I could not tell why) and at times a flood from my heart seemed to pour itself out into my bosom. I thought little of the future. I did not know whether I would ever speak to her or not or, if I spoke to her, how I could tell her of my confused adoration. But my body was like a harp and her words and gestures were like fingers running upon the wires.

One evening I went into the back drawing-room in which the priest had died. It was a dark rainy evening and there was no sound in the house. Through one of the broken panes I heard the rain impinge upon the earth, the fine incessant needles of water playing in the sodden beds. Some distant lamp or lighted window gleamed below me. I was thankful that I could see so little. All my senses seemed to desire to veil themselves and, feeling that I was about to slip from them, I pressed the palms of my hands together until they trembled, murmuring: *"O love! O love!"* many times.

At last she spoke to me. When she addressed the first words to me I was so confused that I did not know what to answer. She asked me was I going to *Araby*. I forgot whether I answered yes or no. It would be a splendid bazaar, she said she would love to go.

"And why can't you?" I asked.

While she spoke she turned a silver bracelet round and round her wrist. She could not go, she said, because there would be a retreat that week in her convent. Her brother and two other boys were fighting for their caps and I was alone at the railings. She held one of the spikes, bowing her head towards me. The light from the lamp opposite our door caught the white curve of her neck, lit up her hair that rested there and, falling, lit up the hand upon the railing. It fell over one side of her dress and caught the white border of a petticoat, just visible as she stood at ease.

"It's well for you," she said.

"If I go," I said, "I will bring you something."

What innumerable follies laid waste my waking and sleeping thoughts after that evening! I wished to annihilate the tedious intervening days. I chafed against the work of school. At night in my bedroom and by day in the classroom her image came between me and the page I strove to read. The syllables of the word *Araby* were called to me through the silence in which my soul luxuriated and cast an Eastern enchantment over me. I asked for leave to go to the bazaar on Saturday night. My aunt was surprised and hoped it was not some Freemason affair. I answered few questions in class. I watched my master's face pass from amiability to sternness; he hoped I was not beginning to idle. I could not call my wandering thoughts together. I had hardly any patience with the serious work of life which, now that it stood between me and my desire, seemed to me child's play, ugly monotonous child's play.

On Saturday morning I reminded my uncle that I wished to go to the bazaar in the evening. He was fussing at the hallstand, looking for the hat-brush, and answered me curtly:

"Yes, boy, I know."

As he was in the hall I could not go into the front parlour and lie at the window. I left the house in bad humour and walked slowly towards the school. The air was pitilessly raw and already my heart misgave me.

When I came home to dinner my uncle had not yet been home. Still it was early. I sat staring at the clock for some time and, when its ticking began to irritate me, I left the room. I mounted the staircase and gained the upper part of the house. The high cold empty gloomy rooms liberated me and I went from room to room singing. From the front window I saw my companions playing below in the street. Their cries reached me weakened and indistinct and, leaning my forehead against the cool glass, I looked over at the dark house where she lived. I may have stood there for an hour, seeing nothing but the brown-clad figure cast by my imagination, touched discreetly by the lamplight at the curved neck, at the hand upon the railings and at the border below the dress.

When I came downstairs again I found Mrs. Mercer sitting at the fire. She was an old garrulous woman, a pawnbroker's widow, who collected used stamps for some pious purpose. I had to endure the gossip of the tea-table. The meal was prolonged beyond an hour and still my uncle did not come. Mrs. Mercer stood up to go: she was sorry she couldn't wait any longer, but it was after eight o'clock and she did not like to be out late, as the night air was bad for her. When she had gone I began to walk up and down the room, clenching my fists. My aunt said:

"I'm afraid you may put off your bazaar for this night of our Lord."

At nine o'clock I heard my uncle's latchkey in the hall door. I heard him talking to himself and heard the hallstand rocking when it had received the weight of his overcoat. I could interpret these signs. When he was midway through his dinner I asked him to give me the money to go to the bazaar. He had forgotten.

"The people are in bed and after their first sleep now," he said.

I did not smile. My aunt said to him energetically:

"Can't you give him the money and let him go? You've kept him late enough as it is."

My uncle said he was very sorry he had forgotten. He said he believed in the old saying: "All work and no play makes Jack a dull boy." He asked me where I was going and, when I had told him a second time he asked me did I know *The Arab's Farewell to His Steed.* When I left the kitchen he was about to recite the opening lines of the piece to my aunt.

I held a florin tightly in my hand as I strode down Buckingham Street towards the station. The sight of the streets thronged with buyers and glaring with gas recalled to me the purpose of my journey. I took my seat in a third-class carriage of a deserted train. After an intolerable delay the train moved out of the station slowly. It crept onward among ruinous houses and over the twinkling river. At Westland Row Station a crowd of people pressed to the carriage doors; but the porters moved them back, saying that it was a special train for the bazaar. I remained alone in the bare carriage. In a few minutes the train drew up beside an improvised wooden platform. I passed out on to the road and saw by the lighted dial of a clock that it was ten minutes to ten. In front of me was a large building which displayed the magical name.

I could not find any sixpenny entrance and, fearing that the bazaar would be closed, I passed in quickly through a turnstile, handing a shilling to a weary-looking man. I found myself in a big hall girdled at half its height by a gallery. Nearly all the stalls were closed and the greater part of the hall was in darkness. I recognised a silence like that which pervades a church after a service. I walked into the centre of the bazaar timidly. A few people were gathered about the stalls which were still open. Before a curtain, over which the words *Cafe Chantant* were written in coloured lamps, two men were counting money on a salver. I listened to the fall of the coins.

Remembering with difficulty why I had come I went over to one of the stalls and examined porcelain vases and flowered tea-sets. At the door of the stall a young lady was talking and laughing with two young gentlemen. I remarked their English accents and listened vaguely to their conversation.

"O, I never said such a thing!"

"Oh, but you did!"

"O, but I didn't!"

"Didn't she say that?"

"Yes. I heard her."

"O, there's a . . . fib!"

Observing me the young lady came over and asked me did I wish to buy anything. The tone of her voice was not encouraging; she seemed to have spoken to me out of a sense of duty. I looked humbly at the great jars that stood like eastern guards at either side of the dark entrance to the stall and murmured:

"No, thank you."

The young lady changed the position of one of the vases and went back to the two young men. They began to talk of the same subject. Once or twice the young lady glanced at me over her shoulder.

I lingered before her stall, though I knew my stay was useless, to make my interest in her wares seem the more real. Then I turned away slowly and walked down the middle of the bazaar. I allowed the two pennies to fall against the sixpence in my pocket. I heard a voice call from one end of the gallery that the light was out. The upper part of the hall was now completely dark.

Gazing up into the darkness I saw myself as a creature driven and derided by vanity; and my eyes burned with anguish and anger.

1. DISCOVERING THE DRAMATIC EXPERIENCE

On first reading, James Joyce's "Araby" seems to be a story of first love. We know, if we have read the story in *Dubliners,* that the setting is Dublin, Ireland, around the turn of the century. Otherwise we can guess that the setting is Irish by the line describing the street-singers who "sang a *come-you-all* about O'Donovan Rossa, or a ballard about the troubles in our native land." On the narrative level, we easily discern that a young boy, nearing manhood, has fallen in love with the girl next door. He is shy, and therefore he does not speak to the girl but watches, hidden, for sight of her. She fills all his dreams and thoughts, and when at last they speak, he promises that if he goes to the bazaar, *Araby,* he will buy her a present. On the following Saturday evening, after his forgetful uncle finally comes homes with money for the fair, the boy takes a train to the bazaar, arriving, however, just as it is closing. The hall is in darkness, the stalls are empty, and the boy, disappointed and angry, fails to get the gift.

The surface action seems simple, but even on casual reading many of the descriptive terms may be bewildering, and the last lines in which the boy sees himself "as a creature driven and derided by vanity" cannot be explained in terms of the summary action. How can the shy boy consider himself vain? To answer this question, the reader must look to the various techniques Joyce employs to tell his story. Beginning with the opening description, we discover that we are apparently dealing with more than a typical love story.

2. DISCOVERING THE AUTHOR'S PRESENTATION

If we determine on close examination that the author has made no direct statement, and that the boy's final frustration culminates in the last two lines of the story, we must consider those lines an indirect statement and look elsewhere for their meaning. An examination of the language in "Araby" points up the fact that the boy could not think in such mature terms, nor with the sophisticated perspective present in the story. As a result, Joyce's use of point of view is important to the reader's understanding of the story.

Point of View

Both in Section One (pages 8–9) and in this section (pages 83–85) we pointed to several advantages and restrictions inherent in the use of the first person point of view. To succeed, the author must make his story credible, and at the same time he must approach his subject in a manner that enables him to achieve maximum dramatic immediacy while remaining free to fully render his theme. The first person limited viewpoint is restrictive, but it also accommodates the subjective approach. In "Araby," Joyce takes advantage of both the objectivity of the observer and the subjectivity of the participant by using a narrator, grown to maturity, who recalls a moment of particular importance in his youth. The story is told in retrospect, and the narrator and the boy are thus merged into the same person. The narrator is, as a result, free to employ a sophisticated, mature level of language and to place the incident in perspective. At the same time, the reader directly experiences the boy's emotion and confusion, but from sufficient distance to make an evaluation. The boy undoubtedly did not understand the meaning of his experience when it occurred. The same boy, grown to manhood and looking back on the experience, does understand it.

This use of a double viewpoint—the boy's and the man's—affects the entire story. First, the narrator can and does comment on the boy's experience. Time has brought perspective and objectivity, and the narrator condenses, intensifies, and evaluates, selecting for his story only those highly concentrated moments that never fade from memory. Secondly, the story's meaning is expanded and deepened by the author's adroit use of a double viewpoint because we feel in the tone and voice of the narrator that the boy's experience continues to be important to the man. For example, when the mature narrator says, "Her name sprang to my lips at moments in strange prayers and praises which I myself did not understand," we see the boy both as an individual and at the same time as representational (see page 85) of a truth only sensed in youth and recognized in adulthood. Thus, the event is given added importance, and this fact profoundly affects the theme or meaning of the story. Finally, the use of a double or reinforced vision enables the author to present the story on both a literal and a symbolic level. The boy is Catholic; the frame of reference and experience are his. The narrator evaluates the boy and his condition by objectifying the boy's experience and rendering it through symbolism and myth. The result is an enlargement of the meaning of an otherwise simple and commonplace experience. It is this enlarged meaning we must comprehend.

Symbolism

From the first line to the last we can discern that the story occurs on several levels. Descriptions of light, sound, and color represent emotions and states of being. The story abounds with ecclesiastic symbols, which finally and ironically merge with the symbolism of the Orient. This fact we discover slowly through a study of the imagery and description.

SYMBOLISM IN SETTING. If we examine the opening description of North Richmond Street in terms of the whole story, we discover that the setting is subject to at least two symbolic interpretations. The first pays close attention to the word "blind" on a metaphorical level. The setting for the story, and the world in which the boy lives, is not just a quiet street in urban Dublin but, as the houses reflect the character of their inhabitants, a street where falsely pious people maintain for their neighbors' approval the outward show of "decent lives." When we note Mrs. Mercer's life of endless gossip over tea, we can guess that the neighborhood thrives on gossip and hypocrisy, and that in this Catholic community devotion to God consists of lip service rather than true faith. The other reading of the opening description interprets the entire setting as a symbol: the street becomes the aisle of a church, the uninhabited house at the end an altar. This reading, coupled with the concept of blindness or unawareness, renders the boy's neighborhood a place where spiritual faith has died.

The concept of spiritual decay is further developed in the next paragraphs, which describe the boy's house and the priest who had died there. Again we look not only at the actual scene as it is realistically depicted but to the ideas that are represented. The priest, a symbol of faith and the clergy, is clearly dead as an active, vital force, but we can speculate about his life. *The Abbot* and *The Memoris of Vidocq* are two novels found in his room. Both were tales of romance and adventure. We can speculate that the priest secretly shirked his duties and escaped into fantasy, or we can interpret the priest as a warm human being who not only made his rounds on his bicycle to help the needy but who communicated with them on a level they could understand. The rusted bicycle pump may be read as a sign of former active service to man and God, or, conversely, as the priest's taking up the *mechanics* of service similar to the vacuous lip service of the street's inhabitants. In either case, the image evoked by the dead priest and his belongings reinforces the interpretation that the street (and thus the boy's world) is a place of spiritual and moral stagnation. The depressing mustiness of the old houses, cluttered with remnants of the past, adds to an atmosphere of decay; and the colors called out—the yellow of the priest's old books and the brown of the houses—become symbolic of corruption and, as we explore the labyrinth of imagery in the story, of betrayal. The reader might expect the sky, like the books, to reflect the lives of the people; instead, its "ever-changing violet," suggesting the color of kings or of church, is in ironic contrast to the dullness and paralysis below. To epitomize the symbolic imagery, Joyce carefully places a "central apple-tree" in the boy's "wild garden"; it is an unmistakable symbol, from the Biblical Garden of Eden, of lost innocence. Into this symbolic setting, Joyce introduces the boy and girl and first love.

SYMBOLISM IN CHARACTERIZATION.   To deduce the full meaning of the nature of the boy's love, we turn again to the story's descriptive imagery. The light, which is first introduced into the setting by the street lamps' lifting their "feeble lanterns" to the sky, assumes the dimensions of a motif in the rest of the story. It represents the feeble vitality and false faith of North Richmond Street's inhabitants and, conversely, suggests the divine light of love and purity. Thus used in the story, light is a medium for the narrator's subtle and ironic commentary upon the girl as the boy sees her and upon the boy, whose spiritual blindness leads him on a quest doomed to failure. This point is made clear in the descriptions of the girl.

As a result of the boy's growing infatuation, he increasingly confuses the image of the girl in a jumble of romantic and ecclesiastical symbols. Torn between lust and adoration, the boy first views the girl as a "figure defined by the light from the half-opened door." Remember that the light inside the house symbolically represents its occupants; the girl becomes a tenuous figure of promise and temptation to the boy, but to the reader and the narrator, she is a quite ordinary product of North Richmond Street, as evidenced by her banal conversation and her preoccupation with the glamour of a carnival. The girl remains nameless in the story, which is both appropriate and ironic; the dream has no substance, and its object, in retrospect, often passes as tenuously as the dream.

Mangan's sister, a figure in the doorway, becomes "a summons to all . . . [his] . . . foolish blood." She becomes a saintly image, transported in the boy's mind into a world of mystical beauty. "Her name sprang to . . . [his] . . . lips at moments in strange prayers and praises" and he is consumed by "confused adoration." The motif of the light, used ironically to comment upon the superficiality of the boy's adoration, occurs again when the boy walks through the "flaring streets" of the market place. The parcels he carries for his aunt become a "chalice" he bears "safely through a throng of foes." Symbolically he becomes an acolyte in a church service, and at the same time his quasireligious thoughts merge with sensual desire and he becomes a knight and Mangan's sister a fair princess. His "adoration" (in itself a religious term) is decidedly confused. Because the season of the year nears Christmas (it is the time of the Advent in Dublin), the boy's religious transference is pathetic, for such romantic rebirth is not possible. Also, the confusion of the devout and the sensual is blasphemous. In any event, nothing, we realize, can endure that originates under blind delusions. One evening the boy goes to the back room where the priest had died and pressing his palms together, murmurs over and over, "O love! O love!" It is a prayer, not to God, but to romantic passion. The boy's confused vision of the girl as both temptress and saint is emphasized by the light motif in the following lines: "The light from the lamp opposite our door caught the white curve of her neck, lit up her hair that rested there and, falling, lit up the hand upon the railing. It fell over one side of her dress and caught the white border of a petticoat, just visible as she stood at ease."

The motif by which the boy's world is illuminated in his imagination foreshadows the coming darkness of failure when, waiting for his uncle to return home with money for the bazaar, he stares at the "dark house where she lived," seeing her as a "brown-clad figure cast by . . . [his] . . . imagination, touched discreetly by the lamp-light at the curved neck, at the hand upon the railings and at the border below the dress." The symbolism of the color brown and the darkness of the houses, like the sensual sugges- tiveness of the petticoat, show that the boy's quest for fulfillment is futile. His spiritual awareness, like that of the people of Dublin, is paralyzed.

The imagery of the first half of the story—the light and dark motif, the ecclesiastical and romantic symbolism—serves as preparation for the final action, the boy's trip to *Araby*. Images from the setting recur as he impatiently waits to set out on his trip. The aunt expresses prejudice when she hopes *Araby* will not be "some Freemason affair." As it grows late, and the boy is conscious only of worldly time, of each passing minute, the aunt refers (ironically to us) to the timeless: "this night of our Lord." The uncle, on returning, prepares to recite the romantic poem about the Arab and his steed, a delay that only stimulates, without the uncle's awareness (the uncle, like the aunt and the rest of the street, is blind), the boy's an- guished drive to get to the bazaar. In the boy's mind, *Araby* has come to embody an "Eastern enchantment." As a result of the inordinate hope he places in the answers and satisfactions the bazaar will bring, the boy faces the fact that his hopes were built on dreams and self-delusions, and the narrative moves to the major symbol of the story.

Araby at first presents itself to the boy only in the glowing letters of the "magic name." Magic, or sorcery, now replaces images of the church. When the boy enters the bazaar, it is closing, and he gazes up into the darkness (the motif of blindness and loss of faith) and recognizes "a si- lence like that which pervades a church after a service."

Once again we can make several interpretations concerning a major symbol, though the effect on the story will be the same. *Araby* can repre- sent a dream of beauty that is shattered by reality, and we have either the converse of the romantic tales or the ugly magically transformed into the beautiful, or we have the sad realization that life is never the beautiful world youth desires and imagines. Another, more desolate, interpretation returns to Christian symbolism in a predominatly Catholic country; *Araby* represents the profane church. The boy would then be guilty of having for- saken the true faith for one of sensual, false pleasure. If this is true, his feeling for the girl is deeply sinful, for he has come close to deifying her in a false temple and has taken on other false gods. Either interpretation must accommodate the boy's discovery that the profane temple, the end of his quest, is corrupt, for "two men were counting money on a salver" and the fall of coins sounds in the stillness. The words *Cafe Chantant* are writ- ten in "colored lamps" (another use of the light image), and in the hall, a symbol of exotic love, a young woman carries on a meaningless flirtation with two men. The boy leaves slowly and hears "a voice call from one end of the gallery that the light was out." We can gather that even the artificial light of the dream and self-delusion is out.

Myth and Archetype

Discovering a few of the many possible meanings of the symbolism in the story necessitates a synthesis, a drawing together of these symbols to discern their larger meaning. In "Araby," we look to the broad concepts that originate in the Christian myth, the quest theme, and the associations pertaining to the Orient.

If we consider the life of Christ, and the ability of his teachings to make life meaningful, and in addition if we understand something of the powerful symbolism that has attached to the Cross and the Church for twenty centuries, it is no wonder we are deeply stirred by the story even though we may not fully understand why. First, Christ promised a deliverance from suffering and a heavenly Paradise to be gained through faith. Behind this promise, and at its heart, lies the Garden of Eden and original sin. Before Adam tasted of the apple he knew immortality and true selfhood. Afterward, he knew sin, death, and shame. He had lost his innocence. He had lost Paradise until Christ came and gave him another chance. But, blighted in spirit, lusting after the worldly, searching for the easy Paradise, man's second chance proves difficult to attain.

The archetypal pattern in which man yearns and searches for deliverance from pain and death runs through all religions and is one of our oldest quests. At the source of "Araby" we also find the quest—for the Holy Grail, for eternal youth, for redemption, for faith in life and hope, for Paradise. This translates into man's search not only for his soul, but for happiness, and when happiness is figured in terms of gaining worldly values rather than those of the spirit, the quest deteriorates. The apple tree becomes a sad reminder of loss, for rules attend the gaining of peace and fulfillment in all myth. Man cannot substitute material for spiritual values. He cannot lust for the flesh as the answer to Paradise, for flesh dies. He cannot, also, quest in the wrong direction, or with a false goal, and hope to find any answer but that of failure. Yet, blind, weak, dark in spirit as he may be, man searches on, for the quest for love, whether carnal or divine, both within and separate from the Christian myth, is one of man's deepest drives.

Within these themes of the quest and the injunctions and promises in Christianity, the boy in "Araby" tries to find fulfillment and happiness. He experiences first love, but ironically, the girl is not even aware of his feeling for her, and because he is shy, and because he is blind, his quest becomes confused between a search for carnal love and a search for spiritual love. He transforms the girl in his imagination into a sensuous, mystical saintly figure—an image both desirable and unattainable. On a personal level the boy pursues a hopeless dream. No mortal could live up to the image he creates in his dreams. His goal from the outset is unattainable. But the boy's quest grows, and he commits a further folly when he transfers his adoration from the girl to the idea of "Oriental enchantment," to an unearthly paradise suffused with exotic perfumes and promises of carnal joy. The word "Araby" derives from Arabia, a mystical land, called variously in different mythologies "the Sheba of the Bible," "Araby the blest," or "Arabia Felix," and consists, essentially, of dreams. As a unique individual experiencing a universal experience, the boy's desire is based on delusion. If the boy, however, is to be considered a representative of youth and of Dublin, we see his plight as a universal condition, and in such case he represents man's succumbing to worldly temptations and losing the spiritual values of redemption, the only values that will bring true fulfillment.

Structure

The closer we come to understanding the meaning of the last lines of the story, the more we realize that the story is not fragmentary, or abrupt, or a mere sketch, but consists of a complete statement symbolically rendered. Plot, as we have discovered, is of little importance in the story. Rather, the structure and the concept of motionless spatiality provide the vehicle for Joyce's statement.

The story, basically a portrait of a boy's journey from blindness to inner awareness, functions much like a wheel. The boy's state of mind constitutes the hub; the spokes—North Richmond Street, Mangan's sister, his aunt and uncle, his trip to *Araby*—make up the conditions of his world. Expressed on a symbolic level, the structure is basically still or static, and the reader experiences the convergence of all the parts. The result, at the conclusion of the story, is a state of rest, for all the elements have interacted to achieve a single effect. It is this single effect that constitutes the theme.

3. DISCOVERING SUBJECT AND THEME

To synthesize the total effect of the story and its resultant meaning, we see the man, the narrator, recalling a moment that seemed at the time to call forth all the promise and dream of youth: romance, an awakening to life. The man, however, also recalls the result of that moment of seemingly endless possibility—the sudden and irreparable disappointment and disillusion. The boy, gazing up into the darkness sees himself "as a creature driven and derided by vanity: and . . . [his] . . . eyes burned with anguish and anger." An examination now of these terms will provide some answers.

Like other elements in the story, the final lines are also subject to multiple interpretation, depending upon the emphasis we place on the narrator. We can say that the boy suddenly realizes the futility of his situation, that he has been duped. *Araby* is a farce. However, he also realizes, which is worse and which results in "anguish," that he has duped himself. Everything he has thought and dreamed and imagined has been based not only on what really existed, but on what he made of it in his own mind. The real was always there, but he transformed it all—his love, his quest to *Araby*—into a nonexistent ideal. He sees the discrepancy, finally, between the real and the dream; and the dream fails, as it must. He therefore is left with nothing.

A further extension of the boy's disillusionment is that he realizes that life is ugly; he must see it as not beautiful, but stagnant and smelling of "ashpits." He has at this point an unexpressed but explicit choice: to correct his erroneous view of the world and turn to true spiritual values, or to retain anger and recognition of deceit as his life's attitude.

The word "vanity," however, elicits other, deeper meanings. Perhaps the word is an allusion to the Biblical "Vanity of vanities; all is vanity," in which man is exhorted to turn from the worldly to the spiritual because the things of this world are without lasting value. If so, the boy at the moment of his despair may realize his self-deception but be incapable of replacing his false values with good ones because, as a member of his society, he has lost the way. The setting of the story indicates he may have lost the way permanently. The narrator, however, seems to know better. His view of the world of Dublin and of the boy's folly is so clear, we can guess he has grown larger and wiser than the world of his boyhood. If this be the case the story consists of a true beginning at its conclusion. If not, it is truly the end. Man is lost. Paradise is lost. The apple tree, symbolic of man's fall from grace, is a continuing condition in spite of Christ's promise of hope.

However, if man can realize the futility of the false dream, as the narrator seems to imply by his tone and his perspective, man can yet reach toward the "ever-changing violet" of the sky. Though the discrepancy between the ideal and the real, the false and the true, will continue to be a problem all through life, man can grow. He does have a choice. And realizing the content of the choices open to him, he has not lost Paradise.

The story, open-ended, offers these and other choices of interpretation. Joyce leaves the reader, like the boy, to decide.

SAMPLE ESSAYS

The following six essays, based on the story "Araby," are designed to serve as models to help you fulfill your writing assignments. Additional essays, which examine other elements in the story, can of course be written. For example, essays applying biography or analyzing structure or dominant metaphor (demonstrated in Sections Four and Five of this book) contain legitimate and useful subject matter. The essays that follow are only a few examples of the many subjects possible.

Before you read on, review the principles of critical writing explained in Section Two. Then study the essays below, which demonstrate the methods employed in narrowing the subject and formulating and developing the introduction, body, and conclusion.

SAMPLE ESSAY 1
USING SUMMARY

INSTRUCTIONS.   The summary essay is particularly valuable to a reader unfamiliar with a work. A good summary not only recounts the high points of the story and plot, but explains how the work is organized and gives its meaning. Summary is not a mere synopsis of the action. In writing a summary, you interpret a work's meaning and significance by synthesizing the points you consider most important and by explaining the relationship of these points to the theme.

To organize the summary essay, carefully read the work to determine its main idea or theme. A statement of the theme with an indication of how the theme is developed will provide you with a thesis, which will focus your essay and suggest its organization. Look at the thesis statement in the summary essay below. By stating that "the discrepancy between the real and the ideal in life is revealed through the boy's progression from first love to disillusion and disappointment," the author not only provides a unifying concept for the entire essay, but gives a significant and meaningful interpretation. A mere listing of the superficial action is of no value to a reader who seeks understanding.

After you have formulated your thesis, list in chronological order the high points in the organizational movement of the work: the opening, the major developments in the body, and the conclusion or resolution. In the short story, "Araby," the high points consist of the setting, the boy's first love, his growing sense of isolation, and his subsequent trip to the bazaar. Listing these points serves two purposes: it enables you to compress the story and to emphasize its development; and it provides you with the major units (or paragraphs) in the body of your essay.

After you have organized your thesis and summary outline and have interpreted each movement in the action, you are ready to write—to fill in your outline with content. The content consists of brief but concise condensations of the action of the story. The content tells your reader what happens. Remember that you cannot relate *all* the action. Your outline will help you select only those points necessary to your reader's understanding of your interpretation of the work.

Study the summary essay below to discover its organization. Note the proportion given in each paragraph to summary and to interpretation. The introduction identifies the work and the author. Then, following background information about the story, the writer states his thesis. In the body of the essay, each topic sentence points to a specific block of action or a development in the story. The content of each paragraph is devoted to a summary of a selected block of action, and the last sentence of each paragraph evaluates and interprets the action described. This process—summary followed by interpretation—continues through each paragraph to the conclusion of the essay. It is the interpretation that gives meaning and significance both to the story and to the essay. In the essay that follows, note the use of quotations and how each aids understanding and imparts a sense of the style and manner of the work.

JAMES JOYCE'S "ARABY":
SUMMARY OF AN EPIPHANY

Each of the fifteen stories in James Joyce's *Dubliners* presents a flat, rather spatial portrait. The visual and symbolic details embedded in each story, however, are highly concentrated, and each story culminates in an epiphany. In Joycean terms, an epiphany is a moment when the essence of a character is revealed, when all the forces that bear on his life converge, and we can, in that instant, understand him. Each story in the collection is centered in an epiphany, and each story is concerned with some failure or deception, which results in realization and disillusionment. "Araby" follows this pattern. The meaning is revealed in a young boy's psychic journey from first love to despair and disappointment, and the theme is found in the boy's discovery of the discrepancy between the real and the ideal in life.

The story opens with a description of North Richmond Street, a "blind," "cold," "silent" street where the houses "gazed at one another with brown imperturbable faces." It is a street of fixed, decaying conformity and false piety. The boy's house contains the same sense of a dead present and a lost past. The former tenant, a priest, died in the back room of the house, and his legacy—several old yellowed books, which the boy enjoys leafing through because they are old, and a bicycle pump rusting in the back yard—become symbols of the intellectual and religious vitality of the past. The boy, in the midst of such decay and spiritual paralysis, experiences the confused idealism and dreams of first love and his awakening becomes incompatible with and in ironic contrast to the staid world about him.

Every morning before school the boy lies on the floor in the front parlor peeking out through a crack in the blind of the door, watching and waiting for the girl next door to emerge from her house and walk to school. He is shy and still boyish. He follows her, walks silently past, not daring to speak, overcome with a confused sense of sensual desire and religious adoration. In his mind she is both a saint to be worshipped and a woman to be desired. His eyes are "often full of tears," and one evening he goes to the back room where the priest had died. Clasping the palms of his hands together, he murmurs, "O love! O love!" in a prayer not to God, but to the concept of love and perhaps even to the girl, his love. Walking with his aunt to shop on Saturday evenings he imagines that the girl's image accompanies him, and that he protects her in "places the most hostile to romance." In the mixed symbolism of the Christian and the Romantic or Oriental myths Joyce reveals the epiphany in the story: "These noises converged in a single sensation of life for me: I imagined that I bore my chalice safely through a throng of foes." He is unable to talk to the girl. Drifting away from his schoolmates' boyish games, the boy has fantasies in his isolation, in the ecstasy and pain of first love.

Finally the girl speaks to the boy. She asks him if he is going to *Araby*. He replies that if he does he will bring her a gift, and from that moment, his thoughts upon the mixed imagery of the saintly light upon her hair and the potential sensuality of "the white border of a petticoat," the boy cannot sleep or study. The word *Araby* "cast an Eastern enchantment" over him, and then on the night he is to go to the bazaar his uncle neglects to return home. Neither the aunt nor uncle understands the boy's need and anguish, and thus his isolation is deepened. We begin to see that the story is not so much a story of love as it is a rendition of the world in which the boy lives.

The second part of the story depicts the boy's inevitable disappointment and realization. In such an atmosphere of "blindness"—the aunt and uncle unaware of the boy's anguish, the girl not conscious of the boy's love, and the boy himself blind to the true nature of his love—the words "hostile to romance" take on ironic overtones.

These overtones deepen when the boy arrives too late at the bazaar. It is closing and the hall is "in darkness." He recognizes "a silence like that which prevades a church after a service" but the bazaar is dirty and disappointing. Two men are "counting money on a salver" and he listens "to the fall of the coins." A young lady, bored with him and interested in two men who are flirting with her, cheapens and destroys the boy's sense of an "Eastern enchantment." His love, like his quest for a gift to draw the girl to him in an unfriendly world, ends with his realizing that his love existed only in his mind. Thus the theme of the story—the discrepancy between the real and the ideal—is made final in the bazaar, a place of tawdry make-believe. The epiphany in which the boy lives a dream in spite of the ugly and the worldly is brought to its inevitable conclusion: the single sensation of life disintegrates. The boy senses the falsity of his dreams and his eyes burn "with anguish and anger."

SAMPLE ESSAY 2
USING SETTING AND ATMOSPHERE

INSTRUCTIONS.   If you are asked to write an essay analyzing the setting and atmosphere in a work, review pages 70–73 and determine, first, how setting and atmosphere contribute to the meaning of the work. Remember that setting is usually a part of atmosphere and that atmosphere consists of the prevailing tone of the work and its resultant meaning or effect. Some works will not warrant an essay devoted to setting and atmosphere; others, like Joyce's "Araby," will be so profoundly dependent upon a particular setting that to ignore its importance will be to miss much of the meaning of the work.

DREAM VERSUS REALITY:
SETTING AND ATMOSPHERE IN JAMES JOYCE'S "ARABY"

Convinced that the Dublin of the 1900's was a center of spiritual paralysis, James Joyce loosely but thematically tied together his stories in *Dubliners* by means of their common setting. Each of the stories consists of a portrait in which Dublin contributes in some way to the dehumanizing experience of modern life. The boy in the story "Araby" is intensely subject to the city's dark, hopeless conformity, and his tragic yearning toward the exotic in the face of drab, ugly reality forms the center of the story.

On its simplest level, "Araby" is a story about a boy's first love.

On a deeper level, however, it is a story about the world in which he lives—a world inimical to ideals and dreams. This deeper level is introduced and developed in several scenes: the opening description of the boy's street, his house, his relationship to his aunt and uncle, the information about the priest and his belongings, the boy's two trips —his walks through Dublin shopping and his subsequent ride to *Araby.*

North Richmond Street is described metaphorically and presents the reader with his first view of the boy's world. The street is "blind"; it is a dead end, yet its inhabitants are smugly complacent; the houses reflect the attitudes of their inhabitants. The houses are "imperturbable" in the "quiet," the "cold," the "dark muddy lanes" and "dark dripping gardens." The first use of situational irony is introduced here, because anyone who is aware, who is not spiritually blinded or asleep, would feel oppressed and endangered by North Richmond Street. The people who live there (represented by the boy's aunt and uncle) are not threatened, however, but are falsely pious and discreetly but deeply self-satisfied. Their prejudice is dramatized by the aunt's hopes that *Araby,* the bazaar the boy wants to visit, is not "some Freemason affair," and by old Mrs. Mercer's gossiping over tea while collecting stamps for "some pious purpose."

The background or world of blindness extends from a general view of the street and its inhabitants to the boy's personal relationships. It is not a generation gap but a gap in the spirit, in empathy and conscious caring, that results in the uncle's failure to arrive home in time for the boy to go to the bazaar while it is still open. The uncle has no doubt been to the local pub, negligent and indifferent to the boy's anguish and impatience. The boy waits well into the evening in the "imperturbable" house with its musty smell and old, useless objects that fill the rooms. The house, like the aunt and uncle, and like the entire neighborhood, reflects people who are well-intentioned but narrow in their views and blind to higher values (even the street lamps lift a "feeble" light to the sky). The total effect of such setting is an atmosphere permeated with stagnation and isolation.

The second use of symbolic description—that of the dead priest and his belongings—suggests remnants of a more vital past. The bicycle pump rusting in the rain in the back yard and the old yellowed books in the back room indicate that the priest once actively engaged in real service to God and man, and further, from the titles of the books, that he was a person given to both piety and flights of imagination. But the priest is dead; his pump rusts; his books yellow. The effect is to deepen, through a sense of a dead past, the spiritual and intellectual stagnation of the present.

Into this atmosphere of spiritual paralysis the boy bears, with blind hopes and romantic dreams, his encounter with first love. In the face of ugly, drab reality—"amid the curses of laborers," "jostled by drunken men and bargaining women"—he carries his aunt's parcels as she shops in the market place, imagining that he bears, not parcels, but a "chalice through a throng of foes." The "noises converged in a single sensation of life" and in a blending of Romantic and Christian symbols he transforms in his mind a perfectly ordinary girl into an enchanted princess: untouchable, promising, saintly. Setting in this scene depicts the harsh, dirty reality of life which the boy blindly ignores. The contrast between the real and the boy's dreams is ironically drawn and clearly foreshadows the boy's inability to keep the dream, to remain blind.

The boy's final disappointment occurs as a result of his awakening to the world around him. The tawdry superficiality of the bazaar, which in his mind had been an "Oriental enchantment," strips away his blindness and leaves him alone with the realization that life and love differ from the dream. *Araby,* the symbolic temple of love, is profane. The bazaar is dark and empty; it thrives on the same profit motive as the market place ("two men were counting money on a salver"); love is represented as an empty, passing flirtation.

"Araby" is a story of first love; even more, it is a portrait of a world that defies the ideal and the dream. Thus setting in this story becomes the true subject, embodying an atmosphere of spiritual paralysis against which a young boy's idealistic dreams are no match. Realizing this, the boy takes his first step into adulthood.

SAMPLE ESSAY 3
USING SYMBOLISM

INSTRUCTIONS. In preparation for writing the essay using symbolism, reread pages 11–14 in Section One.

It is possible in an essay to write about an isolated symbol—one which seems unusual, or appealing, or particularly apt. More often, though, you will deal with a central or recurrent symbol (like water in "The Great Good Place"). If you write about an isolated symbol, your thesis should be a strong statement of the existence of the symbol in the work, and the body of your essay should be composed of statements that actually constitute evidence of the existence of the symbol. As you develop paragraphs in the body of the essay, make clear your reasons for ascribing the symbolic significance you do, show the function of the symbol in the work, and, above all, prove that awareness of the symbol enriches understanding or appreciation of the work. In an essay using a central or recurrent symbol your principal task will be to show how each appearance of the symbol relates to the significance of the total work. (See the student essay "Theme Through Symbol: Water and its Effect Upon George Dane," on page 41, and the essay below.)

THE CENTRAL SYMBOL OF THE CHURCH
IN JOYCE'S "ARABY"

Joyce's short story "Araby" is filled with symbolic images of a church. It opens and closes with strong symbols, and in the body of the story, the images are shaped by the young Irish narrator's impressions of the effect the Church of Ireland has upon the people of Ireland. The boy is fiercely determined to invest in someone within this Church the holiness he feels should be the natural state of all within it, but a succession of experiences forces him to see that his determination is in vain. At the climax of the story, when he realizes that his dreams of holiness and love are inconsistent with the actual world, his anger and anguish are directed, not toward the Church, but toward himself as "a creature driven by vanity." In addition to the images in the story that are symbolic of the Church and its effect upon the people who belong to it, there are descriptive words and phrases that add to this representational meaning.

The story opens with a description of the Dublin neighborhood where the boy lives. Strikingly suggestive of a church, the image shows the ineffectuality of the Church as a vital force in the lives of the inhabitants of the neighborhood—the faithful within the Church. North Richmond Street is composed of two rows of houses with "brown imperturbable faces" (the pews) leading down to the tall "uninhabited house" (the empty altar). The boy's own home is set in a garden the natural state of which would be like Paradise, since it contains a "central apple tree"; however, those who should have cared for it have allowed it to become desolate, and the central tree stands alone amid "a few straggling bushes." At dusk when the boy and his companions play in the street the lamps of the street lift their "feeble lanterns" to the sky of "ever-changing violet" (timid suppliants to the far-away heavens). Since the boy is the narrator, the inclusion of these symbolic images in the description of the setting shows that the boy is sensitive to the lack of spiritual beauty in his surroundings.

Outside the main setting are images symbolic of those who do not belong to the Church. The boy and his companions go there at times, behind their houses, along the "dark muddy lanes," to where the "rough tribes" (the infidel) dwell. Here odors arise from "the ashpits"—those images symbolic to James Joyce of the moral decay of his nation.

Even the house in which the youthful main character lives adds to the sense of moral decay. The former tenant, a priest (now dead), is shown to have been insensitive to the spiritual needs of his people. His legacy was a collection of books that showed his confusion of the sacred with the secular—and there is evidence that he devoted his life to gathering "money" and "furniture." He left behind no evidence of a life of spiritual influence.

Despite these discouraging surroundings, the boy is determined to find some evidence of the loveliness his idealistic dreams tell him should exist within the Church. His first love becomes the focal point of this determination. In the person of Mangan's sister, obviously somewhat older than the boy and his companions, his longings find an object of worship. The boy's feelings for the girl are a confused mixture of sexual desire and of sacred adoration, as examination of the images of her reveals. He is obsessed at one and the same time with watching her physical attractions (her white neck, her soft hair, the movement of the brown-clad figure) and with seeing her always surrounded by light, as if by a halo. He imagines that he can carry her "image" as a "chalice" through a "throng of foes"—the cursing, brawling infidels at the market to which he goes with his aunt. All other sensations of life "fade from his consciousness" and he is aware only of his adoration of the blessed "image." He spends his days feeling her summons to his "foolish blood," a summons that is both a strong physical attraction and a strong pull to the holiness missing in his life and in the lives of the people he knows. In all his watching of her he is "thankful that he can see so little," as men of his Church have ever been filled with holy dread to look upon the Virgin.

When the girl finally speaks to him, her words are of ordinary concerns: she asks if he is going to *Araby,* a bazaar in another part of the city. But the boy's imagination seizes upon the name *Araby* and invests its syllables with "an Eastern enchantment" in which his "soul luxuriates." *Araby* becomes a place where his soul can find the mystical beauty lacking in his own mundane Church. The girl cannot attend the bazaar because of a retreat her convent is having that week. As a consequence the boy feels a summons that has symbolic overtones of a holy crusade: he is determined to go forth to the "enchanted" place and bring back a gift worthy to lay at the feet of his adored one.

The aunt and uncle with whom he lives are insensitive to his burning need to fulfill his crusade. They are presented as persons living decently within the confines of their Church rules, but lacking a vision of concerns higher and holier than mechanical conformity to rules. They do, finally, though, provide the florin to allow him to go to *Araby*.

Alone, he makes his way to the place of Eastern enchantment. When he arrives, he is struck by a "silence like that of a church." This is followed by another image that calls up the image at the beginning of the story, that of the aisle leading to an altar. In this case, it is a hall leading to the booth displaying porcelain vases (chalices for the Eucharist), and flowered tea sets (the flowers on the altar). The great jars guarding the stall can be interpreted as symbols of the mysticism standing guard over the Church.

For the boy, the girl attending the stall, like Mangan's sister, becomes an object of faith. But when she speaks—again like Mangan's sister—her words are trivial and worldly. In a sudden flash of insight the boy sees that his faith and his passion have been blind. He sees in the "two men counting money on a salver" a symbol of the moneylenders in the temple. He allows the pennies to fall in his pocket. The lights in the hall go out; his "church" is in darkness. Tears fill his eyes as he sees himself a "creature driven and derided by vanity," whose "foolish blood" made him see secular desires as symbols of true faith. In this moment of disillusionment he feels that he himself is at fault for being so bemused by his ideals that he failed completely to see the world as it is. He has discovered in his Church and in love (both traditional symbols of ineffably sacred loveliness) only a shoddy imitation of true beauty. Understandably his disillusionment causes him "anguish and anger."

SAMPLE ESSAY 4
USING MYTH AND ARCHETYPE

INSTRUCTIONS.   In writing about myth and archetype as they appear in literature, we must be specific and accurate in our meaning and reference. Reread pages 15 and 16 to review the definitions of these terms and the methods of recognizing their patterns. Remember that myth is rooted in the supernatural; that it originates in stories once held—or still held—to be true by a people or nation; that its common themes center around attempts to explain the meaning of life and death (like the beliefs of Christianity and Buddhism), and to explain natural phenomena once believed to be a divine manifestation of emotions such as pleasure or anger (the Greek god Poseidon raising storms, Zeus hurtling his thunderbolt).

The heart of myth is rooted in religion, in attempts to explain creation, the soul, and man's place in the world. A discussion of myth, therefore, must be preceded by your discovery of its presence in a work; and for your discussion to be meaningful, you must understand the origin or source of the ideas you decide to ascribe to myth. (In "Araby," we perceive the clear presence of a reference to Christianity.)

If you decide to write, or are assigned to write, an essay using archetype, review pages 101–102 to familiarize yourself with the meaning of the word. Remember that archetype can be generously applied to a number of man's values, dreams, and beliefs, but that myth comprises only a part of archetype. Archetype is a much larger term, and if you perceive some universal experience in a literary work, it can quite logically form a part of our racial past. Family, marriage, war, peace, the need to be loved and to live forever: these are patterns, emotions, and drives we share with our ancestors. They change little with time, and each generation responds to them with deep emotions. The presence of archetype in a work gives that work added importance and an essay defining the archetype, its effect and resultant added meaning will be of value to readers who may have responded but have not discerned why.

To write an essay using myth and archetype, determine how their presence influences and reveals the meaning of the work. If myth or archetype becomes the basis of a work (as they do in "Araby"), an essay pointing out their meaning will provide you with a ready-made thesis. Ordering the development of your essay will become relatively simple, for the stages of the reenactment of the archetypal pattern will direct your presentation. If, on the other hand, the use of myth does not form the basis of the entire work, but is only an enrichment of another pattern, your order of development will be somewhat more complex. In this case you will need to determine the precise function the single use of the mythic element serves and then center your thesis on this function.

THE LONELY QUEST OF JAMES JOYCE'S "ARABY"

Probably no other twentieth century short story has called forth more attention than Joyce's "Araby." Some universality of experience makes the story interesting to readers of all ages, for they respond instinctively to an experience that could have been their own. It is a part of the instinctual nature of man to long for what he feels is the lost spirituality of his world. In all ages man has believed that it is possible to search for and find a talisman, which, if brought back, will return this lost spirituality. The development of theme in "Araby" resembles the archetypal myth of the quest for a holy talisman.

In "Araby," Joyce works from a "visionary mode of artistic

creation"—a phrase used by psychiatrist Carl Jung to describe the "visionary" kind of literary creation that derives its material from "the hinterland of man's mind—that suggests the abyss of time separating us from prehuman ages, or evokes a superhuman world of contrasting light and darkness. It is a primordial experience, which surpasses man's understanding and to which he is therefore in danger of succumbing." [1] Assuredly this describes Joyce's handling of the material of "Araby." The quest itself and its consequences surpass the understanding of the young protagonist of the story. He can only "feel" that he undergoes the experience of the quest and naturally is confused, and at the story's conclusion, when he fails, he is anguished and angered. His "contrasting world of light and darkness" contains both the lost spirituality and the dream of restoring it. Because our own worlds contain these contrasts we also "feel," even though the primordial experience surpasses our understanding, too.

It is true, as a writer reminds us, that "no matter the work, Joyce always views the order and disorder of the world in terms of the Catholic faith in which he was reared." [2] In "Araby," however, there is, in addition, an overlay of Eastern mysticism. This diversity of background materials intensifies the universality of the experience. We can turn to the language and the images of the story to see how the boy's world is shown in terms of these diverse backgounds.

There is little that is "light" in the corner of Dublin that forms the world of the story, little that retains its capability to evoke spirituality. North Richmond Street is "blind"; the houses stare at one another with "brown imperturbable faces." The time is winter, with its short days and its early dusk. Only the boy and his laughing, shouting companions "glow"; they are still too young to have succumbed to the spiritual decay of the adult inhabitants of Dublin. But the boys must play in "dark muddy lanes," in "dark dripping gardens," near "dark odorous stables" and "ashpits." Joyce had said of *Dubliners,* the collection of stories from which "Araby" comes, that he intended to "write a chapter in the moral history of my country and I chose Dublin for the scene because that city seemed to me the centre of paralysis." [3] The images of the story show us that the spiritual environment of the boy is paralyzed; it is musty, dark.

Everywhere in his dark surroundings the boy seeks the "light."

[1] Carl G. Jung, *Modern Man in Search of a Soul.* trans. W. S. Dell and Cary F. Baynes (New York, 1933), pp. 156–157.

[2] William Bysshe Stein, "Joyce's 'Araby': Paradise Lost," *Perspective,* XII, No. 4 (Spring 1962), 215.

[3] From *Letters of James Joyce,* Vol. II, ed. Richard Ellmann (New York, 1966), p. 134.

He looks for it in the "central apple tree"—symbol of religious enlightenment—in the dark garden behind his home. The garden should be like Eden, but the tree is overshadowed by the desolation of the garden, and thus has become the tree of spiritual death. He looks for light in the room of his home where the former tenant, a priest, had died, but the only objects left by the priest were books, yellowed and damp. Here, too, the quest has failed. No evidence of spiritual life remains. Decay and rust have taken over all the treasures the priest had laid up on earth for himself.

Into this world of darkness appears a girl, Mangan's sister. Because of her the boy feels a surge of hope that now in her love he will find light. Even though he has "never spoken to her, except for a few casual words," her name is like a "summons to all his foolish blood." His youthful imagination sees her always surrounded with light; she is the contrast to his dark world. She becomes an image to him of all that he seeks. That image accompanies him "even in places the most hostile to romance": the market and the streets, among the "drunken men and bargaining women," amid "the curses of labourers, the shrill litanies of shop-boys." In this unlikely place occurs what Joyce calls an "epiphany," which to him means "a sudden spiritual manifestation," when objects or moments of inconsequential vulgarity can be transfigured to something spiritual.[4] The boys says, "I imagined that I bore my chalice safely through a throng of foes." Plainly he has felt the summons to cherish the holy, the "light," in this dark world of those who are hostile to the sacred.

However, what he feels is beyond his understanding. His love for the girl is part sexual desire, part sacred adoration. He is, he says, "confused."

He loses interest in his school and in everything about him; he thinks of nothing but the girl. He can see her "dark house," "her brown-clad figure touched by lamp-light." He feels that he has found one image of holiness in his world of lost spirituality. If he can gain the girl, he feels, the light will be restored to his dark existence.

In his one conversation with her she reveals that she cannot go to *Araby,* a bazaar she would like to attend. She suggests that it would be "well" for him to go. He speaks impulsively: "If I go I will bring you something." His opportunity has come. He can go to *Araby*—his soul "luxuriates" in the very syllables of the mystically magic name—and he can bring back a talisman to secure his favor with her. The lost light of his world will be restored. Undoubtedly, as

[4] James Joyce, *Stephen Hero* (New York, 1944), pp. 210–211.

a writer suggests, *Araby* is "Arabia, which is associated with the Phoenix, symbol of the renewal of life." [5]

Over half the story is concerned with the delays and frustrations in his plans for his quest, and with his final journey to the "enchanted" place, where the talisman will be procured. Significantly, he must go to *Araby* alone. The train is deserted; when throngs of buyers try to press their way onto the train the porters move them back, saying this "is a special train for the bazaar." All who go on a quest for the high and the holy must go alone.

Arriving, he finds the bazaar nearly empty. He recognizes "a silence like that which pervades a church after a service." The church is empty; it is not attended by the faithful. Two men count money on a "silver salver." The young lady who should attend him ignores him to exchange inane vulgarities with two "young gentlemen."

Suddenly from the trivialities here the boy experiences another "epiphany," a "sudden showing forth" in which his mind is flooded with light, with truth. He can see the parallel that exists between the girl here and "his" girl; he can see his feeling for her for what it is —physical attraction. Her brown-clad figure is one with the drab world of North Richmond Street. Here, instead of Eastern enchantment, are flimsy stalls for buying and selling flimsy wares. His grail has turned out to be only flimsy tea sets covered with artificial flowers. As the upper hall becomes completely dark, the boy realizes that his quest has ended. Gazing upward, he sees the vanity of imagining he can carry a chalice through a dark throng of foes.

SAMPLE ESSAY 5
USING POINT OF VIEW

INSTRUCTIONS.   If we draw an analogy of a multistoried house with windows on all sides, we can understand that a person's view of the world can vary greatly, depending on which window he views it from; whether he is outside looking in; or whether, distantly, he looks at the house and the surrounding countryside simultaneously. Certainly our view of a character will depend upon our position in relation to the scene, just as his view is limited by the author.

Henry James considered the positioning of both characters and narrator crucial to fiction, and in recent years (in fact since his detailed studies of point of view) critics have considered the artist's use of point of view a

[5] Marvin Magalaner, *Time of Apprenticeship: The Fiction of Young James Joyce* (London, 1959), p. 87.

convenient route for entering a work to determine its methods and meanings.

If you are assigned an essay on point of view you should, before you write, do three things: first, determine the literal, technical viewpoint (see pages 8–9); second, decide whether attitudes and ideas expressed in the work indicate an unusual or original variation in the author's use of a standard viewpoint; third, go through the work looking for ways the viewpoint frees or restricts the speaker's vision and understanding of the action of the story (see pages 82–85). You will devote most of your essay to your findings on the third point and in examining the effects angle of vision has on the meaning of the story.

In your introduction to this type of essay, state the point of view. Indicate any variations you may have found. Your controlling idea in an essay on point of view will be the function of the viewpoint in the work as it controls or reveals meaning or theme.

In the body of your essay explain how the viewpoint affects the work. The following questions will help. Does the viewpoint allow for irony? Does it limit sympathy or does it evoke greater sympathy? Does it cause attitudes to be formed? What are they? Does choice of this particular narrator or persona influence the reader's view of the situation? How? Does it control imagery and symbolism?

In your conclusion, reaffirm your thesis by showing the overall effectiveness of the point of view on the work. Did the work gain much or little from its use? Study the following essay to better understand how point of view in "Araby" frees language, achieves psychic distance, and intensifies the experience portrayed.

THE IRONIC NARRATOR
OF JAMES JOYCE'S "ARABY"

Although James Joyce's story "Araby" is told from the first person viewpoint of its young protagonist, we do not receive the impression that a boy tells the story. Instead, the narrator seems to be a man matured well beyond the experience of the story. The mature man reminisces about his youthful hopes, desires, and frustrations. More than if a boy's mind had reconstructed the events of the story for us, this particular way of telling the story enables us to perceive clearly the torment youth experiences when ideals, concerning both sacred and earthly love, are destroyed by a suddenly unclouded view of the actual world. Because the man, rather than the boy, recounts the experience, an ironic view can be presented of the institutions and persons surrounding the boy. This ironic view would be impossible for the immature, emotionally involved mind of the boy himself. Only an adult looking back at the high hopes of "foolish blood" and its resultant destruction could account for the ironic viewpoint. Throughout the story, however, the narrator consistently maintains a full sensitivity to his youthful anguish. From first to last we sense the reality to him of his earlier idealistic dream of beauty.

The opening paragraph, setting the scene, prepares us for the view we receive of the conflict between the loveliness of the ideal and the drabness of the actual. Descriptive words show the narrator's consciousness of the boy's response to beauty and the response of the neighborhood people, who are blind to beauty: North Richmond Street is "blind"; its houses, inhabited by "decent" people, stare unseeingly at one another—and all this is under a sky of "ever-changing violet," in a setting of gardens marred by the "odours of ash-pits" and "dark odorous stables." The boy's own house, which had formerly been inhabited by a priest, is placed in a garden like that of Eden. It is a place of potential holiness, shown to us in the irony of the garden's barrenness and the priest's worldliness: the garden has now only a "central apple tree" and a "few straggling bushes"; the priest had died and left behind him evidence of his preoccupation with secular literature and with collecting money and furniture.

Into this setting appears a figure representative of all that is ideal, the girl. The narrator shows us in a subtly ironic manner that in his youthful adoration of Mangan's sister she is, confusedly, the embodiment of all his boyish dreams of the beauty of physical desire and, at the same time, the embodiment of his adoration of all that is holy. In his dark environment Mangan's sister stands out, a figure always shown outlined by light, with the power to set aflame in him a zeal to conquer the uncaring and the unholy. Her image, constantly with him, makes him feel as though he bears a holy "chalice" through a "throng of foes"—the Saturday evening throng of drunken men, bargaining women, cursing laborers, and all the others who have no conception of the mystical beauty his young mind has created in this world of material ugliness.

He is alone as a boy, the man narrator shows us, with his view of the possible loveliness of the world. Even the aunt and uncle with whom he lives are callous to his burning need to go to the bazaar, which looms in his imagination as a place of mystical Eastern enchantment, to purchase a gift worthy of his loved one. Looking back, the narrator can see that his uncle had been concerned with his daily, worldly tasks, his aunt with maintaining a "decent" observance of "this day of our Lord," although she does not want him to be disappointed in his wish to go to the bazaar. From the vantage point of maturity the narrator can realize that the aunt and the uncle perhaps once possessed an awareness of the romantic, an awareness that has since been clouded by the drabness of North Richmond Street.

Like Stephen Dedalus of Joyce's *Portrait of the Artist as a Young Man,* the boy, then, must seek for the high, the inviolate, by himself. And, also like Stephen, he finds instead the world. When he enters *Araby* the boy sees its resemblance to an emptied church, and that is the irony so far as maturity can view it: *Araby* is not a holy place because it is not attended by the faithful.

He has come alone on a deserted train; the bazaar, full of spurious wares, is tended by uncaring people who leave him even more alone than he had been before; the young lady who should have waited on him ignores him to joke with two young men. The young lady's inane remarks to the young men have a ring in the memory of the mature narrator reminiscent of his adored one's remarks. Both are concerned with the material, the crass.

The narrator can, with his backward look, supply us with two apprehensions: one, the fully remembered, and thus fully felt, anguish of a too sudden realization of the disparity between a youthful dream of the mystic beauty of the world and his actual world; and two, the irony implicit in a view that can see the dream itself as a "vanity."

SAMPLE ESSAY 6
USING CHARACTERIZATION

INSTRUCTIONS. During your study of literature you will undoubtedly be asked to write an essay analyzing some particular character in a play, a poem, or a story. When that moment arrives, review the section on characterization on pages 81–90. Determine from your reading whether the character is major or minor, static or dynamic, and outline both the ways in which the character is revealed and the ways in which the character reveals the meaning of the story.

Your purpose in an essay using characterization will usually center in an explanation of some aspect of the meaning of the work as it is revealed by the actions and attitudes of a specific character. Your task therefore becomes twofold: to analyze the character and, by means of your analysis, to introduce an interpretation of the work. To do this, determine the theme or meaning of the work; then discover the ways your character reveals, embodies, or even obscures the theme. The "ways" become the topic sentences of the paragraphs in the body of your essay.

Study pages 90–91 for other approaches to writing about characterization and read the following essay, which defines the character of the boy in

"Araby." Note the extensive use of point of view and symbolism to explain the boy. A character is revealed by an author in many ways, and your job is to determine those ways and use them as your means of explaining the character. Try always to get at the *consistent principle* (see page 89) that dominates or motivates a character.

FROM INNOCENCE TO KNOWLEDGE: CHARACTER IN JAMES JOYCE'S "ARABY"

In his brief but complex story, "Araby," James Joyce concentrates on character rather than on plot to reveal the ironies inherent in self-deception. On one level "Araby" is a story of initiation, of a boy's quest for the ideal. The quest ends in failure but results in an inner awareness and a first step into manhood. On another level the story consists of a grown man's remembered experience, for the story is told in retrospect by a man who looks back to a particular moment of intense meaning and insight. As such, the boy's experience is not restricted to youth's encounter with first love. Rather, it is a portrayal of a continuing problem all through life: the incompatibility of the ideal, of the dream as one wishes it to be, with the bleakness of reality. This double focus—the boy who first experiences, and the man who has not forgotten—provides for the dramatic rendering of a story of first love told by a narrator who, with his wider, adult vision, can employ the sophisticated use of irony and symbolic imagery necessary to reveal the story's meaning.

The boy's character is indirectly suggested in the opening scenes of the story. He has grown up in the backwash of a dying city. Symbolic images show him to be an individual who is sensitive to the fact that his city's vitality has ebbed and left a residue of empty piety, the faintest echoes of romance, and only symbolic memories of an active concern for God and fellow men. Although the young boy cannot apprehend it intellectually, he feels that the street, the town, and Ireland itself have become ingrown, self-satisfied, and unimaginative. It is a world of spiritual stagnation, and as a result, the boy's outlook is severely limited. He is ignorant and therefore innocent. Lonely, imaginative, and isolated, he lacks the understanding necessary for evaluation and perspective. He is at first as blind as his world, but Joyce prepares us for his eventual perceptive awakening by tempering his blindness with an unconscious rejection of the spiritual stagnation of his world.

The boy's manner of thought is also made clear in the opening scenes. Religion controls the lives of the inhabitants of North Richmond Street, but it is a dying religion and receives only lip service. The boy, however, entering the new experience of first love, finds his vocabulary within the experiences of his religious training and the romantic novels he has read. The result is an idealistic and confused interpretation of love based on quasireligious terms and the imagery of romance. This convergence of two great myths, the Christian with its symbols of hope and sacrifice and the Oriental or romantic with its fragile symbols of heroism and escape, merge to form in his mind an illusory world of mystical and ideal beauty. This convergence, which creates an epiphany for the boy as he accompanies his aunt through the market place, lets us experience with sudden illumination the texture and content of his mind. We see the futility and stubbornness of his quest. But despite all the evidence of the dead house on a dead street in a dying city the boy determines to bear his "chalice safely through a throng of foes." He is blindly interpreting the world in the images of his dreams: shop boys selling pigs' cheeks cry out in "shrill litanies"; Mangan's sister is saintly; her name evokes in him "strange prayers and praises." The boy is extraordinarily lovesick, and from his innocent idealism and stubbornness, we realized that he cannot keep the dream. He must wake to the demands of the world around him and react. Thus the first half of the story foreshadows (as the man later realizes) the boy's awakening and disillusionment.

The account of the boy's futile quest emphasizes both his lonely idealism and his ability to achieve the perspectives he now has. The quest ends when he arrives at the bazaar and realizes with slow, tortured clarity that *Araby* is not at all what he imagined. It is tawdry and dark and thrives on the profit motive and the eternal lure its name evokes in men. The boy realizes that he has placed all his love and hope in a world that does not exist except in his imagination. He feels angry and betrayed and realizes his self-deception. He feels he is "a creature driven and derided by vanity" and the vanity is his own.

The man, remembering this startling experience from his boyhood, recalls the moment he realized that living the dream was lost as a possibility. That sense of loss is intensified, for its dimension grows as we realize that the desire to live the dream will continue through adulthood.

At no other point in the story is characterization as brilliant as at the end. Joyce draws his protagonist with strokes designed to let us recognize in "the creature driven and derided by vanity" both a boy who is initiated into knowledge through a loss of innocence and a man who fully realizes the incompatibility between the beautiful and innocent world of the imagination and the very real world of fact. In "Araby," Joyce uses character to embody the theme of his story.

SUGGESTED ASSIGNMENTS FOR
WRITING ABOUT FICTION

1. Many fiction writers skillfully use characterization to further plot. For example, in *Pride and Prejudice,* Jane Austen brilliantly uses characterization to forward her narrative. Write an essay either on *Pride and Prejudice* or on some other work of fiction that seems to you to employ characterization skillfully. Show how characterization (of one character or more than one) moves the story toward its climax. John Knowles' *A Separate Peace* depends upon the skillful handling of the character of the protagonist to bring out the plot and meaning of the novel. Analyze any unusual, original, or profoundly meaningful character in a work of fiction. Define his nature and his influence upon the meaning of the work.

2. Write an essay assessing the value of point of view in a work of fiction. Does the point of view alter or influence your attitude toward the subject matter? How? How does the use of point of view control thought? Henry James' *The Turn of the Screw* uses the first person narrator (the governess's manuscript) to cause decided opinions to be formed concerning the character of this narrator. Use either this novella or another work that relies upon point of view to control the narrative elements in the work. Examine Hemingway's short story "The Killers" for a technique that approximates the effaced point of view of drama. Consider stream of consciousness techniques found in many modern works (the soliloquy in Faulkner's *As I Lay Dying,* for example).

3. Discuss the importance of setting in a work of fiction. Determine the effects achieved by realistic detail or by a setting that is nebulous and symbolic (Katherine Mansfield's "The Garden Party" or Eudora Welty's "Why I Live at the P. O." or, more elaborately, Lawrence Durrell's *Alexandria Quartet* or Hannah Greene's *I Never Promised You a Rose Garden*). How does the setting influence the work's atmosphere? Analyze the atmosphere in a work of fiction. How does it influence the meaning or theme of the work?

4. Some authors rely upon a highly symbolic presentation of imagery to suggest meanings in their works. In his short story "My Kinsman, Major Molineux" Hawthorne uses laughter as a major symbol. In an essay trace the changing quality of the laughter in the story to show how it controls the meaning. Use other works that rely upon symbolism and analyze the function of the symbols as they influence or control the theme of the work. What is the meaning of the sun as a symbol in Crane's *The Red Badge of Courage?* How does it affect characterization and resolution of plot?

5. Many works of fiction are made into motion pictures or plays. Compare the work in printed form with its visual counterpart. What are the differences? Which succeeds better, and why? Novels made into motion pictures are numerous: Mary McCarthy's *The Group,* John Fowles' *The Collector,* Alan Sillitoe's *Saturday Night and Sunday Morning,* Camus' *The Stranger,*

Malamud's *The Fixer*. Steinbeck's *Of Mice and Men* was made into both a play and a motion picture.

6. James Joyce's short story "A Little Cloud" is a story of contrasts and ironies. Write an essay about this story in which you point out the contrasts. Find in each case the irony inherent in the seeming contrast. The culmination of your findings should point to the theme of the story. If you do not have access to "A Little Cloud" choose another work that demonstrates the artful use of irony. Chekhov's story "Gooseberries," for example, uses contrast and irony.

7. Examine a novel or collection of stories currently on the best seller list. Do you think the work will endure as literature? Set up, in an essay, criteria for excellence in fiction and evaluate the work you choose by those standards. See pages 172–175 for suggestions about writing evaluation.

8. Write an essay examining the techniques an author may employ to render basically morbid or unsavory subject matter aesthetically pleasing. Certainly the protagonist in Faulkner's "A Rose for Emily" performs a morbid act. How does the author prevent the story from being merely disgusting? Look to techniques such as aesthetic distance, tone, point of view, and language for your answers. Many works of fiction deal with potentially objectionable subject matter, but their authors make them into works of art. Among them are Kafka's "The Metamorphosis," Thomas Mann's *The Blood of the Walsungs*, Albert Camus' *The Plague*, William Styron's *Lie Down in Darkness*. Choose one of these or some other work for your subject matter.

9. Write an essay in which you evaluate the style of a work. Your evaluation should not merely judge the excellence of the style; you should show how the author's style enriches the work, or how it intensifies meaning. For example, you could explicate any representative passage of William Faulkner's *The Bear* to show how some of the long, unpunctuated sentences give the sense of timelessness that is an outstanding motif in the novella. Many works employ style as a means of expressing ideas; choose a passage from a work with which you are familiar and, subjecting it to a close analytical reading, show how its style controls meaning or intensifies theme.

10. Physical actions often offer important clues to the meaning or significance of a story. Analyze the importance of plot in Stephen Crane's "The Bride Comes to Yellow Sky." Call attention, in your analysis, to the patterns that affect the story's suspense. Choose some other work of fiction that depends heavily on plot and write an essay explaining the importance to the story of such plot elements as conflict and foreshadowing. Show how the plot arrangement influences the success of the story. You may want to choose a detective or mystery story or a motion picture for the purpose of explaining the importance or effect of the surprise ending.

POETRY

Poetry defies an all-encompassing definition. Coleridge defined it by pointing out that it is composed of the same elements as prose—but with a difference. Aristole said that it contains a higher philosophy than any other art. Emily Dickinson defined it through her own response: "If I feel physically as if the top of my head were taken off, I know this is poetry." Wordsworth said that the difference is in the nature of the poet himself; his superiority to others in sensitivity, in wisdom, and in knowledge of human nature. These writers, along with all the others who have tried to define poetry, would undoubtedly agree that form and metrical language are not the basic differences between poetry and prose.

In Section One of this book we pointed out that all literature presents *experience,* and perhaps it is here that we can find a working definition for poetry. There are differences between the experiences of poetry and those of other forms of writing, but the differences are mainly of degree. In poetry experience is *compressed* and *intensified*. Because of this compression and intensification, poetry possesses greater power than other literature for communicating both experience and abstract concepts.

The method for discovering poems (the dramatic experiences, their presentation, and finally their meaning) is essentially the same as that used for discovering any form of literature. Nevertheless, because the shaping elements in poetry are intensified and compressed, you need to look at the special ways in which those elements apply to a study of poetry.

LANGUAGE

The poet displays an extraordinary sensitivity to words. He chooses words that best express both what he feels or thinks and what he wishes his reader's response to be. You must therefore understand the way in which a poet uses *every word* in his poem. As we mentioned earlier in this book, you must learn both the denotative and the connotative meanings of all words. In studying poetry you must often pay attention to the obsolete meanings of some words. Look, for example, at these lines from Pope's *The Dunciad:*

> heard ev'ry King declare
> His royal Sense of Op'ras or the Fair;
> The *Stews* and Palace equally explor'd.

Precise enjoyment of the satire on kings of the time is impossible unless you know that in the eighteenth century the word *stews,* in addition to the meaning you doubtless know for it, meant *brothels.*

You must note carefully images, metaphors, symbols, allusions; the use of myth and archetypal experience, of ambiguity and irony. Since you are likely to find these devices used in poetry in heightened degree, you must become acutely sensitive to them.

Sound

The language of poetry differs most strikingly from that of prose in its sound. To illustrate, we must define terms like *rhyme, alliteration, assonance, onomatopoeia,* and *repetition.*

Rhyme is the repetition of the vowel and consonantal sounds at the ends of words. The words may be spelled alike, but need not be. Here are rhyming words: *laughter-after, dreary-weary, cheerfully-fearfully.* Rhyme has many variations. When the accented vowel is in the final syllable of the line, the rhymes are called **masculine,** as in these lines from Robert Herrick:

> Whenas in silks my Julia *goes,*
> Then, then, methinks, how sweetly *flows*
> That liquefaction of her *clothes.*

When one or two unaccented syllables follow the accented syllable of rhyming words, the rhyme is **feminine.** Here, from one of Shakespeare's songs, is an example of feminine rhyme:

What is love? 'tis not here*af*ter
Present mirth hath present *laughter*

Although rhyme usually occurs at the end of a line, it may also occur within the line. **Internal rhyme** is the term for the rhyming of words within the same line:

Ah, distinctly I *remember* it was in the bleak *December.*
(Edgar Allan Poe, "The Raven")

In **partial** or **slant rhyme,** the sounds of the rhyming words are similar, but not identical:

Let me not to the marriage of true minds
Admit impediments. Love is not *love*
Which alters when it alteration finds,
Or bends with the remover to re*move.*

Some poets prefer slant rhyme because it allows a sound pattern for short lines without producing a singsong effect, as you may see from these lines in which Emily Dickinson rhymes *heaven* with *given:*

I never spoke with God,
Nor visited in *heaven;*
Yet certain am I of the spot
As if the chart were *given.*[1]

Sight or **eye rhymes** use words or syllables that are spelled alike. In Coleridge's *Christabel* one finds these eye rhymes: *flood-wood, speak-break,* and *worth-forth.* Eye rhyme may also be slant rhyme, as in the lines quoted above in which Shakespeare rhymes *love* with *move.*

Not all poetry is rhymed. Unrhymed iambic pentameter lines, called **blank verse,** are used by many poets. This kind of verse is discussed more fully later.

Alliteration is the repetition of the same consonant sound in several words close together in a sentence or in a line. It is used to intensify emotion and thought. Poe intensified the air of mystery in the line from "The Raven," quoted above, by repeating the *r* sound. Throughout *Don Juan,* Byron relies upon alliteration for coalition of sound and sense. For example, he repeats the sounds of *t, s, r* and *z* to underscore the witty satire of these lines from that poem:

Wordsworth's last quarto, by the way, is bigger
Than any since the birthday of typography;

---

[1] Emily Dickinson, "I Never Saw a Moor," *The Complete Poems of Emily Dickinson,* edited by Thomas H. Johnson (Boston: Little, Brown and Company, 1960).

A drowsy, frowzy poem, call'd *The Excursion,*
Writ in a manner which is my aversion.

If you become aware of alliteration, it will help you grasp those aspects of a work the poet may want to intensify.

Assonance is the repetition of the same or similar vowel sounds within words (for example, *woo* and *wound, deep* and *free, long* and *lawn*). Poets use assonance often. It, like alliteration and rhyme, is pleasing in itself, and in addition it provides sense by sound in a subtler way than either of the other two. As an instance, note how we can hear the lament in these lines from Ben Jonson's *Cynthia's Revels,* not only because of the meaning of the words, but also because of the measured pace of the long vowel sounds within the words:

> Yet, slower yet, oh faintly, gentle springs;
> List to the heavy part the music bears,
> Woe weeps out her division when she sings.

There is alliteration also in the lines above, but more than that sound, it is the assonance that imparts the sense of woe.

As you read poetry aloud, let your voice sound out the assonance in order to determine the emotional quality of lines.

Onomatopoeia is the term applied to words whose sounds suggest their meanings. Examples are *swish, crack, pop.* Although the use of onomatopoeia is limited, it can be effective. Perhaps the best-known use of this device throughout an entire poem is in Poe's "The Bells." Another notable example occurs in Milton's epic poem *Paradise Lost,* when Satan returns to Hell and boasts in full assembly of his success in corrupting man, expecting praise from his angels, and receives instead "A universal hiss, the sound / Of public scorn." The many *s*'s, with the use of the onomatopoetic word *hiss,* suggests the sound serpents make and presages the form into which Satan and his followers are being transformed.

Repetition is another way of creating sound patterns that are pleasing to the ear. Words, phrases, lines, or entire stanzas are repeated for a variety of purposes, including intensification, emphasis, contrast, and rhythmical continuity. Repetition is much used in songs and ballads, both for its "catchy" quality and for its ability to call attention to a motif. Jonson's lines from *Cynthia's Revels,* quoted above, contain a repeated word, pleasing to the ear and suggestive of the sense of the lines. The lines immediately following those already quoted repeat one word four times, providing by the repetition intensification as well as euphony:

> Droop herbs and flowers,
> Fall grief in showers;

>   Our beauties are not ours;
>   Oh, I could still,
>   Like melting snow upon some craggy hill,
>   Drop, drop, drop, drop,
>   Since nature's pride is now a withered daffodil.

Wallace Stevens' poem "The Emperor of Ice-Cream" [2] uses the same line, "The only emperor is the emperor of ice-cream," to end both of its two stanzas. This particular repetition highlights the poem's theme, making it less difficult to understand.

Rhythm and Meter

Sir Philip Sidney said that the "well-weighed syllable" not only "delights," but also has "majesty." The syllables of lines of poetry follow one another in a particular order; they flow at a particular pace. To disturb the flow and pace of words in lines of poetry is to destroy their delight and their majesty. Consider these lines from Coleridge's "Kubla Khan":

>   In Xanadu did Kubla Khan
>   A stately pleasure-dome decree:
>   Where Alph, the sacred river, ran
>   Through caverns measureless to man
>   Down to a sunless sea.

Now consider a rearrangement of the lines:

>   Kubla Khan decreed a stately pleasure-dome in Xanadu, where
>   Alph, the sacred river, ran through caverns incapable of measurement by
>   man down to a dark sea.

The rearranged lines make the same statement, but clearly there is a wide difference between the two, principally in their order and pace.

Order and pace in poetry make its **rhythm,** which is the regular recurrence of grouped, stressed and unstressed syllables in alternation. All speech has rhythm because of the stress we place on syllables. Even the rearranged lines of Coleridge's poem have rhythm, but because they cannot be measured according to a pattern they do not have a metrical flow, and therefore are not poetry. Rhythm in poetry can be *measured.* To determine the **meter** of lines of poetry you will need to train your ear to hear which syllables should be stressed, which unstressed. Stress falls naturally upon some syllables because of their pronunciation; if you are uncertain, use the dictionary. Webster's *New World Dictionary,* for example, gives this marking of stress for the word gymnasiast:

---

[2] Wallace Stevens, "The Emperor of Ice-Cream," *The Collected Poems of Wallace Stevens* (New York: Alfred A. Knopf, Inc. 1954). Reprinted by permission.

jim-ná-zi-ast

Sense, with pronunciation, determines the stress of monosyllabic words and of syllables in polysyllabic words in a sentence, as in this prose line: Give me ă cúp ŏf cóffĕe, pléase. Poetry should be read aloud to determine where stress best falls.

Rhythm is measured in feet. Each **foot** contains a determined number of *stressed* (ˊ) and *unstressed* (˘) syllables. Six kinds of feet are common to English verse:

1. the *iambic* foot, or *iamb*—one unstressed syllable followed by a stressed (˘ˊ)
2. the *trochaic* foot, or *trochee*—one stressed syllable followed by an unstressed (ˊ˘)
3. the *dactylic* foot, or *dactyl*—one stressed syllable followed by two unstressed (ˊ˘˘)
4. the *anapestic* foot, or *anapest*—two unstressed syllables followed by a stressed (˘˘ˊ)
5. the *spondaic* foot, or *spondee*—two stressed syllables (ˊˊ)
6. the *pyrrhic* foot, or *pyrrhic*—two unstressed syllables (˘˘)

The succession of stressed and unstressed syllables in lines of poetry are separated by vertical lines to show the number of feet in each line:

Ĭn Xán| ă dú |dĭd Kúb |lă Khán

A line may contain only one foot or as many as eight feet; however, most lines have more than two and fewer than six. These are the names for lines with various numbers of feet:

monometer—a line containing one foot
dimeter—a line containing two feet
trimeter—a line containing three feet
tetrameter—a line containing four feet
pentameter—a line containing five feet
hexameter—a line containing six feet
heptameter—a line containing seven feet
octameter—a line containing eight feet

The two most commonly used lines in English poetry are the iambic pentameter and the iambic tetrameter. The line above from Coleridge's "Kubla Khan" is iambic tetrameter. Following is a line of iambic pentameter from Milton's *Paradise Lost:*

Ănd swíms| ŏr sínks, |ŏr wádes, |ŏr créeps, |ŏr flíes

A poem may have variation of rhythm; beats may be dropped, for instance, especially at the ends of lines; or one kind of foot may appear within a line consisting principally of another kind of foot. Despite variations, however, the line is called by the kind of foot that predominates. Note the trochaic foot that begins a line of iambic pentameter in Pope's "Windsor Forest":

Pleás'd in | the si | lent sháde | with emp | ty práise

This change of foot allows the poet to stress the word "pleas'd."

Another kind of change will give a falling rhythm to a line, as in this one from Matthew Arnold's "The Forsaken Merman":

Dówn | to the depths | of the séa

The line is anapestic trimeter, but the single stressed syllable beginning the line makes our voices fall thereafter to impart a meaning that fits the sound of the line.

Poets often vary the meter of their poems to fit the effect they wish to make. *Paradise Lost,* for example, is basically iambic pentameter, but it has many such variations. This line from that work uses a single stressed syllable, a spondee, a trochee, and two anapests, in that order:

Húrl'd | héadlóng | flám ing | from th'ether | eal ský

The three strong syllables at the beginning of the line call attention to the description of the manner in which the action is performed.

As you read poetry, note variations from the predominant meter of lines. They are clues both to the effects the poet desired and to the meanings he intended.

Scansion, the marking of stress and of numbers of feet, has no dogmatic rules. A reader must rely upon his ear to detect the slightly stressed, heavily stressed, or unstressed syllables. Readers interpreting the sound and sense of lines will sometimes mark the meter differently. Some readers, for example, would scan Milton's line above as predominantly anapestic:

Húrl'd | héadlong flám | ing || from th'ether | eal ský

Your scansion is as valid as another's if you can support it according to principles of added pleasure in sound and added fusion of sound and sense. We justify our scansion of Milton's line by saying that the strong beginning, with a rapidly paced falling ending, better suits the act described. Readers who scan according to the second method might say that they prefer the pause after the word *flaming.* The pause, or *caesura,* as it is called, is indicated by two vertical lines. It is a useful device in lines. You can often detect the need for a caesura by punctuation, as in these two lines from John Donne's "Holy Sonnet X":

Óne short | sleép past, || we wáke | eter | nally,
And Deáth | shall be | no móre: || Deáth, || thou shalt díe!

The two lines contain three caesuras in addition to the ones naturally indicated by the punctuation at the ends of the lines. These pauses call attention to certain words and ideas, as you can see.

Pauses occurring at the ends of lines make what are called **end-stopped** lines. All these lines from Wordsworth's "The Solitary Reaper" are end-stopped:

> Behold her, single in the field,
> Yon solitary Highland lass!
> Reaping and singing by herself;
> Stop here, or gently pass!

In contrast, the **run-on,** or **enjambed,** line does not pause at the end. A later line of this same Wordsworth poem is run on:

> O listen! for the vale profound
> Is overflowing with the sound.

Producing a different effect from the end-stopped, the run-on line has a continuous flow. Remember not to pause when reading a run-on line of poetry.

Not all poetry has meter. Poetry written with rhythmical language, but not with meter, is called **free verse.** These four lines of free verse are from Edgar Lee Masters' "George Gray":

> To put meaning in one's life may end in madness,
> But life without meaning is the torture
> Of restlessness and vague desire—
> It is a boat longing for the sea and yet afraid.

Free verse is useful to poets for expressing significant ideas in language like that of conversational speech. After Walt Whitman used free verse with remarkable effects, many early-twentieth-century poets also used the form. Although many poets still use free verse, there has been a swing back to metrical language because of its great value.

As you learn the kinds of meter and to scan lines you increase your ability to understand and appreciate what a poet is doing with his work. Merely to know the technical terms and to be able to scan a few lines will do little to enlarge your power for apprehending the richness of a poem unless you understand that rhythm and its relationship to sound and sense is an intrinsic element of a poem. This relationship forms a basic part of the total meaning and effect of a poem. To gain full appreciation of sound and rhythm, read poetry aloud. Note where you place stress. Note rising and falling rhythms. Note rapidly paced or slowed syllables. Determine the reasons for their being as they are. Note in poems how all devices of sound and of meter reinforce meaning and pleasure.

THE FORMS AND CONVENTIONS OF POETRY

There are no rigid rules compelling poets to put the lines of their poems into one of the accepted **forms.** The sense in which the term form is used here refers to the organization of the rhythmic units in a line of poetry and to the organization of the stanzas of a poem. (For other uses of the term "form" see Glossary.) Traditionally, however, poets have continued to use established forms. Probably they do so for one of two reasons. We can imagine that a poet may simply like a form—it appeals to his aesthetic sense—and he uses it for this reason alone. More likely, though, he chooses a form because tradition has proved that certain kinds of things can be said best in certain forms. Probably a poem can reveal itself best by progressing in a certain way. To test the validity of this idea, let us look at the more common forms and a few examples from them that show their successful use.

A **couplet** is two successive rhymed lines. Some couplets are **closed;** that is, the thought is complete within the two lines, as in this couplet from Dryden's "Absolom and Achitophel":

A man so various that he seemed to be
Not one, but all mankind's epitome.

Dryden's lines lend themselves well to a closed couplet. The statement seems to express a truth that is applicable to a kind of individual we all have known, and it *needs* to be put into a short, quotable, easily remembered form. Other couplets are **open;** the thought runs on to the next line or lines, as in these from Blake's "The Tiger":

Tiger! Tiger! burning bright
In the forests of the night,
What immortal hand or eye
Could frame thy fearful symmetry?

Blake's lines require more than two lines to complete the idea expressed in them. A readily apparent reason for the use of rhyming couplets is that the very simplicity of the form forces the reader to an immediate awareness of the deeper emotions of dread and wonder inherent in the seemingly simple question of the lines. The poem will deal with a profound philosophical question; it demands a simple form to set it starkly before the reader. Another reason is that the balance of the form allows for the contrasts that are introduced.

Two closed lines of rhymed iambic pentameter are called a **heroic couplet.** Alexander Pope used the form in "The Rape of the Lock," from which these lines come:

> The hungry Judges soon the sentence sign,
> And wretches hang that jury-men may dine.

The biting satire of these lines demands a short conversational sentence (which the form gives) to make its point effectively.

The arrangement of lines of poems into **stanzas** gives them shape and produces different effects. The stanza functions as a kind of paragraph, completing a unit of the whole poem and laying the foundation for a continuance of its pattern in other verse "paragraphs" to follow.

After the couplet, the next smallest stanza is the **tercet,** three rhymed lines. It is useful for allowing progress of an idea or of a narrative in short advances. Thomas Hardy's "Lines on the Loss of the Titanic" [3] is composed in tercets. Here are the eighth and ninth tercets of that poem:

> And as the smart ship grew
> In stature, grace, and hue,
> In shadowy silent distance grew the Iceberg too.

> Alien they seemed to be;
> No mortal eye could see
> The intimate welding of their later history.

Notice how the first quoted tercet leads into the idea of the next one. Notice also that the first prepares for the "welding" in the following one. Short stanzas, such as this, make progress but also permit linking of ideas.

Terza rima, a stanza of Italian origin, consists of a series of tercets in which the second line of each tercet rhymes with the first and third lines of the following one (*a b a, b c b, c d c,* and so on). Dante used this form in *The Divine Comedy* and Shelley in "Ode to the West Wind." Here are the first two tercets of Shelley's poem:

> O wild West Wind, thou breath of Autumn's being,
> Thou, from whose unseen presence the leaves dead
> Are driven, like ghosts from an enchanter fleeing,

> Yellow, and black, and pale, and hectic red,
> Prestilence-striken multitudes: O thou,
> Who chariotest to their dark wintry bed
> The wingèd seeds. . . .

A successful result of form here is that the short forward progression of the stanzas is admirably suited to the movement of the "fleeing" leaves. In addition, this kind of progression is appropriate to the growing concept of

---

[3] Reprinted with permission of The Macmillan Company from "The Convergence of the Twain: Lines on the Loss of the Titanic" by Thomas Hardy, from *The Collected Poems of Thomas Hardy*. Copyright, 1925, The Macmillan Company.

the leaves as symbols of the speaker's "ideas," which are also carried by a movement outside themselves.

A **quatrain** in a stanza of four lines, usually rhyming *a b a b* or *a b b a*. It may be composed of two couplets. With an additional line beyond the tercet the poet can extend his thought somewhat more fully than in the two shorter stanzas; it is also suited to less formal expressions than they are. The quatrain is often chosen for the ballad (illustrated here by the first stanza from the anonymous ballad "Fine Flowers in the Valley"):

> She sat down below a thorn,
>> Fine flowers in the valley,
> And there she has her sweet babe born,
>> And the green leaves they grow rarely.

Another kind of quatrain is the **elegiac stanza,** which rhymes *a b a b* and is composed in lines of pentameter length. The elegiac stanza is used for subjects of serious import. Gray's well-known "Elegy Written in a Country Churchyard" uses the form. Note the sober effect of the iambic pentameter lines of the opening stanza of that poem:

> The curfew tolls the knell of parting day,
>> The lowing herd winds slowly o'er the lea,
> The ploughman homeward plods his weary way,
>> And leaves the world to darkness and to me.

Three widely used forms are **rhyme royal, ottava rima,** and the **Spenserian stanza,** having seven, eight, and nine lines respectively. Chaucer was the first to use rhyme royal in English. Its iambic pentameter lines rhyme *a b a b b c c*. Here, from Chaucer's *Troilus* and *Criseyde,* is a stanza of rhyme royal:

> Criseyde was this lady name al right:
> As to my dom in al Troyes cité
> N'as non so fair; for, passing every wight,
> So angelik was hir natif beauté,
> That lik a thing immortal seemèd she,
> As is an hevenissh parfit creatúre
> That down were sent in scorning of natúre.

Ottava rima is iambic pentameter, rhyming *a b a b a b c c*. Byron used it in *Don Juan*. It is of Italian origin, and Byron admired it when visiting Italy. He said he chose it for *Don Juan* because he meant the poem to "be a little quietly facetious upon everything." The form does allow for the "playfulness" he desired, and yet the form demands, too, that Byron control his playfulness. Notice both qualities in this stanza of ottava rima from *Don Juan:*

If ever I should condescend to prose,
    I'll write poetical commandments, which
Shall supersede beyond all doubt all those
    That went before; in these I shall enrich
My text with many things that no one knows,
    And carry precept to the highest pitch:
I'll call the work "Longinus o'er a Bottle,
    Or, Every Poet his *own* Aristotle."

The Spenserian stanza has eight lines of iambic pentameter, followed by one line of iambic hexameter (an **Alexandrine**), rhyming *a b a b b c b c c.* It was named after Edmund Spenser, who used it in *The Faerie Queen.* Stanza LXI from that work follows:

And more, to lulle him in his slumber soft,
A trickling streame from high rock tumbling downe,
And ever drizling raine upon the loft,
Mixt with a murmuring winde, much like the sowne
Of swarming bees, did cast him in a swowne:
No other noyse, nor peoples troublous cryes,
As still are wont t'annoy the wallèd towne,
Might there be heard: but carelesse Quiet lyes,
Wrapt in eternall silence farre from enimyes.

Note how the extended lines permit the slumbrous sound effect the poet wishes to incorporate within the stanza. The form permits also the full development of vivid imagery for which *The Faerie Queen* is famed.

    Conventions in poetry, as in all art, are accepted usages, styles, features, or methods. Some poetry conventions have precise rules, like the sonnet convention, but others have only generally agreed upon features. We will discuss here some of the most commonly studied conventions.

    The **epic** is a long narrative poem celebrating the deeds of a traditional hero, who is often of a semidivine nature. Beyond this requirement there are no precise rules for epics, but they customarily observe several conventions. They are based, for example, upon legends or myths; *The Iliad* and *The Odyssey* of Homer are based upon ancient Greek folklore, and Milton's *Paradise Lost* is based upon legends from the Bible. Epics begin customarily with an **invocation** to the muses, asking for aid so that the poet may sing the story in inspired fashion. The narrative begins **in medias res** (in the middle of the action); *The Odyssey* begins at a point of heightened dramatic interest in which Odysseus faces the most disheartening obstacle to his return home. Epics then use **flashbacks** to give background material, introducing them at points where they will add meaning or have greater effect. Sometimes the flashbacks are of the kind called

retardations—that is, the story cuts off sharply at a high point of interest and a long explanatory section is inserted before the story takes up again. One such retardation occurs in *The Odyssey* when Odysseus' faithful old nurse Eurycleia recognizes his scar and, as the audience waits in suspense, wondering whether she will give him away before he wishes to be recognized, we hear the story of how Odysseus received the scar. Another feature of the epic is the use of **epithets** (stock words or short phrases applied characteristically). Epithets from *The Odyssey* are "rosy-fingered dawn" "grey-eyed Athena," "brave Odysseus," "Penelope of the white arms." Milton's *Paradise Lost* contains epithets like "darkness visible," "Eternal Father," and "Fair Consort." Epithets are a stylistic device that makes vivid the imagery of the epic poem and helps the audience identify characters. The **epic simile,** sometimes called the **Homeric simile,** is an extended comparison, which likens one thing to another at such length that it becomes virtually a short narrative, as in this comparison, made when Athena's aegis takes form in the hall above the evil suitors (from Robert Fitzgerald's translation of *The Odyssey*) [4]:

> And the suitors mad with fear
> at her great sign stampeded like stung cattle by a river
> when the dread shimmering gadfly strikes in summer,
> in the flowering season, in the long-drawn days.
> After them the attackers wheeled, as terrible as falcons
> from eyries in the mountains veering over and diving down
> with talons wide unsheathed on flights of birds,
> who cower down the sky in chutes and bursts along the valley—
> but the pouncing falcons grip their prey, no frantic wing avails,
> and farmers love to watch those beakèd hunters.
> So these now fell upon the suitors in that hall.

Catalogues are another epic convention. Heroic deeds and heroes are listed to enlighten the listeners concerning the great deeds of their forbears. One such listing occurs in *The Odyssey* when Odysseus descends into Hades, where he talks with many of the other Greek heroes. Epics are divided into two kinds: the **primary epic,** designed to be sung to a people whose ancient forbears are celebrated in the poem, and the **literary epic,** designed to be read by those who enjoy literature. Primary epics are those like *The Iliad* and *The Odyssey* of Homer, the Anglo-Saxon epic, *Beowulf,* the Spanish *El Cid,* and the French *Song of Roland.* Examples of the literary epic are Milton's *Paradise Lost* and Vergil's *Aeneid.*

The **sonnet** is fourteen lines, usually of iambic pentameter, with varied rhyme schemes. The **Italian,** or **Petrarchan, sonnet** is divided into an

---

[4] From Homer, *The Odyssey,* translated by Robert Fitzgerald. Copyright© 1961 by Robert Fitzgerald. Reprinted by permission of Doubleday & Company, Inc.

octave (eight lines) rhyming *a b b a a b b a* and a **sestet** (six lines) rhyming *c d e c d e;* the **English,** or **Shakespearean, sonnet** is divided into three quatrains and a couplet rhyming *a b a b, c d c d, e f e f, g g.* In addition, many sonnets show a thought development corresponding to the divisions of the fourteen lines. For example, some Italian sonnets present a generalization in the octave and a specific example in the sestet; or they present a problem in the octave and a solution to the problem in the sestet. Following is a fairly conventional Italian sonnet, Milton's "On His Blindness":

> When I consider how my light is spent
>> Ere half my days in this dark world and wide,
>> And that one talent which is death to hide
>> Lodged with me useless, though my soul more bent
> To serve therewith my Maker, and present
>> My true account, lest He returning chide,
>> "Doth God exact day-labor, light denied?"
>> I fondly ask. But Patience, to prevent
> That murmur, soon replies, "God doth not need
>> Either man's work or his own gifts. Who best
>> Bear his mild yoke, they serve him best. His state
> Is kingly: thousands at his bidding speed,
>> And post o'er land and ocean without rest;
>> They also serve who only stand and wait."

The English sonnet may give an image in the first quatrain, intensify it in the two quatrains to follow, and solve the problem in the couplet. Following is a sonnet of this kind; it is Keats' "When I Have Fears":

> When I have fears that I may cease to be
> Before my pen has gleaned my teeming brain,
> Before high-piled books, in charactery,
> Hold like rich garners the full ripened grain;
> When I behold, upon the night's starred face,
> Huge cloudy symbols of a high romance,
> And think that I may never live to trace
> Their shadows, with the magic hand of chance;
> And when I feel, fair creature of an hour,
> That I shall never look upon thee more,
> Never have relish in the fairy power
> Of unreflecting love—then on the shore
> Of the wide world I stand alone, and think
> Till love and fame to nothingness do sink.

Sonnets may, on the other hand, be handled in original and unusual ways; Gerard Manley Hopkins, for example, altered the sonnet in striking ways, and Yeats' "Leda and the Swan" is a brilliant variation of the traditional sonnet form.

The **ballad,** traditionally, is a story told in song, which has been passed down from generation to generation. **Literary ballads** were written later; two famous examples are Keats' "La Belle Dame Sans Merci" and Coleridge's *Rime of the Ancient Mariner.* One convention observed in ballads is **incremental repetition,** which is the repetition of some lines with a variation so that the narrative is advanced as in these stanzas from "Lord Randal":

> "O where hae ye been, Lord Randal, my son?
> O where hae ye been, my handsome young man?"
> "I hae been to the wild wood; mother, make my bed soon,
> For I'm weary wi' hunting, and fain wald lie down."

> "Where gat ye your dinner, Lord Randal, my son?
> Where gat ye your dinner, my handsome young man?"
> "I dined wi' my true-love; mother, make my bed soon,
> For I'm weary wi' hunting, and fain wald lie down."

> "What gat ye to your dinner, Lord Randal, my son?
> What gat ye to your dinner, my handsome young man?"
> "I gat eels boiled in broo; mother, make my bed soon,
> For I'm weary wi' hunting, and fain wald lie down."

> "What became of your bloodhounds, Lord Randal, my son?
> What became of your bloodhounds, my handsome young man?"
> "O they swelld and they died; mother, make my bed soon,
> For I'm weary wi' hunting, and fain wald lie down."

> "O I fear ye are poisoned, Lord Randal, my son!
> O I fear ye are poisoned, my handsome young man!"
> "O yes! I am poisoned; mother, make my bed soon,
> For I'm sick at the heart, and I fain wald lie down."

Ballads also use a **refrain** (a repeated line or stanza), often a nonsense refrain, which does not seem to have a connection with the story being narrated. Some think that oral passing down of ballads accounts for the nonsense refrains. To preserve the convention many more modern literary ballads include the nonsense refrain. The story of the ballad usually starts abruptly at the climax of the narrative and is concluded abruptly also, without comment from the author or singer. Ballads are popular, a possible reason being that they often tell a story of archetypal experience, one that strikes a chord of remembered experience for many kinds of human beings.

A **dramatic monologue** is a poem in which one person speaks either to someone else or to himself. Often a short narrative is brought out in the course of the monologue, and almost always the speaker reveals his true character. Robert Browning's are perhaps the best-known poems of this kind. In "The Bishop Orders His Tomb at Saint Praxed's Church," for example, the speaker, a dying bishop, tells his nephews (his sons?) the kind of tomb he would like to have, and in so doing reveals himself as a greedy, sensual person. The speaker of a dramatic monologue differs from the speaker of other poems in that he seems never to be the poet himself but rather a character in an episode. Another characteristic of the dramatic monologue is that the speaker addresses an unseen and unheard person. We must infer a listener's presence from remarks made by the speaker (as, for example, we infer the presence of the envoy who has come to arrange a marriage with the daughter of his master and the duke who is the speaker of Browning's "My Last Duchess"). Many of Edgar Lee Masters' poems from *Spoon River Anthology* are dramatic monologues, and T. S. Eliot's "The Love Song of J. Alfred Prufrock" is a variation of the form.

Metaphysical poetry is a term used to describe the poetry written by John Donne and those who followed his style, among whom were Andrew Marvell, George Herbert, and Abraham Cowley. In protest to the mellifluous Elizabethan love poetry, these poets wrote lines that were in language more like conversational speech, contained unusual metaphors, and often had irregular meter. They used **conceits,** exaggerated figures of speech designed to astonish, like Donne's comparison of a lady to fish bait. To make the figure of speech metaphysical they compared objects, persons, or images to things cosmic, or supernatural, or religious. Here is an example of a metaphysical conceit from Donne's "The Good-Morrow":

> My face in thine eye, thine in mine appears,
> And true plain hearts do in the faces rest;
> Where can we find two better hemispheres
> Without sharp north, without declining west?

The lovers in the poem are so close that the eye of each is reflected in the eye of the other; the reflected orb is then compared to a hemisphere, but a perfect hemisphere, unlike ordinary geographic divisions of the earth's surface. Metaphysical poetry, although in a sense ridiculing other love poetry, is also love poetry. However, its expression instead of being tender or complimentary in a conventional way is intellectualized.

Blank verse is composed of stanzas of unrhymed iambic pentameter. It is perhaps the most widely used of any verse form in English. Brought into England in the sixteenth century, it later became the standard in that country for drama. Shakespeare used it in his plays; Milton used it in *Paradise Lost;* Wordsworth used it in *The Prelude*. Blank verse accommodates so many variations that it continues to be popular. Modern poets use the form freely without evoking reminiscences of famous uses before theirs. No one, for example, reading Wallace Stevens' "Connoisseur of Chaos" would be forced to think of Wordsworth's *The Prelude*. A few lines from each of these poems will illustrate this. First, from *The Prelude:*

> Life's morning radiance hath not left the hills,
> Her dew is on the flowers. Those were the days
> Which also first emboldened me to trust
> With firmness, hitherto but slightly touched
> By such a daring thought, that I might leave
> Some monument behind me which pure hearts
> Should reverence.
>
> (Book VI, 51–57)

And from "Connoisseur of Chaos": [5]

> A. Well, an old order is a violent one.
> This proves nothing. Just one more truth, one more
> Element in the immense disorder of truths.
> B. It is April as I write. The wind
> Is blowing after days of constant rain.
> All this, of course, will come to summer soon.
>
> (IV, 21–26)

Modern poets do, however, use any of the traditional forms they wish. Sometimes they deliberately choose a very old convention precisely because they wish to evoke memories of an earlier poem for purposes either of contrast or of irony. Both contrast and irony result when the conversational language and commonplace imagery of much modern poetry is put into one of the traditional fixed forms, as this last tercet of Robert Frost's "Provide, Provide" [6] demonstrates:

> Better to go down dignified
> With boughten friendship at your side
> Than none at all. Provide, provide!

Some modern poets use traditional forms, but experiment with them, mixing stanzas of different forms, or changing rhythms from one stanza to another, or rhyming in unusual ways.

On the other hand, some modern poets reject all traditional forms

---

[5] Wallace Stevens, "Connoisseur of Chaos," *The Collected Poems of Wallace Stevens* (New York: Alfred A. Knopf, Inc., 1954). Reprinted by permission.

[6] Robert Frost, "Provide, Provide" from *Complete Poems of Robert Frost.* Copyright 1936 by Robert Frost. Copyright © 1964 by Leslie Frost Ballantine. Reprinted by permission of Holt, Rinehart and Winston, Inc.

and strive for new ways to express a world of changing customs, language, and values. *Free verse,* mentioned earlier (see page 131), is one way poets free themselves from older traditions. Although free verse does use rhythmical language it adheres to no fixed metrics. A line containing six feet, for example, could have six different kinds of feet. It would be unusual, however, to see so great a freedom. Poets ordinarily change rhythm for a sound reason—to intensify meaning, to understate, to match sense with sound. Here, from Eliot's "Burnt Norton," [7] are five lines of free verse:

> Time present and time past
> Are both perhaps present in time future,
> And time future contained in time past.
> If all time is eternally present
> All time is unredeemable.

Try to scan the lines and notice how difficult it is after the first line to decide where the divisions for marking feet should go. Note, too, however, that the language is rhythmical. Part of the musical quality comes from repetition, part from parallel syntax (parallel arrangement of words).

Poets free themselves from older traditions in countless ways. They invent new forms, they modify the old. Exciting poetry is being written today in both experimental and traditional forms. The criterion for excellence is not the form the poem chooses, but that elusive combination of talent and sensitivity that permits him to make of language a poem.

Knowledge of forms and conventions is not useful only to poets and scholars; you will find you need it when you write your essays about poetry because it gives you practical and precise terms with which to discuss poems. In addition, many otherwise puzzling elements become clear to you when you know the form or convention within which the poet shapes his work.

We have stressed in our discussion of poetry that the elements poets use to shape their poems create certain effects. Nevertheless, any one device is effective only in so far as it contributes to the whole poem. Correctly interpreting either an element of a poem or the whole poem is based, of course, upon knowledge of the technicalities of poetic creation, but interpretation increases in value as you correlate your own experience and sensitivity with the poet's shaping. Thus, as you apply your knowledge you are increasing not only your own enjoyment of poetry but your ability to help others enjoy it more.

---

[7] T. S. Eliot, "Burnt Norton," *Collected Poems 1909–1962* (New York: Harcourt, Brace and World, Inc.) Reprinted by permission.

DISCOVERING A POEM

We have chosen two poems as models to demonstrate how the discovery method presented in Section One of this book, combined with analysis of the specific devices used in shaping poems, can give insights into, and thus prepare you for writing essays about, poetry. We will work first with one of Shakespeare's well-known sonnets and then with a poem by a modern writer, "The Rival" by Sylvia Plath.

POEM ONE
SONNET CXLVI

Poor, soul, the center of my sinful earth,
Thrall to these rebel powers that thee array,
Why dost thou pine within and suffer dearth,
Painting thy outward walls so costly gay?
Why so large cost, having so short a lease,
Dost thou upon thy fading mansion spend?
Shall worms, inheritors of this excess,
Eat up thy charge? Is this thy body's end?
Then, soul, live thou upon thy servant's loss,
And let that pine to aggravate thy store;
Buy terms divine in selling hours of dross;
Within be fed, without be rich no more:
    So shalt thou feed on Death, that feeds on men,
    And Death once dead, there's no more dying then.
               William Shakespeare

1. DISCOVERING THE DRAMATIC EXPERIENCE

The experience of this poem is one of the most dramatic and, at the same time, one of the most philosophic that can happen to human beings. It is the confrontation of a man with his soul. An internal experience, it presents a speaker considering the low estate to which his soul has fallen. He then questions his soul to learn both how this came about and what can be done about it.

2. DISCOVERING THE AUTHOR'S PRESENTATION OF EXPERIENCE

In order to make the dramatic experience of "Sonnet CXLVI" vital we must examine the means the poet uses to make the experience reveal something about human nature or the human condition. This examination will consist of analyzing the elements of technique that Shakespeare uses to give the experience universality.

Words

The words seem simple, yet the usages of many are puzzling. Why, for example, is the soul called the center of "my sinful *earth*" (line 1)? A little work with the dictionary indicates that one meaning of the word *earth* is the substance of the human body or the human body itself. Obviously, the poet speaks of the soul as the center of man's body. *Thrall* (line 2) originally meant "a slave or bondsman." So the soul is a slave to the body. The next word whose usage puzzles is *charge* (line 8)—how can worms eat up a soul's *charge?* The word *charge* comes from the Late Latin *carricare,* meaning "to load or fill to usual capacity." We begin to understand that worms will eat finally all that the body had managed to gather to itself. A final word, *aggravate* (line 10), needs explanation. Its usual meaning is "to make worse," which makes us wonder why the poem speaks of "making worse" a *store* or that which is stored up. Again, the derivation of the word helps. It was used in Shakespeare's time in its original sense of "to make heavy." That which was stored up is "made heavier," or added to.

Some words of the sonnet have connotative meanings differing from their denotative meanings. As is usual, connotative meanings in this sonnet must be grasped by a reader's sensitivity. Those meanings will be clearer after other elements are noted.

Point of View

The words of the sonnet are spoken by a persona in first person, and the entire poem consists of words of direct address. A speaker addresses his soul. Point of view here, however, presents a more complex problem than in most poems. The complexity arises from the difficulty in deciding precisely who or what the speaker is. Can we say a man addresses his soul? What part of the man? Line nine speaks of the persona as "thy servant," meaning the servant of the soul. Is this the body? Does the body address the soul? Or does the mind of the speaker address his soul? Or does the soul, as the "center of man," direct an inward reflection? The last seems most likely. When we consider the end of the sonnet, it seems that the soul of the speaker directs his mind to make the observations that lead to this conclusion.

Imagery and Symbolism

The imagery of this sonnet is organized around a dominant metaphor, that of a house. Throughout, the poem refers symbolically to the body of man as a house. In line 4 it speaks of the "walls" of the house. In line 6 it calls the body a "fading mansion." Dwelling within the house is the soul: a dweller who is a "slave" to the house itself. Real estate terms reinforce the dominant metaphor: the soul has only a "short lease" on the house. The dweller, then, is not a permanent tenant of the mansion; he simply leases it for a short time. Costs of upkeep are mentioned: line 4 speaks of the cost of "painting . . . [the] . . . outward walls"; line 10 speaks of the costs of increasing the stores within the house. As we read through the poem we become aware that this single metaphor governs the thought of the entire sonnet. The image forces us to visualize the dweller within the house—the soul—pining, suffering dearth (famine) (line 3), while all the means are spent to enhance the appearance of the body or to increase its store of material things. The image makes us see that the mansion, however well kept up outwardly, is fading. We see it dying now, and we are forced to project our thoughts into the future to see it completely crumbled and consumed by worms.

Imagery controls the point of view of the sonnet. The terms of direct address in which the poem is cast form another image. Our imaginations expand upon the concept of the sonnet as we are compelled by imagery to see the abstraction as the poet saw it.

Myth and Archetypal Pattern

To discover an archetypal pattern in this sonnet we must look for factors of the experience that are an instinctual expression of man's basic nature. We all know that members of the human race have always been concerned with life and death; and only the smallest amount of research tells us that the origins of the concept of soul are concealed in prehistory. The human mind has always had a deep philosophical regard for the ultimate fate of the soul at death. In large measure our recognition of the experience is instinctual also. Thus, the poet communicates with us at both the conscious and the subconscious level. We are aware in the sonnet of an individual's meditations upon the tendency of humankind to expend the means at hand on bodily concerns at the expense of the spiritual. But, because the experience itself is one embedded deeply in the *unconscious* of the human race, our minds seize upon the experience with full awareness of its universality.

Structure

Analysis of the prosody of "Sonnet CXLVI" shows that it is composed of fourteen basically iambic pentameter lines. Scansion of the two opening lines, however, will show how a variation from this meter prevents a singsong monotony:

Poór soúl, ‖ the cén | ter ŏf | my sín | fŭl eárth,
Thráll tŏ | thĕse réb | el powérs | that thĕe | ar ráy

The poem opens with a strong spondee followed by a caesura, making the words of address stand out. The lines then contain an iamb, a pyrrhic, and two more iambs, then a trochee and four iambs. Five lines of the sonnet (7, 10, 11, 12, 14) are strict iambic pentameter. Of the remaining lines, three have only two syllables varying the meter and seven have only one. Reading aloud reveals effects other than the prevention of monotony that these slight variations bring. For one, we recall that the entire sonnet is speech, and we realize that for its language to resemble natural speech it cannot be cast in pure metrical lines. English speech is basically iambic pentameter, with humps and bumps, with stops and starts—and this is the rhythm of "Sonnet CXLVI." Another effect is achieved by the placement of the variations, in each case, at the beginning of the lines. Lines opening with a spondee or a trochee have a falling meter. Thus, emphasis is given to the important words at the beginning of the lines; and the falling away of emphasis after the opening controls the interpretation we give the words.

The poem is in traditional English, or Shakespearean, form: three quatrains rhyming *a b a b, c d c d, e f e f,* followed by the couplet rhyming *gg.* Further, this sonnet follows convention by presenting its image in the first quatrain, intensifying it in the second, and reaching a heightened climax of the image in the third; by having a turn of thought at the third quatrain; and by imposing an epigrammatic comment upon the imagery and its representational thought in the concluding couplet.

With these fundamental elements of the structure of the poem we have the materials that will enable us to understand what the poet does with it. Individual readers will use the materials in different ways, but everyone must have knowledge of them to obtain a starting point for bringing his own insights to understanding and enjoyment of the sonnet.

Voice and Tone

When one concentrates on the unseen but very clearly heard speaker of this sonnet, he becomes aware that the individual speaking is on familiar terms with his soul. This is not a persona who is thinking fleetingly and for the first time of the state of his soul. The tone in the opening two lines is one of genuine curiosity. At the turn of thought the tone seems to have gained in confidence, as if the speaker had received answers. Finally, with the couplet, the confidence grows to assurance. The answer has been certified.

Statement

Until the turn of thought in the third quatrain, the statement in this sonnet is in the form of question. The questions, however, are rhetorical, and their implied answers have the force of assertions. Is it not true, they ask, that man spends all he has on the material and neglects the spiritual? The thought changes in the third quatrain to suggest that if this is true the soul should reverse the process and let the body pine to bring an increase for itself. The statement of the couplet is a paradox: if the soul should cause the death of the body it will cause at the same time its life. Study of this paradox brings enriched understanding of all terms of the sonnet. We will come back to this point later.

3. DISCOVERING SUBJECT AND THEME

Our first reading showed the dramatic experience of "Sonnet CXLVI" to be that of a speaker's confrontation with his soul. Our interest thereafter centers on precisely how the confrontation is structured. In different phases of step two we saw that the situation is structured in traditional English sonnet form, organized around the "key design" of an image showing man's body as a decaying mansion within which resides a dying soul. The language used by the speaker reveals his puzzled state: he cannot understand why the all-powerful soul, the controlling force of man's life, permits the body to take for its own selfish uses all the energies and drives of the whole man. The language, the point of view, and the structure of the poem we saw as a design to present a problem of universal scope and to offer a solution to that problem.

Style and point of view demonstrated that men can view their bodies and souls as entities: the actions and conduct of men determine the eventual outcome of both body and soul.

The organizing principle of the dominant metaphor made clear the precise way in which man causes death for both his body and his soul. Man, the metaphor revealed, spends his means and his energies for the adornment of or the sensual nourishment of his body. In this lifelong preoccupation he thinks little of his soul. As a result his soul dies within him. Man spends his time "painting . . . [his] . . . outward walls so costly gay," the speaker tells his soul, and the very telling makes him stop at this moment of confrontation to wonder why he concerns himself with making his body beautiful when the nature of that body is to possess beauty for only a short "lease." It fades, then dies, and eventually comes to the ugliness of being eaten by worms.

All the means of shaping the poem—the point of view of one familiar with his soul, addressing it in familiar diction in the terms of a dominant metaphor concerned with the familiar imagery of houses, structuring the address within the traditional English sonnet form of problem and solution in the rhythm of English speech—reveal the subject as an archetypal expression of man's universal interest in that part of his being that transcends the physical.

Individual conclusions as to what the sonnet says about this subject, what its theme may be, as always will vary. For instance, one reader could give a prose paraphrase like this: " 'Sonnet CXLVI' says man can achieve immortality only if he makes his principle concern the enrichment of his spiritual life." Another could say, " 'Sonnet CXLVI' is an affirmation of the Christian concept of the belief in the resurrection of the body and the immortality of the soul." Whatever a reader says, his increased understanding of the poem will give validity to his particular interpretation.

SAMPLE ESSAYS

SAMPLE ESSAY 7
USING STATEMENT

INSTRUCTIONS. In Section One, pages 17–20, you read about the importance of statement. You probably recall that the author may make comments in his own person (direct statement), through a persona (the voice in Shakespeare's "Sonnet CXLVI") or through a character in the work (indirect statement). Whether stated by the author or by a persona speaking indirectly for the author, statement in a work can provide a concise and reliable method of getting at some aspect of the meaning of a work. If the statement is made ironically, of course you will look to the meaning that lies under the surface of what may appear to be a deceptively simple remark. Some poems, like the sonnet, will often conclude with a statement. In fiction and drama, a key line of dialogue or description may contain a statement that reflects much of the meaning of the entire work. Such statements are crucial and provide worthwhile subject matter for essays.

A statement is much more concrete than an idea, for a statement is restricted and will occur as a written passage; its meaning, however, may be as encompassing in scope as a general idea, present and only implied in the content of a work. Characters may embody ideas; so, too, may dominant symbols, images, and specific actions. Your discovery of ideas, like your discovery of statements themselves, provides subject matter for essays. The approach to both (to a specific statement or to a general idea) is through analysis and proof. You must show through evidence found in the work that your interpretation is sound.

Your purpose in writing essays of statement of idea will be to explain for your reader the meaning of the statement or idea and its importance to the work. In the introduction, quote the statement (synthesize the idea) unless its length is prohibitive. If the passage is long, make reference to it as specifically as possible. Show how the statement is important to the work, and in your thesis sentence, indicate how the statement or idea reflects various meanings in the work. The body of your essay will contain a discussion, point by point, of the meaning and importance of the statement or idea. In the conclusion summarize the artistic function of the statement (show how its placement within the specific context of a passage clarifies, deepens, or synthesizes meaning) and briefly review its place in the work. If the statement contains a major theme, your essay will increase in effectiveness if you can succinctly state that theme. Similarly, if your subject is an idea, review its place in the work and relate its importance to the theme.

The essay below analyzes the last two lines of Shakespeare's "Sonnet CXLVI." Note that the explanation of the statement contained in the last two lines clarifies the meaning of the entire poem. In other works the statement may not warrant such detailed explication. In such cases, use the statement as a means of exploring other aspects of the work. Reread the essay about Odysseus on pages 34–38 to review this technique, then compare its method with that of the essay below.

SHAKESPEARE'S "SONNET CXLVI":
THEME THROUGH STATEMENT

During the Elizabethan period in England the sonnet came into vogue. Cohering into four clusters—abab, cdcd, efef, gg—the new English or Shakespearean form tended to shift in thought in three places and conclude tersely in a final heroic couplet. The last two lines often functioned as an answer to either an argument or a question. Shakespeare, one of the greatest writers of the sonnet, followed this form in his "Sonnet CXLVI." In the first eight lines the narrator, in direct address, chides his soul. In the next four lines he exhorts his soul to solve by act and attitude the dilemma of its condition. The last two lines form the statement:

> So shalt thou feed on Death, that feeds on men,
> And Death once dead, there's no more dying then.

Framed in an ironic reversal, the couplet culminates the sonnet's profound philosophical discourse upon the ultimate meaning of death.

The sonnet opens with the narrator or persona asking his soul —the conscious, acting, eternal part of himself—why it suffers from neglect, why it has chosen to direct all its energies and devotion to its "outward walls," to physical life and material possessions. Substituting worldly for spiritual values, the narrator continues, is "costly": the body will die, and with it all material gains; the soul (the mind and spirit), on the other hand, ignored and neglected for a lifetime, will never have grown in wisdom and vision.

On a philosophical level, the persona is protesting materialism. On a spiritual level, however, the persona is concerned with a much larger question, the meaning and consequence of death. Man, fearing death and the unknown, ignores the mind and cherishes the tangible existence of the body; ironically, in doing so, he kills his soul and still loses his body. This irony forms the dilemma the persona seeks to solve. He says: "Then, soul, live . . . to . . . Buy terms divine;/Within be fed, without be rich no more." These lines exhort the soul to forget the vanities of the body and material ambition for they are transient; instead, concentrate on the riches of the mind and spirit, for they live forever.

The rewards accruing to a spiritual and intellectual life are told in the final statement and constitute a skillful and double-edged solution to defeating both the fear and reality of death. The dimension, the ambiguity, and the power of the final couplet derive from a basic premise supporting the existence of two worlds, this one and the one after death. The couplet answers the dilemma of two kinds of dying, spiritual and physical, and promises rewards on more than two levels of living. Physical life is pronounced inferior to a state of enlightened awareness, though, on an even higher level, a spiritual life on earth becomes significant as preparation for another, eternal life in which the soul continues into infinity. The statement, centered in these levels of living and dying, negates physical death and asserts the vitality of this life and the tenuous, but definite promise of the next.

A sense of fulfillment through spiritual awareness, the statement declares, can be achieved through ignoring the body and thereby cancelling its importance as an ultimate end. So doing, the soul (man's consciousness) can successfully overcome the fear of physical death and live fully, assured of its immortality. It can "feed on Death, that feeds on men," that is, it can, by ignoring death, defeat it, for by losing its importance in the mind death loses its control over daily life. On another, ironic level (for the narrator's soul *is* miserably shackled in materialism) the narrator slyly asserts that for the soul to be freed the body must first die. The invitation is explicit: mortal death results in eternal life.

Finally, the narrator states in the last line that ". . . Death once dead, there's no more dying then." This line concludes the poem with a wry contention that is equally serious and humorous: when the soul no longer fears Death (as a concept), death no longer exists, for dying, while still alive, is only a state of mind; further, when the body dies, the soul will not have to fret about repeating the process, for the body dies only once.

Thus in the final statement, through a fictitious conversation between a man and his soul, Shakespeare seriously proposes a method for living wisely and fully, and he provides several answers to the question of death, asserting ultimately that man worries too much about what he can do nothing about, and does too little about that over which he has control. If man must die, so be it; in the meantime, live wisely. Seldom do fourteen lines contain such levels of thought, and for this reason, we still read "Sonnet CXLVI" today.

SAMPLE ESSAY 8
USING DOMINANT METAPHOR

INSTRUCTIONS.   To be properly understood, metaphor (like simile, allusion, symbol, and other types of figurative language) must be considered a part of imagery. The term imagery derives from "image": a reflection, a model, or representation of a person. As a critical term, image still denotes a literal representation, but in literature the writer uses a word or group of words to elicit a sensory experience or a mental picture of an object. "Shining red apples" is an image; it calls to mind a specific, known object, and the image is conceptualized visually by its shape and color. "The apple of the mind," however, is a figurative image—a metaphor— for the meaning of apples has been extended. We pay attention in poetry and prose works to images, and when they are used figuratively to suggest or represent other objects or abstract ideas they become, properly, figures of speech. We speak of figures of speech or collections of images in a given literary work as imagery.

You have already read about symbols and allusions in Section One (for information about writing essays using these subjects see page 109, using symbolism, and page 208, using allusion). Allusions and symbols, like metaphor and all figures of speech, have a common purpose: aiding the artist in communicating directly a rich, complex experience incommunicable in ordinary prose. Imagery enriches writing through suggestion and implication; it renders the texture of language dense with potential emotive and sensory response by creating simultaneously several levels of meaning. The ways in which the author gives his work this density of meaning is your greatest concern when writing about imagery, and the effect or meaning of figurative language in a work provides you with your thesis.

We write about imagery to make known to the reader the meanings to be derived from a close examination of the work's language. Several types of essays are possible. You can write about the world of the work, both physical and imaginative, which the images evoke; or the patterns or clusters of images as they reveal or portray a particular meaning, action, or character. You can analyze the imagery as it elicits responses based on myth or archetype; or the interaction of the imagery to produce a particular effect. You may choose one image or figure of speech, and if its meaning is obscure or highly complex, explain the function, meaning, or overall effect on the work or on other imagery. A dominant image that functions as a motif will, if pointed up and explained, significantly aid your reader's understanding.

In writing about metaphor, remember that it compares two quite different things without stating the comparison. In a metaphor, an ordinary word will have ascribed to it the qualities of another, seemingly very different word. For example, "My mind is a bright, shining apple" is a metaphor. Often, however, the author will only imply the subject. "My mind" is clearly the subject in the metaphor above, but in "Sonnet LXXIII," for example, the subject is omitted when Shakespeare writes:

> That time of year thou mayst in me behold
> When yellow leaves, or none, or few, do hang
> Upon those boughs which shake against the cold,
> Bare ruin'd choirs, where late the sweet birds sang,
> In me thou see'st the twilight of such day
> As after sunset fadeth in the west . . .

In these lines old age is the subject. Not only is the subject unstated, but the metaphor is extended. Therefore when you begin your study of a passage, determine whether the metaphor contained in the passage is simple or extended. A simple metaphor occurs in isolation and has no referent in the lines preceding or following it. An extended metaphor, on the other hand, will function as the controlling image in a passage or, as in many of Shakespeare's sonnets, in the complete poem. If the metaphor is extended, divide it into its two parts, the **tenor** and the **vehicle.** The terms tenor and vehicle were devised by I. A. Richards. According to him, the tenor is the idea being expressed or the subject of the comparison. The vehicle is the image by which the idea is conveyed. For example, the main idea, or the tenor in the metaphor of the passage above, is old age. The vehicle is a series of images of late fall or winter that carry the idea. After determining the tenor and the vehicle, determine the ways the many vehicles or images are used to convey or express the main idea through unusual comparisons.

In Shakespeare's "Sonnet CXLVI" the tenor of the first extended metaphor is man's soul and body. The vehicles or images used to make the comparison are the occupant or renter, and a house. The meanings to be derived from such a seemingly simple comparison are many, as the essay that follows will demonstrate.

Pointing to the differences between two similar things may result in worthwhile observations, but as a general rule you will encounter and so study comparisons made between two very dissimilar things—an idea and the images used to describe it—and your task in analysis is to determine how the idea is enriched with unexpected, multiple meanings as a result of the comparison. Explaining those meanings becomes the purpose of your paper. Study the essay below about a poem with which you are now familiar. Note that the introduction states the subject and theme of the poem and the body analyzes the meanings to be derived from the two major metaphors. Note also, and this is the great advantage of figurative language, how Shakespeare compresses his many complex and vividly expressed ideas into a few lines. In the essay, the explanation of the metaphors is written in straight or literal prose and consequently requires hundreds of words. Even so, the metaphors' meanings are still not completely realized. Skillful use of metaphor, understandably, is the mark of a highly accomplished writer.

DOMINANT METAPHOR IN SHAKESPEARE'S "SONNET CXLVI"

In "Sonnet CXLVI" Shakespeare develops his argument by means of two interlocking metaphors. The first compares man's body or physical world to a house within which the soul, the occupant, is trapped. This metaphor dominates the first eight lines and poses, in two questions, the problems that result when man devotes his life to materialism. The solution and final proposal for escaping entrapment are expressed within a second, extended metaphor, which is the chain process of lesser concepts or conditions (physical life, physical death) being subjugated philosophically, or being "eaten" by other concepts larger and more powerful (spiritual life, the eternal soul). Through the interaction of these two metaphors, which merge finally into an ironic reversal, Shakespeare expresses his profound ideas about life and the ageless dilemma of death.

The first question posed in direct address by the narrator to his soul chides the soul's failure to distinguish between two kinds of well-being: the material and the spiritual. The owner of a house, or man's soul, is spending so much time and money making his house beautiful and impressive from the outside that within, in the spirit, he is exhausted and impoverished. He "suffers dearth" and "pines within"; he is spiritually and intellectually starved. With a figure of speech, in which the house is the body and the soul its occupant, the metaphor becomes meaningful on several levels, for "outward walls" may refer either to the physical body or, more abstractly, to material-ism. This ambiguity enlarges the meaning of the poem and serves as preparation for the second question.

In lines 5 through 8 the meaning of the house and its occupant is expanded as the narrator addresses his soul a second time, asking why, when it has "so short a lease" it spends "so large cost" upon a "fading mansion." The soul, the narrator asserts, is only a renter, a temporary occupant. Ownership of any kind is one of man's crip-pling, pathetic illusions, for the body will die and with it the need for all worldly possessions. Ironically, worms, not the soul, are the true heirs of "this excess," this fleshly home the soul so covets. Explicit in the narrator's metaphorical question is the argument that the soul is immortal, and the proposal that follows suggests a neat reversal as a solution to the soul's confinement and the seeming dilemma of the body's death. The reversal is accomplished by means of the motif of life or living, which acts as a transitional, unifying device throughout the poem.

The word "live" contains three meanings in the poem. In the first four lines the soul lives, or resides, in the body. "Live" in this sense is pejorative; the soul does not thrive or grow, it only exists. In lines 5 through 8 we discover, ironically, that the body is really living on the soul; that is, the body thrives at the soul's expense. Further, the body at its death becomes food for worms, and the worms eat, or live on, "this excess." In lines 9 through 12 the poem shifts in tone, and a transition from a negative to a positive or affirmative view of life is accomplished in large part through the introduction of the third meaning of "to live," which connotes an attitude or way of life. The term becomes less literal and more conceptual, though the soul is exhorted to live on or "use" the body as a means to a higher life. The double meaning of the term "to live" ("Then, soul, live thou upon thy servant's loss") blends with the concept of devouring, or feeding, and line 12 concludes, "Within be fed, without be rich no more." To live, to be fed, to feed: these terms unify the poem, add complexity of meaning to the metaphor of the house, and become a clear transition into the second dominant metaphor.

The final heroic couplet culminates with the second metaphor, clearly implied in the first eight lines and stated in line 12. Because the soul will be consumed by the body if its devotion to materialism continues, and because the body proves to be vulnerable (subject to consumption by worms), the final lines of the poem suggest, through the metaphor of devouring and being devoured, a way to reverse the process so that the soul can triumph even over Death (literal death and Death in the abstract). The solution is both simple and profound: the soul, by turning to higher, spiritual values, negates the importance of the body. The soul then grows in power, transcending the death of the body. Transcended, it loses its fears of dying, and therefore its fear of the concept of Death. The soul can thus "feed" on Death that causes such anxiety in man, for Death exists or "feeds" on men only because the body is mortal. Thus in the final line, ironic and transcendental both, we see that when the fear of Death is overcome "there's no more dying then": if the soul transcends the body, Death is defeated, for Death is only a state of mind and the body can only die once. The metaphor follows: worms consume the body; the body is consumed by the soul; the soul, grown in power and magnitude, consumes Death and so triumphs. Death, devoured, becomes the equal of worms.

Through dominant metaphor Shakespeare presents an ingenious plan for defeating Death and for using eternal values as a means for man to transcend his own mortality.

SAMPLE ESSAY 9
USING FORM OR CONVENTION

INSTRUCTIONS.   To write about the form or convention of a work of literature you must become aware of the traditional uses of the particular form or convention you are to analyze. As we use the term here, form refers to the fixed forms of works of literature. Do not confuse this meaning of form with the other meaning, which refers to the structure and texture of a work. Your instructor will make clear which sense of the term you are to consider (see Glossary).

The term conventions (the accepted modes of procedure in any art) refers in literature to accepted devices (like the soliloquy in drama, the stream of consciousness mode in prose fiction, the pastoral mode in poetry) used by authors for many ages. At times the terms form and convention are interchangeable; for example, the sonnet, which began as a convention, became a fixed form and is referred to by either term. Most of the literary terms in this book may be considered conventions, because they represent accepted modes of procedure used in the creation of works of literature. If you are asked to write an essay on form or convention, your task will be to show the integral relationship of the form of the work to its texture and content. In short, you must show that an unmistakable relationship exists between the external shape of a work and its internal shape (see also pages 132–142). You should take as your thesis either a point concerned with the underlying reasons an author might have had for choosing to write within a certain form or convention (what the form or convention does to enrich the work) or a point concerned with an author's particularly brilliant use of a particular form or convention.

As you develop paragraphs in the body of your essay, analyze different aspects of the convention as they are shown in the work. As you write, clarify the more difficult aspects of the form or convention as they are exemplified in the work. Show how interrelated parts of the convention are especially effective. Your conclusion should be an emphatic evaluation of what the use of the convention does for the work.

THE FORM AND CONTENT OF SHAKESPEARE'S "SONNET CXLVI"

The content of Shakespeare's "Sonnet CXLVI" is conceived in the dramatic terms of man's universal desire for eternal life. This dramatic content interlocks with the staid form of the English sonnet in a manner that makes them interdependent. This interdependence extends as well to the sound and movement of the sonnet. The material of the poem progresses from question to amplification of question to suggested answer, and finally, to answer. The progression falls quite naturally into the traditional English sonnet division of three quatrains and the conclusive couplet. Each of the three quatrains represents a development in thought. Further, each successive quatrain presents a surging wave of sound and movement paralleling the increasing strength of the content development.

The problem is stated in the initial question of the first quatrain: Why does man allow his soul to die? In the second quatrain a corresponding development intensifies the question: Was man's body created expressly to cause the death of the soul? There is the tragic implication here that the very nature of man poses an insoluble problem. However, with a slight change of thought, the third quatrain suggests a possible negative answer to the questions of the preceding quatrains. It intimates that the soul can live if it allows the body to die. Then, with an incisive change of thought, the couplet presents the final solution: the soul, by refusing to accept death, defeats death. This triumphant solution is arrived at only by the steadily increasing strength of the thought development.

Scansion shows that the rhythm and sound of the first quatrain pose the initial question in arresting tones:

> Poor soul, ‖ the cén | ter of | my sín | ful earth,
> Thrall to | these réb | el powers | that thée | array,
> Why dost | thou pine | within | and súf | fer dearth,
> Painting | thy out | ward walls | so cost | ly gay?

The spondee of the first foot, stressing almost equally the words "poor" and "soul," makes dramatic and intimate the terms in which the speaker will address his soul. The persona asks his question metaphorically. He speaks of man as a house, his soul a slave held captive therein, and his body a dying structure, which nevertheless is gaily adorned. The terms used by the speaker are both intimate and sympathetic; the tones are equally intimate and sympathetic. The strength of line 1 diminishes after these strong words of direct address until the soul is named "center," in a stressed tone, of the "sinful earth" (the body), also stressed. After line 1 there are only two heavily stressed syllables in the first quatrain—that which refers to the soul—"thrall" (slave), and the action word, "painting." All lines of the quatrain end with the falling accents of iambs, so that the intimate accents of sympathy in the words of address are followed by accents of sorrowful concern as the falling state of the soul is described in falling metrical accents.

The variation of metrics throughout the sonnet lends a conversational rhythm to the language, as the lines of the second quatrain show:

> Why so | large cost, ‖ having | so short | a lease,
> Dost thou | upon | thy fad | ing man | sion spénd?
> Shall worms, ‖ inher | itors | of this | excess,
> Eat up | thy charge? ‖ Is this | thy body | y's end?

Here are the uneven accents of familiar conversation. In addition, the homeliness of the metaphor is aided by the use of short, blunt words like "lease," "spend," "eat," "charge." Heavily stressed words of the quatrain are "why," "dost," "worms," and "eat." Thus, the metaphorical question is stripped of nonessentials to stand out starkly in our imaginations.

Earlier we had seen the fallen state of the soul; here we see a projection of the future state of the body—a crumbled ruin, consumed by worms, the true inheritors of the costly mansion.

The third quatrain shows greater variation than the preceding ones, as it exhibits a change of thought. Because the suggestion is unexpected, the accents must change unexpectedly. This quatrain suggests the possible solution that the soul can control human action, that it can permit the body to die as it spends means upon itself for "terms divine." Scansion reveals its wide variation of meter:

> Then, soul, ‖ live thou | upon | thy ser | vant's loss,
> And let | that pine | to ag | gravate | thy store.
> Buy terms | divine | in sell | ing hours | of dross;
> Within ‖ be fed, ‖ without ‖ be rich ‖ no more.

The many spondees of this quatrain make dramatic its suggestion. "Then, soul," the speaker begins in strong tones of discovery. He proceeds to offer his solution in lines filled with many strong accents, the last of which is composed completely of accented syllables: "Within ‖ be fed, ‖ without ‖ be rich ‖ no more." There are also many pauses in this last line—after the words "within," "fed," "without," "be rich," and "no more." This heavy occurrence of caesuras slows the pace of the line so that phrases take on a powerful and measured voice stress, bringing out the thought with clear, forceful emphasis.

With the couplet comes the conclusive solution traditional to the English sonnet, but rather than being expressed in the usual, somewhat general terms, the concluding lines emerge dramatically. It is as though the paradoxical solution occurs to poet and reader at the same instant:

> So shalt | thou feed | on Death, ‖ that feeds | on men,
> And Death | once dead, ‖ there's no | more dy | ing then.

Strong, monosyllabic words, spoken in strong, heavily accented tones, state—in an unexpected twist of thought—the triumphant conclusion: if the soul permits the body to die, death itself is slain. If death is slain, there is "no more dying." The forceful accents of the couplet ring with the paradoxical truth that both body and soul can then continue to live.

SAMPLE ESSAY 10
USING STYLE

INSTRUCTIONS.   An essay about the style of a work should be exceptionally illuminating to your readers. Choose as your thesis some aspect of the language of a work that seems of actual significance in controlling either response to the work or interpretation of it. Your purpose is to show how your own feeling about a work has been influenced by its style. As you organize your essay be sure to assemble quotations that let your reader see in operation the points you are making about the style of the work.

In your introduction lead up to your thesis sentence by giving generalized statements concerning the aspect of the language of the work with which you will be dealing. Let your thesis sentence state clearly what relationship style bears to the work as a whole.

The body of your essay should deal with specific elements that illustrate this function. Analyze the diction. Is it colloquial, unusual, highly allusive? Analyze the tone. Is it a distinctive factor, one that is an integral part of the meaning of the work? Analyze sentence structure: are the sentences short or long; are they characteristically terse, rambling, lucid? Analyze the use of metaphor as it appears to be a distinguishing mark of the language. As you develop each of these factors show how each relates to your central idea of the function of the style in this particular work.

In your conclusion point out how an analytical look at the style of the work deepens understanding and appreciation of it.

STYLE AS ARGUMENT:
SHAKESPEARE'S "SONNET CXLVI"

Despite the complex philosophical thought Shakespeare expresses in "Sonnet CXLVI," he seems as free as someone who makes his inward meditations in a natural sequence of thoughts. He even seems not to consider an audience for his words. This appearance of freedom results in part from the style of the sonnet. Three aspects of the style—diction, figures of speech, and tone—vivify and make familiar the context of this poem.

The diction of "Sonnet CXLVI" is common and homely. Although certain words seem to be used in an uncommon way, learning that these uncommon words ("charge," "aggravate," "thrall," "earth") had meanings in an earlier time that they do not have today shows that they too form a part of the common diction of the poem. The word "earth," used to designate the body, is extremely plain, but, oddly, is the most vivid word that could have been chosen to make explicit the lowliness of the body in comparison to its "center," the soul. Here, also, "center," describing the importance of and the controlling position of the soul in relation to the body, is both the simplest and the most striking word for these purposes. In addition, in the opening quatrains, the choice of questions for the mode of address to the soul makes for the most familiar, homely way of conversing with one's soul. The use of "thy" and "thou" adds to the familiarity. There are no elevated words; death is called simply that, "Death," and the destruction of the body is described in literal terms: it is eaten by worms.

Phrases, too, are formed of commonplace terms: the speaker of the sonnet talks of "large costs," of "eating up a charge," of a "servant's loss," of "buying terms divine," of "being fed." Clauses are short and bluntly to the point, as these examples will show: "Within be fed, without be rich no more"; "So shalt thou feed on Death, that feeds on men." Most of the sentences forming the grammatical sense of the sonnet are either simple or compound, making for straightforward, sincere expression. The entire diction of the sonnet moves freely, despite the depth of its thought, to give a familiar air to the drama of an individual's probing of his soul.

For this philosophical probing the poet chooses, not high-sounding, intellectual figures of speech, but the homely metaphor of a house. Commonplace phrases like "painting the walls," adding to "the store," and having a "short lease," build pictures that add to the natural air of the whole. It is natural, too, at the concluding thought in the couplet to visualize the homely figure of the soul's feeding on death, as worms have fed on the body. This paradox, showing that death is a necessity for the soul's life, is at once epigrammatic and familiar.

Familiar also is the tone in which the diction and the figures are delivered. The language of "Sonnet CXLVI" is conversational, as though the individual who talks with his soul has done so many times. He and his soul are not strangers. "Poor soul," he begins in commiserating accents, and puts his questions with the air of one sincerely concerned by his respected friend's plight. And he seems genuinely puzzled that the friend would allow that inferior entity, the body, to take over all that they possess for its own selfish adornment or pleasure. The turn of thought comes naturally, as the speaker suddenly seems to have received an answer to his questions. At this point the tone becomes confident, as though the speaker is talking to an equal. Conditions can change, he states. Although still using his friendly, familiar tone, he, nevertheless, gives a command: stop permitting this waste that leads to your death, and reverse the process. "Buy terms divine in selling hours of dross," he commands.

The final break of the sonnet is not a shock; we do not hear the epigrammatic solution in the couplet expressed in grandly general terms. Instead, soul and speaker seem to speak as one as they tell us here in familiar tones and language that in reversing the process of shameful waste, the soul can thus "feed on Death that feeds on men."

DISCOVERING A POEM

The following free verse poem presents a sharp contrast to Shakespeare's sonnet. It is not so tightly structured and its references, imagery, and style are contemporary. Both poems, however, are basically concerned with the same subject; both use direct address in which the persona speaks to an abstract concept.

POEM TWO
THE RIVAL [8]

If the moon smiled, she would resemble you.
You leave the same impression
Of something beautiful, but annihilating.
Both of you are great light borrowers.
Her O-mouth grieves at the world; yours is unaffected,
And your first gift is making stone out of everything.
I wake to a mausoleum; you are here,
Ticking your fingers on the marble table, looking for cigarettes,
Spiteful as a woman, but not so nervous,
And dying to say something unanswerable.

The moon, too, abases her subjects,
But in the daytime she is ridiculous.
Your dissatisfactions, on the other hand,
Arrive through the mailslot with loving regularity,
White and blank, expansive as carbon monoxide.

No day is safe from news of you,
Walking about in Africa maybe, but thinking of me.

1. DISCOVERING THE DRAMATIC EXPERIENCE

At the paraphrasable level, Sylvia Plath's poem "The Rival" consists of a monologue in which a persona speaks to someone she seems to hate. She compares the person with the moon, stating that he deprives her of life, that he is cruel and indifferent and oppressive. A first reading indicates that the person addressed may be a lover or husband, and a love relationship is easily assumed because the tone and language, the intimacy and misery of the persona's voice reveal familiarity, obsessive attraction, and anger. The persona obviously considers herself the victim of a spiteful lover.

This or a similar interpretation seems satisfactory until we hear the deeper tones of the persona's voice, until we examine the specific relationship she establishes between the moon and the rival, and until we ask ourselves why she calls the person who causes her such anguish the rival. If the poem contains statement it is to be found in the title, and until we can identify the rival and establish the rival's relationship to the persona, we have discerned little but the surface meaning.

2. DISCOVERING THE AUTHOR'S PRESENTATION

To discover the rival's identity and the reasons behind the persona's obsessive preoccupation with the rival, we turn to the structure of the poem and to its imagery and symbolism; together they reveal the meaning of the poem by evoking deep archetypal responses.

Structure and Imagery

In "The Rival" both the structure and the imagery controlling the meaning of the poem form an interlocking pattern of comparison and contrast. The structure is one of development and reversal. In the first half of the poem the persona uses the image of the moon to define the rival. She states, "If the moon smiled, she would resemble you." Round and shining in the night sky, the moon dominates the first stanza as a concrete image and basis of comparison. In stanza II the mood subtly shifts; we see only the moon's pale light shining into a room and the reality of the rival fades line by line to a nebulous concept. Between the first and last half of the poem the controlling image undergoes a dramatic change: night fades to day; the moon becomes "ridiculous" in the bright blue sky, and the sunlight, "white and blank," dominates the poem as its central image and as the vehicle personifying the rival.

The poem derives its structure from a changing impression: the dominant image is at first the moon, but with a gradual transformation, the sun becomes the dominant image. As the moon fades and the sun rises the identity of the rival dissolves from concreteness into abstraction. In the first half of the poem the rival is human; in the second half the rival's human identity disintegrates with the passing of the night only to re-emerge with day, transformed into a brilliant, overwhelming presence. Resplendent in strength and power with the blazing sun its vehicle, the rival becomes ascendant, dominating, and omnipresent.

Comparison and contrast, the outer shell of the organization of the poem, structures the symbolic development of "The Rival" and exposes, through metamorphosis, moon and sun as major symbols.

Symbolism and Myth

The moon, dominating the first part of the poem, is symbolically complex, for it represents the seemingly contradictory concepts of life and death. Aware of the mysterious relationship between the lunar cycle and the physiological cycle in woman, man concluded thousands of years ago that the moon mysteriously controlled the seasons, births, and harvests. Thus with time the moon came to symbolize resurrection and rejuvenation. Yet man recognized, too, the moon's inconstancy as its face emerged then slowly disappeared. As a result, tradition identified the moon, especially during its invisible phase, with the Land of the Dead. Influencing both birth and death, even today the moon is equated with the human condition, and in this sense the moon in "The Rival" imparts a deep mystical significance. It not only conjures thoughts of the rival but mirrors the persona's state of mind: "abased" by the moon and subject to its influence, the persona is torn between the rejuvenating vitality of life and the equally strong compulsion toward death.

Symbolically, the image of the moon also embodies the passive aspects against which the rival is first compared and then contrasted. As a minor duplication of the sun, the moon is diminished, passive, and feminine. It influences life only on our own planet and shines only from the sun's reflected light. Feminine, volatile, associated with the night, the moon is maternal, enveloping, protective and dangerous. "Her O-mouth grieves at the world" echoes knowledge of the endless cycle of birth and death. The rival, in contrast, incapable of grief, is "unaffected." Thus when the persona compares the rival to the moon, describing it as "beautiful but annihilating," she imparts to the rival a mystic, foreboding quality that gradually reveals its identity.

Because its pale light only half illuminates objects, the moon is associated with the world of the imagination, with fantasy and dream. In the second stanza the persona says that the rival, like the moonlight, makes "stone out of everything." The moonlight freezes images; the rival destroys life. Emerging from the moonlight as a spiteful, feminine presence, the rival returns the persona's aversion and reciprocates the fixed, magnetic attraction that binds them together. In the same way that the moon must take its life from the sun, the rival's life depends upon its taking the life of the persona. Thus the statement that both the moon and the rival are "great light borrowers" lifts the poem's meaning from an expression of personal irritation to an archetypal consciousness of death.

The persona herself is most clearly revealed through the symbolic significance of the moon. Symbolizing the strengths and dangers of the world of appearances and imagination, the moon reflects the persona's state of mind: she conceives the poem under the influence of the moon, and the rival is revealed to her in the moonlight. He "ticks" his fingers with malicious impatience and the persona feels herself "wake to a mausoleum." "Beautiful," "annihilating," eternally attentive, the rival emerges with quiet finality as the symbol of death. The poem becomes, as a result, not a mere argument between lovers, but a visionary experience and, narrowly, a visionary's perception of death.

Structurally, the poem is divided between images of light and dark. The moon seems "ridiculous" as it pales in the bright solar light of reason and objectivity, but the rival, instead of vanishing with the moon, becomes stronger and more pervasive. It merges with the sun to assert its reality and its power. The rival, "white and blank," becomes a presence as destructive as "carbon monoxide." The fact that the passing of the night does not dissipate the influence or presence of the rival reveals the moon as a symbol of the death-wish. Its urgent, increasingly powerful appeal reveals death not only as the rival of life, but as the victor. Conceived in fantasy, death thrives; prevailing over the bright light of reason, it walks victorious.

Archetype

The response of man to the moon and to death is universal, primitive, and instinctual, for man has always been deeply concerned with the nature and meaning of birth and death. From this basic concern spring most myths and all religions. Further, the desire for self-destruction as a form of sacrifice has been the basis for ritual since the dawn of man. Death, conceived as mystery, becomes compelling in its promise of supreme liberation. The light and dark principle are reversed; death becomes the source of light. In "The Rival," the blinding light in the poem's conclusion goes far back to the principle that punishment and death are the way to order, to clarity, and to light. As a result, an interpretation of "The Rival" as a visual image of the persona's state of mind becomes possible; as such, the poem constitutes a record of the persona's desire for death and ultimate release. Thus the love relationship: death is also the rival for the persona's love.

3. DISCOVERING SUBJECT AND THEME

Symbols occur in clusters and their positioning controls their meaning. An interpretation of the symbol cluster in "The Rival" (moon, death, sun) indicates that the true subject of the poem is death, that the identity of the rival is death. The rival is a contestant for the persona's life, ambiguously promising release from suffering, mysteriously promising life through death. Obsessive, compelling, and destructive, the rival is both loved and hated as it represents variously repression and release, life and death, light and darkness. The poem is a personal and subjective confrontation—a structured record of the poet's state of mind.

SAMPLE ESSAYS

SAMPLE ESSAY 11
USING VOICE AND TONE

INSTRUCTIONS.   Before writing the essay on voice or tone ask yourself several questions about the work: Who narrates the fiction or speaks the words of the poem? What does tone reveal about the persona's attitude toward the subject matter of the work? Does the persona or speaker seem disinterested or does he seem to wish to make a point? Do the voice you hear and the tone you detect form an argument? Reread pages 8–10, 16–17, and 73–76, to review the definitions of voice and tone and their application to works of literature.

In the introduction to your essay lead up to the controlling idea by giving your reader the answers to the questions in the preceding paragraph. Also include sufficient factual information to make clear the situation. State your thesis in the introduction and remember that it should be concerned with the way in which understanding the voice or tone of a work increases understanding or appreciation of the whole work. Develop the body of the essay by giving specific examples of voice or tone. Analyze each example to show that it conforms to your central idea of what constitutes the essence of the overall tone. Comment about the person whose voice you hear; what is revealed about him? Point out meanings gleaned from perceiving the voice and tone. Your conclusion could summarize, and, in addition, comment upon the role in the work of voice and tone.

Notice, in this connection, how the conclusion of the sample essay that follows attributes a controlling function to voice and tone.

THE REVEALING VOICE
OF SYLVIA PLATH'S "THE RIVAL"

"The Rival" is a love poem, even if an unconventional one; in fact, we might call it a "love-hate" poem. The voice we hear is that of an embittered woman who addresses a lover or husband in caustic tones, thereby revealing the ambivalence of her feelings for him. The speaker seems to feel that the loved one is a rival, both to the moon and to her. His rivalry to the moon is spoken of in shifting tones; his rivalry to her is spoken of in increasingly bitter tones. Let us move through the poem to see how the speaker's tone reveals the stifling effect this competition has upon her.

The poem opens like a conventional love poem. The lover is compared favorably to the moon: the moon would resemble the lover if the moon "smiled." This statement lets us assume that the lover does smile. So traditional lovers' symbols—"the moon" and "smiles" and "beauty"—are used in the first few lines. But the lovers' symbols, we soon hear, are to be reversed. The tone shifts from the conventional in a startling fashion. Both the moon and the lover "leave the same impression / Of something beautiful, but"—and here we are drawn up sharply—"annihilating." *Annihilating,* the ability to cause death, is attributed to the moon and to the lover. The comparison is no longer favorable. We hear the abrupt shift to criticism. Both the moon and the lover are "light borrowers." We assume the physical fact that the moon borrows her light from the sun. But what of the lover? From what or from whom does he borrow "light"? From the cutting quality of the speaker's tone we can tell that she feels herself deprived of light in the lover's "borrowing." They are, then, competitors for light, or—to extend the symbolism—for life itself.

This extension of symbol grows naturally out of the poem. There is a reference to death in all the five-line stanzas, and only the two lines following the three longer stanzas are free from references to death. Stanza I calls the lover "annihilating"; stanza II says the speaker wakes to him, and life with him, as to a "mausoleum"; stanza III satirically refers to his letters to her as "expansive as carbon monoxide." The tone grows increasingly bitter until even his letters "arriving through the mailslot" spread a poison that is death to her.

The bitterness turns to carping. The annoyance the persona feels at the lover's "ticking fingers on the marble table, looking for cigarettes," leads her to call him "spiteful as a woman." She has chosen

the ultimate insult, one calculated to deprive him of his essential mas-
culinity.

In stanza III she names herself a "subject" of his. Thus we can
detect her bitter love for him and her obsessive attachment to him.
Her attachment is as inescapable as death.

The last two lines of the poem say "No day is safe from news of
you, /Walking about in Africa maybe, but thinking of me." These
lines, with their caustic accusation, do much to reveal the true state of
the feelings of the speaker. Obviously, as *he* walks about in Africa,
she thinks of *him!* Even though he were as far away as the moon she
would think of him!

The seventeen lines of the poem do not reveal the cause for the
unhappy situation that exists between the lovers. They reveal only
that the persona cannot, even in bitterness, exorcise his image from
her mind and heart. Voice and tone in "The Rival" are powerful elements in making a speaker reveal the opposite of that which she
wishes her words to indicate.

SAMPLE ESSAY 12
USING BIOGRAPHY

INSTRUCTIONS.   Before writing the essay using biography seek out
all the information you can about the author. Facts relating to his physical, mental, and emotional experiences will help you judge his intentions.
All an author feels, sees, does, and says can help you decide how his experiences have influenced his writings. (You should know before you attempt
this kind of essay that there are people who deny the validity of using biographical information as an aid in interpreting a work. However, since
there are also those who advocate its use, you should know the procedures
for it.)

As you study an author's life try to find a unifying pattern that reveals his characteristic response to the experiences of his life. If you write
about the influence of biography on a work you should be familiar with
the greater part of all that an author has written. You could not make a
logical correlation between an author's life and his ideas in a work unless
you can see that his experiences seem to have had an important influence
in more than one work.

Of course your thesis will show how an author's entire life experiences (or some pervading influence derived from them) illuminates the
work of art. You might, for example, show how Shaw's preoccupation with
Fabianism influenced the content of *Major Barbara,* or how Coleridge's

addiction to opium evoked the fascinating but repellent imagery of *The Ancient Mariner,* or how Byron's relations with his half sister formed the inspiration for his dramatic poem *Manfred.* Organization of the essay should trace evidences of the effects resulting from the causes you assign, following a pattern either of sequential appearances or of lesser effects leading to the greatest. Note that the following essay traces in sequential order evidences of the predominant facet in Sylvia Plath's temperament.

SYLVIA PLATH'S POETIC TEMPERAMENT:
THE PERSONA OF "THE RIVAL"

The salient fact to note about Sylvia Plath is that she was, always, a poet. From early childhood she showed the habits of a mind that functions poetically. All her poetry shows that her mind seized the external experiences of her life and drew them within to let them later explode into expressions of a deeply realized awareness of the features of the world about her. But, in addition to this awareness, she was aware also of her other self, the woman. Her poem "The Rival" is an expression of fully realized awareness, and it is partly for this reason that we recognize the persona in this poem as the poet herself. The problem is to decide to whom the poet speaks. She addresses an ambiguous "you," who could be one of several persons or things: the "you" could be someone she loves, or someone she hates, or time, or death.

Some knowledge of Sylvia Plath, the person, will help us resolve this problem. The important facts (for our purpose) are these: She was born in Boston in 1932 of parents of Prussian and Austrian descent, both teachers. She loved poetry and wrote little poems from an early age, publishing her first poem when she was eight. She also studied art from an early age and was always considered creative and brilliant. She entered Smith College on a scholarship and graduated *summa cum laude.* After winning *Mademoiselle's* college fiction contest, she served as guest editor for them. At Smith she won poetry prizes and was elected to the honorary society for the arts and to Phi Beta Kappa. At twenty she attempted suicide. Following this attempt she was given psychiatric treatment. In 1952 she met and married the English poet Ted Hughes. A biographer states that they "lived on next to nothing." They lived alternately in London and in America. Of this marriage two children were born, a daughter and a son. Husband and wife both began to publish extensively. Miss Plath was often ill with flu during these years. During the last year of her life, a time of difficulty for her, she wrote a great many poems. In 1963 she committed suicide.

Knowing that Miss Plath attempted once to end her life and later accomplished that act, and seeing the many references to death in "The Rival"—"annihilating" (line 3), "making stone out of everything" (line 6), "mausoleum" (line 7), "marble" (line 8), "dying" (line 10), "carbon-monoxide" (line 15)—one is tempted to say that here speaks a woman who is, like Keats' persona, "half in love with easeful death." And perhaps the speaker in the poem *is* somewhat in love with death; but if she is, it is against her will, for "The Rival" shows a full awareness of the world, and a rejection of the death images. It also shows that the rival is death, or thoughts of death, which intrude upon the act of creation.

Again biography aids our interpretation: in notes prepared for the BBC, Miss Plath commented that her new poems were "all written at about four in the morning—that still blue, almost eternal hour before the baby's cry, before the glassy music of the milkman, settling his bottles." We can picture her on the occasion of the composition of "The Rival." The moon, coming into her room, awakes her. As she lies in bed, thinking it is too early to rise, she begins the activity that is always hers upon awakening: she composes a poem. The moon is beautiful, the poem says, but "annihilating." The thought of death occurs simultaneously with thoughts of the moon and its mythic power to drive men mad.

Many of Sylvia Plath's poems show this intrusion of death into her awareness of the things of life. For example, in "Poppies in October" she sees the colors of the sky as "a sky palely and flamily igniting its carbon monoxide"; in "Death & Co." she sees babies in their hospital gowns with "the flutings of their Ionian / Death gowns"; and in "Ariel," speaking of riding her horse, she describes herself as "The dew that flies / Suicidal, at one with the drive / Into the red / Eye, the cauldron of morning." Thus, the moon is "annihilating." It makes the poet, in the very act of creating this poem, think of the death-wishes that have obtruded upon so many of her creations.

The "O-mouth" of the moon grieves at the world, the poet says (line 5), but her poetic self is unaffected. Poetic inspiration, in other words, will not come, when that other self, the woman who cannot escape the thoughts of death, comes to disturb the composition of a poem. Instead of writing, the poet feels herself groping for a cigarette on the marble table. She wishes to rise, to create, but sensitive awareness of the coldness of the marble table brings thoughts of death again.

However, a lifelong possession of the personality that is a poet's makes this poet reject the thoughts of death. Day arrives, and the moon is "ridiculous." Thoughts of death are ridiculous. The poet is dissatisfied with that night person, that moon-blinded person who cannot hold back the dark thoughts of death. An awareness of a daily occurrence, the arrival of the mail "through the mailslot" (line 14), makes her acutely aware that the moon also arrives with regularity. Even though day with its daily tasks, which replace for this poet the hours when she can create, will be here soon, the moon's return is inevitable. During the prosaic hours of the day the moon will be on the other side of the earth, in Africa, "but thinking of me" (line 17), waiting to return with thoughts of death. The moon, symbol of death—the rival—*will* return. The poet must create *now*.

SAMPLE ESSAY 13
USING COMPARISON AND CONTRAST

INSTRUCTIONS.   In your reading of literature you will often discover a poem, story, or play that derives its basic meaning from a comparison or contrast between two or more subjects. Consider two images in a poem, two characters in a story, two uses of setting in a play. Their differences, used in sharp contrast, may produce important effects in technique and theme; their similarities, used to complement and reinforce a particular, unifying idea or technique, may point directly to a major idea or theme. Realize, too, that a metaphor, seemingly singular, functions as an implied analogy between two objects or concepts. On a larger scale, the comparison and contrast between plot and structure, between what characters say and do, between idea and image, between the form of a work and its function—or, on an even larger scale, the similarities and differences between two separate works or authors—are fit subject matter for essays.

There is an important difference you should note between analysis and comparison and contrast: analysis is an examination of the parts of a single subject; comparison and contrast is an examination of the similarities or differences between two subjects. Essays of comparison and contrast have a double subject; your first and most important task when using a double subject will be to establish your objective, to determine what, precisely, you want to emphasize. Draw up a list indicating similarities and differences between the two subjects. The list will not only constitute the topic sentences in the body of your essay, but will help you discover some unifying principle or central idea for your essay. Discovering a unifying, central idea helps you establish some *common basis* for your comparison. A simple comparison of Faulkner's *The Sound and the Fury* with Sophocles' *Oedipus Rex* would be sheer folly: the subject is not only too broad, but contains no principle, no central reason for inquiry. A comparison or contrast of these two works, radically separated in time and genre, would become meaningful, however, if you wanted to show changes in the concept of tragedy. You must discover a reason for your comparison and contrast and then use that reason or purpose as a guide in selecting your method of organizing and presenting your material.

Following are three basic methods of organizing the essay of comparison and contrast, each of which has several possible variations. Which one you use will depend on the complexity of the points you wish to make and the emphasis you wish to place on one of the two subjects.

Use One Subject To Clarify Another   If your reader is familiar with one of your two subjects, you can lead him to an understanding of the second by first presenting the more familiar subject and then making repeated reference to the familiar as you explain the unfamiliar. In writing about "The Rival," you might first review the meaning of the moon as a symbol, then in succeeding paragraphs disclose the essence of the rival through a point-by-point reference to the moon.

Use Two Familiar Subjects To Clarify an Unfamiliar Concept or Principle   Determining your reader's familiarity with subject matter is largely a matter of judgment, and the rule here applies equally to all writing: never depend upon a reader's ability to understand fully. In this second plan, as in the first, you must discuss all relevant points and analyze both familiar subjects. Use two familiar subjects (two novels you think your reader might have read, two images he will have recognized in a poem, two familiar characters from drama) to explain an unfamiliar principle or truth that can be derived from the similarities or differences between two or more subjects. This form of organization is appropriate to many works of literature. An essay on Sylvia Plath's "The Rival" could be structured in this manner to demonstrate how the unfamiliar principle of the poem (the theme) is revealed in the poet's comparison and contrast of the moon and the rival.

Use a Familiar Principle To Explain the Meaning of Two or More Unfamiliar Subjects   Your reader will often be more familiar with the general principles of literature than with specific works of literature. If you feel this is the case, use a familiar principle in your essay as the guiding or controlling point of reference from which you explain specific aspects of a work or works. For example, an essay guided or controlled by a discussion of familiar literary techniques such as point of view, verse form, or imagery, could easily show how the moon as a symbol of the rival is both a person and a concept, thus rendering purposefully ambiguous the symbolic meaning of the rival.

The following essay about Sylvia Plath's "The Rival," is structured like the poem itself, by comparison and contrast. This essay uses the second method described above.

CONTRASTIVE ANALYSIS
IN SYLVIA PLATH'S "THE RIVAL"

Sylvia Plath structures her poem "The Rival" within a wide, generalized metaphor. In the first two stanzas she compares the moon, as symbol, with an enigmatic, ambiguous rival, which exists on one level as a person, and on another as a force or concept of destruction; in the last two stanzas she contrasts the moon with the rival. The poem's total effect derives from the use of comparison and contrast in its basic structure and in the imagery dominating the theme. Understanding the poem, which is expressed on various levels of conflict, becomes a problem-solving activity, for to understand the theme, one must identify the rival and sense its lunar, eerie hold over the speaker.

The poem opens with an explicit condition—the personification of the moon—in which the speaker draws her initial comparison through direct address to the rival. The smiling moon, she states, resembles the smiling rival; both are beautiful, and both are destroyers, deriving their energy not from inner resources, but by drawing light or strength from others. The moon only passively reflects the sun's light; the rival only reflects the life force of others. The implication on one level, of the rival as a person, is clear: the rival somehow, whether emotionally, creatively, or intellectually, is depriving the speaker of her life and strength. Further, the comparison grows to an indictment as the speaker personifies the moon as a round mouth grieving at the world whereas the rival smiles indifferently upon human need and suffering. Thus the first comparison isolates the rival from the speaker, indicating a psychological separation as remote as the moon is from the earth. Such alienation is reflected in the speaker's tone, in the conflict between caustic anger and obvious obsession as voice and diction further sharpen, through contrast, the meaning of the moon and the rival's relationship to the speaker. The speaker is moon-struck. Expressed in terms of witchcraft and the supernatural, both moon and rival have cast a love-spell, and caught within the opposing forces of aversion and compulsion, the speaker is helpless.

The destructive, obsessive element controlling the poem continues into the second stanza in an implied comparison between the spirit or remembered presence of the rival and the visual and psychological effects of moonlight. The scene becomes more abstract, the confrontation more intense as the moonlight, like the rival, is equated with death. The traditional gift of light is reversed; the speaker turns the concept of life toward death, contending that the rival's only gift to her is a cessation of life. The rival merges with the moonlight to represent the cruel lover, a rival contesting not only her right to live her own life, but a rival, in fact, who is in active contention for her life.

The second half of the poem is contrastive: with daylight the moon fades before the life-giving power of the sun, but the rival increases in power. As night merges into day the rival changes from an enigmatic, waiting figure to a pervading, overwhelming presence. The rival, gaining ascendancy, separates from the death symbolism of the moon and asserts itself as Death, as a confident contender or rival for the speaker's life.

The poem, a texture of contrasts, presents a subtle, almost imperceptible drama, a narrative of impending death. In tone the speaker reveals her aversion to death, her will toward life, and, conversely, her love of death, her weariness with life. The rival's hold over the speaker's natural will toward life is the death-wish. Death is the speaker's spiteful lover.

SAMPLE ESSAY 14
USING EVALUATION

INSTRUCTIONS.   In many respects the essay of evaluation can be viewed as the most important kind you will be asked to write. Understanding the reasons for past judgments on those works acknowledged as great provides you with the tools to evaluate new works not yet subject to the test of time. This assumption implies, of course, that standards of excellence do exist, and that the application of these standards to works of literature, through comparison, will give rise to valid decisions about quality. Your ability to make judgments based on objective criteria and to substantiate your judgment by logical, defensible reasoning will mark you as a mature, independent, and experienced reader.

To evaluate the quality of a work, we apply various standards based on artistic rather than personal or ideological grounds. We ask: (1) Does the work reveal some basic, universal truth about the human condition? (2) Does the work succeed in eliciting our belief, and does its meaning afterward continue to be important? (3) Does its form or overall plan embody the theme or meanings and seem complete and aesthetically whole? (4) Does the work, in short, seem beautiful, complete, vital, and important?

Answering these questions forms the basis of your evaluation. You may emphasize the successes or the failures in a work, for seldom will works of art be perfect. Your main purpose, however, will lie in subjecting a work to the above questions, which essentially, if answered affirmatively, constitute a definition for art. These questions do not entertain judgments based purely on personal preference or on political issues. You may like a work because its statements about a political stance seem accurate; you may like a work because you like the subject matter. These criteria, however, are not considered valid for judging *art*. You must, instead, turn to aesthetic concerns. You may discuss specific aspects of a work: the successes or failures, as you see them, in style, tone, imagery, point of view, structure, characterization. Remember that a work may fail in one way but remain successful as a whole, and that a work may succeed brilliantly in several respects but seem slight or disappointing in its total effect.

A work can logically and profitably be evaluated from either of two distinctly different approaches. The first is objective, the second subjective. An evaluation can be (1) an objective appraisal based on the contents of a work; or (2) a subjective, personal reaction and an expression of appreciation or of dislike. Both types of essays, if well written, find their purpose in revealing artistic values in a work. The objective appraisal looks to the details in the text; the subjective appraisal, sometimes referred to as the impressionistic approach, finds its purpose in communicating what the critic (you as the reader) feels in the presence of the work.

It is true that all criticism judges worth, because even the most objective analytical approach will inevitably be most seriously concerned with explaining the profound, the complex, and the successful. Evaluation differs in degree, and we may clarify the difference by asserting that evaluation states whether a work is good or bad and tries to prove why, whereas analytical criticism attempts an interpretation or explanation of the work's essential meaning. In theory the two are far apart; in practice they come close.

In organizing an essay of evaluation, state in your introduction those points or criteria you intend to use in your evaluation. State also, as your central idea, your overall conclusion about the work's value. In the body of your essay, apply each point or criterion to the work and use them to discuss the success of the work—its power, style, subtlety, logic, humor. Remember to maintain your purpose, which is judging worth; do not allow your essay to become an analysis of the work's meaning. Your conclusion may, in this type of essay, be very brief. Emphasizing or summarizing your total impressions will usually be sufficient.

Study the essay below to better understand how the subjective and objective approaches may be blended. The reaction to the poem is clearly personal and subjective; the criteria for judgment, however, are objective because the writer ultimately looks to the work itself for proof or substantiation.

THE MAN IN THE MOON:
DEATH IN SYLVIA PLATH'S "THE RIVAL"

Reading Sylvia Plath's poems provokes a direct, emotional experience, for it opens a view into an anguished but brilliantly original mind. Her poems are deeply personal, yet their value is unmistakable, for they speak past personal experience and tap a world of intuition and insight most of us only vaguely sense. Our failure may be due to the limitations of sanity, or to our fear of going beyond safe thoughts into those other dark, lunar fantasies of instinctive truth. In any event, Miss Plath's poems consist of emotions experienced and recorded so precisely that they become startlingly profound. Her poem "The Rival" provides an excellent example of her technique of tapping ancient fears and compulsions and rendering them new and original through her own insight into the use and meaning of symbols and idiom.

The poem derives much of its vitality from the uniqueness of Miss Plath's approach to her subject. She develops her poem by comparing the rival with the moon. At first the reader assumes the rival to be a lover or husband, and the comparison, read in the context of a quarrel, is strikingly biting and original. The moon, usually associated with passivity and the feminine principle, effectively points up the rival's cruelty (he is unaffected by the world) and devastatingly, in the second stanza, the speaker emasculates him (he is "spiteful as a woman"). As an attack, within a love-hate reference, the poem succeeds as imaginative, effective insult.

In the second part of the poem, however, an unusual shift occurs both in subject and in tone. The rival, controlled in the first half of the poem by the restriction of the moon image, escapes its reference and floods the daylight half of the poem, a pervasive presence, dominant, and effectively out of control. From the night, from dream, and into the day, spreading across the face of the earth, the symbol of lover changes to the symbol of death, yet the control is always tight in its reference and the poem remains personal while reaching out toward a universal statement. The reader's response deepens from enjoyment of original phase to involvement in the poem's basic concern.

The form and development of the poem demonstrate craftsmanship in originality and brevity, but equally significant in the poem's total effect is the striking, almost eerie presence of the speaker. The reader senses tragedy first hand not only in the tone (the depression, the obsession with death) but in the actual breathing presence of the speaker's torment, her brilliance, and her wavering sanity that is revealed within her voice and her vision of reality. The poem is not an intellectual exercise in expression but a revelation of a state of mind, frozen with intensity in words that mirror the moment of its existence. Pain and unendurable emotional tension breathe life into the words of "The Rival." This presence, combined with the clear artistry of form, makes the poem a vivid, startling insight into a particular human mind.

Demented but intensely real, lifting the ancient symbols of moon, sun, and death out of the past and into the present, placing them meaningfully intact into the twentieth century with its carbon monoxide, its mailslots, and implied modern suburbia gives the poem vast and meaningful reference. The old is rejuvenated, and like the moon itself, the poem speaks of timeless concerns within the framework of the modern mind and idiom. Turned slowly, like a moon in space, the poem glitters with the complexity, the compression, and the old-new levels of meaning that constitute true poetry.

SUGGESTED ASSIGNMENTS FOR WRITING ABOUT POETRY

1. Poets use myth not only to enrich the meaning of their works but as the subject of their poems. Some poets use traditional myth; others form their own individual mythologies. In T. S. Eliot's *The Waste Land*, we find allusions to pagan cults based on vegetation; Yeats and Blake devised their own personal myths. Analyze the use and importance of myth in Hart Crane's "For the Marriage of Faustus and Helen," in which two quite different characters from ancient myth dance to jazz; compare the use of myth in two sonnets: Wordsworth's "The World Is Too Much with Us" and Edgar Allan Poe's "Sonnet—To Science." Read several poems (Blake's "I Saw a Chapel," or Yeats' "The Wild Swans at Coole") based on personal mythology and describe the depth of meaning derived from private references and visions.
2. Make a close textual analysis of a short but complex poem. Analyze an element of technique to reveal meaning. Use the discovery method described on pages 26–28 and 141–142 to find the shaping device used by the poet. Wallace Stevens' "The Emperor of Ice-Cream," Robert Frost's "The Road Not Taken," H.D.'s "Heat," and many other short poems make excellent subjects for this study.
3. Some poems communicate immediacy and meaning through visual patterns. Look at George Herbert's "Easter Wings," a poem shaped like two pairs of angel wings; determine whether the visual pattern aids meaning. Read E. E. Cummings' "next to of course god america i"; what do you make of his extraordinary use of typography and punctuation? Does it aid meaning? Does it confuse the sense of the poem? Select one or more poems laid out in unusual visual patterns. Analyze their effect by comparing their visual, rhythmical, and logical meanings.
4. Write an essay that evaluates the corrective purpose of a verse satire

(Pope's "The Rape of the Lock," Dryden's "Mac Flecknoe," Thomas Hardy's "In Church," Blake's "London"). Show how the compression and intensification of poetic lines make effective the corrective purpose of the satire.

5. Free verse is precisely that—free. It does not have to conform to any rule of rhyme, meter, or stanza. The poet must, therefore, achieve form without resort to traditional fixed forms, and to be successful he must, in each of his poems, pay more attention to rhyme, meter, and line arrangement than if he were writing, for example, a sonnet. The verse may be free but the poet is not. Examine several free-verse poems to discover the calculated skill with which the poems are structured and realized. Write an essay examining the form in one of the poems you select. Read Whitman's "When Lilacs Last in the Dooryard Bloom'd," Theodore Spencer's "Epitaph," W. H. Auden's "Musée des Beaux Arts," and William Carlos Williams' "Poem." Select a poem from your campus literary magazine. Analyze its form and judge its merit as free verse.

6. Compare two poems by two poets who use one of the fixed forms. Show how the form is functional for any age, even though there have been changes in language and ideologies. For example, compare a sonnet by an Elizabethan poet with a sonnet by a modern poet, or compare two sestinas of different ages: Swinburne's "Sestina" and Donald Justice's "Dream Sestina."

7. Consider the allegory in many of Christ's parables (Matthew 13:24-30) and analyze its use. Analyze Sir Walter Raleigh's "What is our life?" or George Herbert's "Redemption." Find poems using allegory in modern poetry and analyze their meaning. How does the allegory function in the poem's basic premise and structure? Read about allegory in the Glossary, page 224.

8. Write a character sketch of the speaker of a dramatic monologue. Use one of Browning's dramatic monologues, Eliot's "The Love Song of J. Alfred Prufrock," Tennyson's "Ulysses," or another. Your essay should show the unfolding development of character as it is revealed by ambiguities of statement or unconscious revelations made by the speaker. Essentially you will be writing an essay of explication; you will explain the meanings of statements uttered by the speaker.

9. Analyze the metaphor or other figurative language in a poem of your choosing. Consider poems like Elizabeth Jennings' "Delay" or Ogden Nash's "Very Like a Whale." Review the rules for writing about metaphor (pages 150–155); in addition, consider the use of personification in a poem like James Stephens' "The Wind." How does the use of metaphor add complexity and clarity to the poem's meaning? How does metaphor add immediacy?

10. Correlate the sound and the sense of a poem. Show how the use of a particular meter and rhythm, when correlated to the sound values of the poem, intensifies the meaning of the language. Almost any poem is good for this purpose, but excellent examples are Ben Jonson's "To Celia," Gerald Manley Hopkins' "The Windhover," Yeats' "The Second Coming," Wallace Stevens' "Sunday Morning," and Keats' "Ode on Melancholy."

DRAMA

Unlike other forms of fiction, drama is written primarily to be performed, a characteristic that offers the playwright both advantages and disadvantages. No other form of literature, for example, offers such an opportunity for immediacy and vitality: the dramatic experience literally comes to life before the eyes of the audience. For this immediacy, the playwright pays a price. He is limited to what the characters can say and do on stage. He cannot omnisciently enter the minds of his characters. He cannot step forth in his own person to make evaluative comments. He cannot, as the creator, give interpretative descriptions of the appearance or the inner state of his characters. Finally, the playwright's convictions about the human condition can only be inferred from what we hear the characters say or see them do as they move and speak on stage, making visible and audible the thoughts, the feelings, and the sensory impressions of the work.

Despite its original design for performance, drama has always been enjoyed as literature, and today many people study or read for pleasure the Greek tragedies, the plays of Shakespeare, and modern drama, without having seen any of them. There are advantages in reading plays not found in viewing them; for example, playwrights often put into their stage directions interpretative comments that would be lost upon a theater audience. In the description of the stage setting for *Desire Under the Elms,* for example, Eugene O'Neill says the two elms outside the farmhouse look "like exhausted women resting their sagging breasts and hands and hair on its roof." Although no designer could fashion elms so that an audience would see them in this impressionistic manner, a reader can view them in his imagination precisely as the author does. In the introductory sections of a play, playwrights often include comments about their characters, comments that help actors and directors understand how a certain character is to be interpreted, and which show that playwrights expect and want their plays to be read. Here, for example, is George Bernard Shaw's description of Lady Britomart in *Major Barbara:*

> Withal a very typical managing matron of the upper class, treated as a naughty child until she grew into a scolding mother, and finally settling down with plenty of practical ability and worldly experience, limited in the oddest way with domestic and class limitations, conceiving the universe exactly as if it were a large house in Wilton Crescent, though handling her corner of it very effectively on that assumption.

Obviously, the theater audience lacks the opportunity given the reader to see inside this character's mind to learn what made her as she is.

There are further advantages to reading plays, too. When you read a play, it becomes in part your own creation. You can assign the emotional connotations you wish rather than being dependent upon a particular actor's inflection of voice. You can visualize scenes and actions as your own taste directs rather than being forced to view the play as a particular director wants. Remember, however, that reading plays is no substitute for viewing good productions whenever you can. Reading and viewing plays are different aesthetic experiences. The point is that you can enjoy both.

Since critical reading and writing about drama as literature will form the basis for most of your class assignments about drama, the material that follows is designed to help you analyze and enjoy the plays you read.

Kinds of Plays

As a basis for understanding the nature of drama, its history and structure, let us first classify the general kinds of plays. Traditionally, we recognize the tragedy, the comedy, the tragicomedy, and the melodrama.

TRAGEDY.   Over two thousand years ago Aristotle analyzed the elements that distinguished **tragedy** from other kinds of writing. The rules he set down have served as a starting point for discussions of tragedy ever since; but it is still difficult to define precisely what tragedy is. Even after you have read a great many tragedies you will discover that rules applying to one play will not apply to another. But let us begin with Aristotle, who said:

Tragedy, then, is an imitation of an action that is serious, complete, and of a certain magnitude; in language embellished with each kind of artistic ornament, the several kinds being formed in separate parts of the play; in the form of action, not of narrative; with incidents arousing pity and fear, wherewith to accomplish its catharsis of such emotions.

Poetics

In the sense that Aristotle used the term, *imitation* does not imply that the dramatist copies something. Instead, he creates a work of art in which he imitates an *action;* that is, he *re*-creates life by showing men in action. The creation is "serious" because it attempts to present *truth* about human nature and about life as it is for human beings. As the tragic dramatist sees it, his truth is "complete" in that it is structured within the limits of the acts of the play and has a clearly discernible "beginning, middle, and end." Aristotle's statement that all of the presentation must be "of a certain magnitude" implies that the vision of the human condition presented should be of universal scope and that the tragic hero should possess character of great nobility. "He is better than ordinary men," Aristotle says, and his actions must "reveal moral purpose."

The language, too, says Aristotle, must be of high order to achieve the magnitude tragedy demands. It must exhibit moral purpose; the poetry must have meter and rhythm of excellence; the diction must have "perfection of style."

Finally, the events of a tragedy must arouse "pity and fear" to effect a "catharsis." You can comprehend the kind of events that will excite pity and fear if you realize that "pity" in this sense does not mean mere pathos, but rather implies the deeper sense of compassion experienced by spectators as they share disaster with a tragic hero. But precisely what Aristotle meant by "catharsis" has occupied scholars throughout the ages. They have said variously that the term means "purgation," "purification," or "exaltation." All these interpretations indicate that to experience pity and fear for another (even a stage hero) in some way lifts our minds above a too narrow concern with our own troubles.

Aristotle's definition was based, of course, upon the tragedy of his time. Whether later tragedies can be judged by the same definition is difficult to decide. The theater of a given time reflects its society, and as societies change, the events of plays will reflect this change. But as our views of man and of his universe change, should the nature of the tragic hero change also? And should the effect of tragedy upon a different kind of audience be different?

There are those who argue that there have been no tragedies written since the Elizabethan period—and further, that none can be written, since a society that fails to see nobility in the spirit of man cannot produce a tragic hero. They further argue that modern skepticism concerning the existence of a supernatural power and concerning the possession by man of freedom of will makes it impossible for us to see a hero's moral disintegration as a condition that disturbs an uncaring universe.

On the other hand, some argue that we can produce tragedies provided we change our ideas concerning the tragic hero. They argue that we cannot continue to be concerned with high-born men of noble character and of noble birth whose downfall affects a whole nation. Instead, they say, our tragic hero must come from the ranks of "little people"—the ordinary citizen, whose character, too, is ordinary.

However we decide this question, we must, if dramatists write plays intended to be tragedies, consider them as tragedies and formulate ideas of the characteristics shared by the best of them. Surely, the despair of some serious writers at their view of modern man and his position in the universe is itself a matter of sufficient "magnitude" to create a tragedy. Most modern tragedy contains this quality of despair. Although in modern tragedy the consequences of the events selected for the play need not affect a whole nation, they must represent universal human problems, which the tragic character must battle with full awareness of their magnitude. Events we consider sorrowful do not make subjects for tragedy. In life, we speak of a "tragic" automobile accident; this kind of sorrowful event is not a subject for tragedy because it does not represent a struggle between the tragic hero and some force of his own nature. The hero of modern tragedy, like the hero of classical tragedy, does not suffer passively. He struggles, either against some force of his own nature or against the overwhelming forces of his society.

Because many modern tragedies lean heavily on psychology and sociology, modern spectators do not so much sympathize or empathize with modern tragic heroes as they *study* them. Often the effect upon modern spectators is one of "alienation" rather than one of sympathy. Sometimes, however, because of an intellectual effect upon the spectator, he will struggle in sympathy with the protagonist in his battle against the forces of his nature.

One could say that modern tragedies do not deal with man's physical or material condition; instead, they deal with his spiritual condition. Thus, like classical and Elizabethan tragedies, they make us think upon eternal truths. Modern tragedies good for study are Yeats' *Purgatory,* O'Neill's *Desire Under the Elms,* Strindberg's *Miss Julie,* Anouilh's *Antigone,* Lorca's *Blood Wedding,* Gorky's *The Lower Depths,* Ibsen's *The Wild Duck,* Miller's *Death of a Salesman,* Williams' *The Glass Menagerie,* and many others.

In your essays about tragedy, ancient or modern, approach your analysis with the seriousness that a consideration of the eternal verities demands. If you judge a modern work as either a valid or an invalid example of tragedy, be sure to show what criteria you are applying for your judgment. Are you using Aristotle's rules? Are you rejecting them to substitute others? Are you, perhaps, only modifying them?

COMEDY. We know that a **comedy** is something that makes us laugh. But the nature of laughter and its cause are another matter. The French philosopher Henri Bergson, for example, said that "laughter is corrective." His theory holds that the function of comedy is to reform the ills of human nature through ridicule. Psychologist William McDougall expresses it in a slightly different way. For him, laughter is "an antidote to sympathy": comedy prevents us from becoming discouraged at the shortcomings of man. Some scholars even argue that the effect of laughter in comedy is akin to the effect of catharsis in tragedy: we are in some way "lifted" above our narrow, personal concerns. When we laugh at the shortcomings of others, we are, in other words, lifted above our own shortcomings.

There are so many forms of comedy (just as there are so many forms of laughter) that the term seems not to be inclusive enough for all the kinds of plays included in this category. Comedy, like tragedy, originated in Greece. Street processions with ludicrous masks and costumes reveled in honor of the god Dionysius. The paraders carried bawdy signs and sang bawdy songs. These revels led to the bawdy **satyr** plays. In the intervening centuries since then comedy has developed many new forms ranging from **slapstick** to **satire.** There is **light comedy,** like A. A. Milne's *Mr. Pim Passes By,* in which there is little conflict, but much humor of situation. There is **romantic comedy,** like Rudolf Besier's *The Barrets of Wimpole Street,* which relies upon a romance, witty dialogue, and humorous situations. There is **straight comedy,** like Jean Giraudoux's *Amphitryon 38,* which takes an ironic view of the difficulties human beings bring upon themselves. There is **poetic comedy,** like Christopher Fry's *The Lady's Not for Burning,* which has as its appeal not only dramatic poetry of excellence, but also the high spirits of its characters. There is **high comedy,** like Oscar Wilde's *The Importance of Being Earnest,* which criticizes social manners. There is **satiric comedy,** like Ben Jonson's *Volpone,* which combines wit with biting criticism of evil. There is **musical comedy,** like Richard Rodgers and Oscar Hammerstein II's *The King and I,* which uses engrossing narrative, appealing music, and witty dialogue. There is **farce,** like Shakespeare's *A Comedy of Errors,* which relies upon response to humorous situation and unexpected twist of thought—and like the movies of the Keystone Cops, which rely upon response to an external, slapstick humor.

All these various forms of comedy appeal to the intellect, making us realize that man is often not the noble hero of tragedy, but a blundering fool. Comedy makes us see the limitations of man; it also shows us that we should not despair because of our limitations, but should laugh at them.

TRAGICOMEDY.   Because all tragedy contains elements of the comic and all comedy contains elements of the tragic, the need arose for a different term to classify plays showing this interrelationship. During the Renaissance, Sir Philip Sidney gave them the name **tragicomedies.** In a tragicomedy there is no tragic hero, and the moral thought is not concerned with a fall caused by a "flaw" in an otherwise noble person. Although the theme of the play is serious, scenes of pathos are mixed with scenes of humor or irony in the presentation of that theme. H. D. F. Kitto, in his book *Greek Tragedy,* noted the "absence of a tragic theme" in some of the tragedies of Euripides, especially *Iphigeneia in Taurus.* In the Elizabethan age, Shakespeare included comic scenes in his tragedies as a matter of course, both for relief and for the amusement of the groundlings, and at the end of the Elizabethan era, Ben Jonson was writing savage satires on evil that definitely contain elements of tragedy. Further, because many critics believe that tragedy has not been written since the Elizabethan period, tragicomedy is the designation they give to all the serious drama of the eighteenth, nineteenth, and twentieth centuries. For study of tragicomedy, you can read plays like Brecht's *Mother Courage,* Shaw's *Arms and the Man,* Molière's *Tartuffe,* Ionesco's *Rhinoceros,* Pirandello's *Six Characters in Search of an Author,* and Chekhov's *The Cherry Orchard.*

MELODRAMA.   Written solely for entertainment, **melodrama** is popular because of its engrossing narrative, exciting action, entertaining dialogue, and rapid-paced events. Audiences can identify with the characters of melodrama, who are often placed in troublesome situations from which they are always happily released. Melodrama does not concern itself with man's spiritual nature, but with his physical and material well-being. The protagonist is usually an ordinary person in a complicated situation. The characters are usually either all good or all bad. Unlike tragedy, melodrama does not concern itself with the illumination of the human condition.

Melodrama is not so popular now in the theater as it was in the nineteenth century, but it is still popular for movies and television plays. The stereotyped "westerns" may be considered melodramas, as may psychological "thrillers," and mystery dramas. In recent times, many of the nineteenth-century melodramas have been revived, and contemporary audiences go to them for the fun of hissing at the villain and cheering the hero.

Brief History of Drama

Now that we have defined and discussed the various classifications of plays, let us briefly review the history of drama, the better to understand the plays of all ages.

GREEK DRAMA.   In the sixth century B.C., drama as we know it evolved from open-air festivals held in Greece to celebrate Dionysius, the god of wine. Out of the music and epic recitation of the festivals, out of the saytr plays came a new form, one that gave dignity to the dance and spectacle. These original plays were based on ancient Greek beliefs and myths, and the audiences who came to the open-air arenas clearly knew the stories before they saw the plays performed. The occasion, on which three dramatists competed for high honors, was not one for novel entertainment, but one for profound contemplation of religious beliefs.

Structure   Thespus, who produced the first Greek tragedy, used one actor; Aeschylus added a second and Sophocles introduced a third. Sophocles is also credited with developing the dramatic plot, a method of telling the story by action rather than by narration. In his *Poetics* Aristotle pointed out the reason for the characteristic structure of a division into scenes and acts when he said, in discussing tragedy: "But most important of all is the structure of the incidents. For tragedy is an imitation, not of men, but of action and of life, and life consists in action."

This was the profound discovery: "life consists in action." As we perform the actions of our lives, they fall naturally into a pattern of small scenes. We talk with one person, then another; we experience moments of danger, pain, happiness, boredom; we move about performing acts of consequence or of triviality; we laugh; we cry. But each small scene is part of the larger pattern of our lives. We play out our lives in episodes, but collectively those episodes lead to consequences of greater or smaller importance.

As Aristotle suggests, then, life itself is the model for the structure of plays. This does not mean that all plays are "true to life"; but realistic or not, all plays do mimic actions of the kind men perform or are capable of performing. As the encounters in our own lives influence the encounters that follow, the smaller scenes of plays influence the larger pattern. However, unlike life, which is essentially unstructured, a play cannot be a haphazard collection of "influences." Playwrights must so construct their plays that each encounter, each conversation serves a function in the play. As Aristotle put it, a play constitutes "a whole, the structural union of the parts being such that, if any one of them is displaced or removed, the whole will be disjointed and disturbed." If a playwright builds his scenes in such a way that each is necessary to the whole, his play will rise as a structure of significance, and his collection of small human encounters will reveal something about human nature or about the human condition. Before you can perceive this totality, however, you will have to look carefully at the small units.

Playwrights choose their small units carefully, making sure that each has a *function* in the large pattern of the whole. Sometimes you will be asked to write an essay showing the function of a particular scene of a play. When you receive such an assignment, think in terms of "influences" that follow as a result of this particular encounter; think, too, of encounters preceding it that *caused it* to happen. From this you can see that the scene functions according to a pattern of *cause* and *effect,* rounding out conclusions in the larger units of the play, the acts.

Scenes serve many useful functions in a play. For one, they explain the situations and conditions that exist as present action and dialogue are to take place. Such scenes are called **expository scenes.** For another, they introduce necessary information in a brief, dramatic fashion. For this function many playwrights use messengers, conversations between any minor characters, or spoken meditations of principal characters. These scenes are called **messenger scenes.** Scenes also function transitionally, allowing the reader or viewer to slide easily from one scene and one bit of action into a greatly changed scene. These scenes are called **transition scenes.** Other scenes, which function to further the action or to complicate it, are called **development scenes.** They carry the plot along to the **climax scene,** where the action is at its highest peak of interest or excitement. Finally comes the **denouement,** functioning to round out the action, to tie up all loose threads, to satisfactorily put an end to action. These scenes, when tied together by action that relates each to the others, make the completed pattern of all the acts.

Traditionally the Greeks (and later the Romans and the English) structured their plays in five acts, each of which contained one or more of the various kinds of scenes described above. Plays are constructed around a conflict, and the five acts, as described below, function either to advance, retard, or resolve the conflict.

Act I contains exposition scenes, which introduce settings, characters, and situations and hint at the conflict. In Sophocles' *Antigone,* for example, the first scene provides the following information: Antigone and Ismene, daughters of Oedipus, hear Creon announce his succession to the throne of Thebes after the repulse of an assault on Thebes by the Argive army. Their brothers, Eteocles and Polyneices, have been killed, each by the sword of the other; Eteocles has been buried with honor, but the sisters hear Creon declare death to anyone who buries Polyneices, who led the

Argive attack against Thebes. The point of conflict is introduced when we hear that Antigone intends to obey religious law and bury her brother's body, in defiance of civil law. A definite interest-catching scene occurs when a sentry enters to tell Creon that someone has buried Polyneices.

Act II traditionally contains **rising action** (complication of the conflict). By this time all background material has been presented and the play proceeds with **present action.** Sometimes a device called the **exciting force** is used to complicate the action. In *Antigone* this force might be considered the sentry's terror as he brings in Antigone after he has caught her again bestowing burial rites on Polyneices. Because Creon has accused the sentry of being the offender, the sentry is compelled to find the guilty one to save himself. In the rising action of this scene, Antigone defies Creon and he condemns both her and Ismene to death. This sentence and, in addition, the information that Antigone was to have been the bride of Haimon, Creon's only surviving son, leads into the further action.

Act III usually continues the rising action in the play until a **turning point,** or **crisis,** occurs. This is a point at which matters force an issue. Here the leading character, or **protagonist,** faces an important test. Earlier he has met more than one lesser crisis and has either conquered it or has been defeated in it. Now he faces the greatest test of all. In *Antigone* the leading character faces this great test when Antigone learns that Creon's precise sentence is that she be entombed with only a small amount of food.

Act IV contains **falling action.** There is no lessening of dramatic interest, since interest increases as the action approaches the climax. In *Antigone,* the protagonist, on her way to the tomb, blames her parent's incest for her fate.

Act V contains the **catastrophe.** Events leading to the catastrophe are set in motion by the **tragic force,** which usually occurs late in Act IV or in Act V. In *Antigone* Creon's nature might be considered the tragic force. Teiresias, the blind prophet, accuses Creon of causing calamity by his pride. Angrily Creon accuses Teiresias of being bribed, whereupon the blind prophet predicts that Creon must pay with "corpse for corpse, flesh of your own flesh." Creon leaves to free Antigone, but he is too late. Antigone has hanged herself, and Haimon has stabbed himself in trying to stab Creon.

Classical Conventions From the beginning, drama, like all art forms, began to develop its own conventions, many of which are still in effect. Actors, for example, have always spoken in uncommonly loud tones to project their words to everyone in the audience; **soliloquies** and **asides** have always been used to provide audiences some knowledge of what characters are thinking; music has from the first been used to heighten dramatic effect, and dialogue has often been poetic.

Greek drama also had some special conventions. No more than three speaking characters, for example, ever appeared on stage at one time, and men played all the female roles. Actors wore facial masks and loose, flowing robes. With several thousand spectators seated in tiers of seats around the arena, the nuances of facial expression and vocal inflection would have been lost; thus, actors wore masks symbolic of the dominant emotion they were portraying. Because *what* was said in Greek plays was of the greatest importance, both chorus and actors spoke very loudly. Greek plays always employed the chorus. With Aeschylus the chorus functioned as hardly more than an oratorio, but Sophocles made an actor of the chorus. The utterances of the chorus were odes, sung or chanted as the members of the chorus moved across the stage in a stately dance. When they were silent, the chorus remained on the stage, standing at the back, prepared to make their comments concerning the action and speech of the other characters. The choric utterances reflected the conventional beliefs of the time, but were not necessarily statements of the meaning the dramatist intended with his play.

Another convention of the Greek theater, so closely observed that Aristotle called it a "principle," was the observance of the **unities** of action and of time. Aristotle said that in the action of a tragedy there must be nothing haphazard but all must make a complete whole. The time limits of a play, he said, should be no more than one revolution of the sun. Another convention of Greek plays (later referred to as the unity of place) was the limiting of plays to one setting. By convention, Greek plays showed no violence on stage. You will recall that *Oedipus Rex* fulfills all these requirements: all the action takes place before the palace of Oedipus in a single day; Oedipus blinds himself off stage; Jocasta hangs herself off stage, and we hear of both these violent actions from a messenger.

Because Aristotle set forth so succinctly in his *Poetics* what the best Greek dramas should contain, it would be to your advantage to become familiar with that short work. Then study the *Poetics* in conjunction with several Greek tragedies. Particularly good for introductory study are the tragedies *Oedipus Rex* and *Antigone* by Sophocles, *Agamemnon* by Aeschylus, *Medea* by Euripides, and the comedies *The Frogs* and *Lysistrata* by Aristophanes.

ROMAN DRAMA. Roman drama originated with the Greeks. Translations of Greek plays and plays modeled upon Greek tragedies or comedies were given in Rome for entertainment at festivals, funerals, or dedications. Roman drama displayed little originality, unless we consider native to the Romans the "Fescennine verses" (ribald performances in varied rhythms presented at harvests and other occasions of merriment). Plays good for study are Plautus' comedies *Cistellaria* and *Casina* and Seneca's tragedies *Thyestes* and *Medea*.

MEDIEVAL DRAMA.   Medieval drama developed differently in different nations. Folk festivals were celebrated all over Europe, and English drama started with dramatizations of church services. Biblical stories were presented, as were **mystery plays,** based on the life of Christ, and **miracle plays,** based on the lives of saints. These plays became so elaborate that they had to move outside the churches. Lay members began to take part in the performances, and gradually the general populace became responsible for productions. The **morality plays** of the fifteenth and sixteenth centuries were dramatized allegories embodying principles of right and wrong. The anonymous *Everyman* is a good morality play to study.

Comedies and tragedies appeared in England about the middle of the sixteenth century. For study read the first English comedy, *Ralph Roister Doister,* by the schoolmaster Nicholas Udall and the first English tragedy, *Gorboduc,* by Sackville and Norton.

ELIZABETHAN DRAMA.   The new learning of the Elizabethan era led to a period of richness for literature. Drama flourished in this age of rediscovery of the classics and of patronage of literature by noblemen. The new movement of *humanism* (belief in man's possibilities to achieve perfection) was the inspiration for the creation of brilliant literature for the stage.

Elizabethan drama was not presented at religious festivals as Greek drama was. During this period permanent theaters were constructed, and people attended them for entertainment and instruction. Elizabethan drama, based at first on classical themes, moved away from religious myth and began to incorporate native elements and national history. This essential change from classical drama, coupled with the humanistic insistence upon the rightness of expressing human passion, provided the impetus necessary for drama to begin to emerge as a distinctive form. Playwrights of great creative power, like Shakespeare, added their talents to make this age one of great richness for drama.

Structure and Conventions   Elizabethan drama retained the basic five-act structure of classical drama and the basic plot structure (rising action, falling action, climax, and denouement). It discarded many of the classical conventions, including the unities of time and place. The action in many of Shakespeare's plays, for example, extends over a long period of time, and the settings are frequently changed. *Macbeth* has such varied scenes as a plain, a heath, a palace at Forres, Scotland, Macbeth's palace at Inverness (with scenes there in the court, the hall, the dining hall, and other palace rooms), and even a scene in England. Like the Greek plays, Elizabethan plays had all male actors, and all plays were written in verse. Unlike the Greek plays, however, they mixed comic matter with serious; subplots followed the main plot line; low-born characters sometimes had prominent roles. A wealth of plays exists for study in this period; among them are Thomas Kyd's *The Spanish Tragedy,* Christopher Marlowe's *Doctor Faustus* and *Tamburlaine the Great,* John Webster's *The Duchess of Malfi,* George Peale's *Edward the First,* Ben Jonson's *Volpone* and *The Alchemist,* and, of course, the plays of Shakespeare.

SEVENTEENTH-CENTURY DRAMA.   In the seventeenth century the quarrel between Puritanism and the theater led to the Act of 1642, which forced the closing of the theaters, thus causing a decline of drama. Nevertheless, the art was not entirely dead; scattered plays, most designed only to be read, continued to be published in England. By the time of the Restoration, drama was flourishing again. Plays of this century good for study are Dryden's *Aureng-Zebe,* and examples of Restoration drama, like Wycherly's *The Country Wife* and Congreve's *The Way of the World.*

EIGHTEENTH-CENTURY DRAMA.   Plays changed little during the first half of the eighteenth century. The appearance of the novel caused a decline in interest in dramatic literature. English tragedies in this era were modeled after French tragedies, but somewhat later in the century comic operas became popular. Burlesque and farce, and somewhat later, the sentimental comedy drew appreciative audiences. Good for study are John Gay's *The Beggar's Opera,* Oliver Goldsmith's *She Stoops to Conquer,* and Richard Sheridan's *The Rivals.*

NINETEENTH-CENTURY DRAMA.   During the nineteenth century, drama underwent a natural decline, perhaps because novels satisfied the people's appetite for literature. Nevertheless, a few great plays (mainly in verse) were written in this period. Many were of the type called **closet plays,** so named because they were considered more suitable for reading than for acting. Among those good for study are Goethe's *Faust,* Shelley's *Prometheus Unbound,* Browning's *Strafford,* and A. C. Swinburne's *Atlanta in Calydon.*

After mid-eighteenth century the three-act play appeared, and in the nineteenth century the one-act play. The three-act play has continued to gain favor until it is now considered the standard for full-length plays. The dramatic plot pattern, however, remains very much the same as the five-act Greek model.

The one-act play differs from longer plays in the tightness of its structure. The action starts very near the climax, and the play usually concerns itself with no more than three characters and no more than one incident. The incident usually illuminates sharply the main character. Like a short story, a one-act play telescopes background and beginning situations and lets present action focus on the illuminating incident. One-act plays make particularly enjoyable reading.

MODERN DRAMA. Modern drama has so many forms and each has been influenced by so many diverse factors that to establish the development of any is to point backward in many directions at once. For example, the sources of a play of the absurd like Samuel Beckett's *Waiting for Godot,* include, among others, the philosophy of Nietzsche, expressionism, naturalism, and the Italian Commedia d'ell Arte. The origins of a verse drama like Yeats' *Purgatory* include both classical and Elizabethan drama and, in addition, some of the influences named for Beckett's play.

Modern drama is usually considered to have begun with Henrik Ibsen. His influence began to be felt as early as 1880 and steadily grew for a period of twenty years or more. His method of realism and his expression of the social needs of the time made his plays a daring new force. Another profoundly felt influence was that of the famous Moscow Art Theater. They wished, in the words of one of its founders, Stanislavsky, "to declare war upon all conventionalities of the theater." The new writers wanted to write plays that mirrored the newer generation and its criticism of the life of their time. But it was probably Ibsen's *A Doll's House* and *Ghosts* that were the most influential in bringing about naturalistic drama. Plays of this kind show characters molded by the customs and beliefs of their culture and by their natural instincts. Very often naturalistic plays criticize the society that produced modern man. They show that the inciting forces bringing misfortunes to men are not villains like Iago, but society itself or the psychological make-up of men (*A Doll's House* deals with the problems an individual woman has in fulfilling her personality in a stereotyped society; *Ghosts* deals with the problem of syphilis).

Many of our playwrights picture the humankind of our age as lost, believing in Nietzsche's despairing cry (1885) that "God is dead." In naturalism we get a rejection of a spiritual world. On the other hand, many of our playwrights forcefully attack this view, denying a fatalistic or deterministic philosophy. These latter playwrights see the spirit of modern man as capable of nobility and emphasize this spirit as a positive force. But, whatever the philosophical views of the playwright, all show life "as it is" to them, even if the showing means that realistic detail must be distorted.

You should not think of the writers of naturalism as using only a "realistic" method. Ibsen's later plays began to be highly symbolic and allegorical. Shaw, Chekhov, Strindberg, and Pirandello, too, may be read on many levels. Thus, although we think of drama after these playwrights as the theater of protest against realism, there existed in the work of many of the "realists" elements of the contemporary revolution in the theater.

When you write about the "realism" of a play be sure to distinguish between, say, realistic details of dialogue (speech that sounds like the conversation of ordinary people) and of actions (actions such as real people would perform) and a realistic *presentation.* Ibsen's play *Hedda Gabler,* for example, has many such realistic details of speech, setting, action, and dialogue, but it is a *symbolic presentation*. This is revealed in the play when you perceive that the symbolic representations—objects (like Hedda's hair), actions (like Hedda's shutting out the light and throwing away fresh flowers), and persons (the womanly Thea)—although realistic in detail, are all symbols that point to meanings.

Many of us are completely bewildered at our first reading of the plays that followed the plays of realism. In much of contemporary drama characters do not seem real; actions seem unmotivated; dialogue seems incomprehensible. We wonder helplessly what the plays can possibly mean. If you have felt this bewilderment, it will help you to learn the origins of this kind of complex drama. Although the sources go back to antiquity, an immediate source is German expressionism, which sprang up in Germany at the turn of this century. This movement profoundly influenced much contemporary drama. The term comes from the fine arts; it seems to draw a parallel between the art of certain writers and the art of painters like Van Gogh, Cezanne, and Matisse. Because the expressionist playwrights were writing in revolt against conventional drama forms, the outstanding features of their plays are revolt, distortion, and caricature. Expressionism was in sympathy with pacifism, socialism, and bold reform. It was also related to the world-wide experimentation in the arts that marks our century. Expressionists were like the cubist and surrealist painters, and like the experimentalist novelist James Joyce. The expressionist playwrights were deeply influenced (as the naturalists were) by Nietzsche. Although the expressionist view of the universe and of the condition of man in the universe is essentially grim, it is also comic, because, the expressionists say, an image of man trying to see himself as important in a hostile universe has comic elements. This kind of comedy is called "black" or "cruel" comedy. German expressionist plays are plays of ideas and psychic situations, represented by symbolic images and elements; action is suggestive of the inner working of the mind (for example, Georg Kaiser's play, *Alkibiades Saved,* shows how the figure of speech, "the thorn in the flesh," leads to idealism. Because the thorn in his foot prevents Sokrates from taking part in athletic activity, he remains quiet to meditate the values of his culture. The problem of the play is made visible as a happening.) Sounds are important in these plays, and so is silence. This particular aspect of expressionism foreshadows the deep concern of writers of the absurd with the loss of human communication.

Another very direct influence came to contemporary drama with the plays of the German playwright Bertolt Brecht. Brecht developed in the twenties what we now called the *epic theater*. Rejecting the catharsis of classical and Elizabethan drama, Brecht insists upon "demonstration of thesis" as the most important function of drama. In his theory of *alienation* he says that plays should not involve the emotions of the audience, but should "alienate" those emotions so that viewers might use their intellects upon the subject matter. To achieve this alienation, Brecht suggests that actors stop the action of the drama at emotional points to address the audience directly. Brecht's *Baal* is a play of expressionism showing a rejection by the poet protagonist not only of the conventions of drama but also of the society in which he lives. Not desiring audience identification with his problems, and completely lacking idealism, Baal turns from one sexual orgy to another to show his complete contempt for society.

Despite his theories, Brecht's characters, especially those of his later plays, are so well drawn that audiences feel full emotional sympathy for them. It was such playwrights as Samuel Beckett, Eugene Ionesco, Harold Pinter, Edward Albee, and other writers of the absurd who achieved portrayal of true alienation.

All the elements of the *theatre of the absurd* can be seen in earlier forms of drama; however, playwrights of this genre highlight elements of the absurd. Martin Esslin, who first gave the genre its name, gives, among others, these antecedents for this kind of drama: the *mimus* (clowns of ancient Greece and Rome who burlesqued people and events), the Commedia d'ell Arte, Shakespeare's clowns, the German expressionists, the Dadaists, Mallarmé, Büchner, early Brecht, Charlie Chaplin, the Keystone Cops, Buster Keaton, and the Marx Brothers movies. In his book *The Theatre of the Absurd* Esslin says that the theme of these plays is in the "sense of metaphysical anguish at the absurdity of the human condition." Thus, these plays do show anguish, but they also show absurdity. Characters are nonrealistic; they are symbolic beings who go through meaningless actions and utter senseless words, both of which are symbolic of their state. Plot, in the traditional sense, is absent; nevertheless, the speech and action in the best of these plays present a unified center of action. Although the basic theme of all may be the same, each explores an area of contemporary life with a perception that makes it stand out from others in the genre. For example, in Beckett's *Waiting for Godot* we see the strange combination of hope and despair that motivates men held in a static condition. Two tramps, Estragon and Vladimir, wait on a country road for someone who never comes. That wait constitutes all the action. Three other characters enter, but no news of Godot comes. There is comic pantomine and there is endless talk, which begins in the philosophic but careens off into the nonsensical. We never learn whom they wait for; Godot could be a friend, or a political or military person who could bring aid, or he could be God. Although the two say often, "Let's go," they do not move. The play seems meaningless on the surface; however, at its end we can perceive that an aspect of the modern human condition has been piercingly examined. With a play like this the reader wavers in his response; he does not know whether to laugh or to cry.

Plays of this sort are *antirealistic;* they are *anti-theater.* They rebel against both the conventions of society and of the theater. They present a completely new approach to drama, and a completely new approach to the problems of life. To summarize, this kind of drama has these characteristics: acute awareness of the human condition, absence of plot or story, nonrealistic characters, a rejection of language as a meaningful means of communication, a combination of laughter and despair, alienation of the audience, a picture of the inner workings of the mind, and ultimately, an attempt to understand man and his condition. For study in this genre you should read, among others, Beckett's *Waiting for Godot* and *Endgame,* Ionesco's *The Chairs, Rhinoceros,* and *The Leader* (on page 193 of this text), Edward Albee's *Zoo Story,* Harold Pinter's *The Caretaker.*

Another kind of modern drama, **verse drama,** is in some ways a return to earlier forms and in other ways a presentation of life somewhat like the methods of expressionism or the absurd. A play like Yeats' *Purgatory* has the elements of rhythm and the intensity of language that make poetry; in addition, it has, with its use of metaphor, the ability to present a world both of reality and of anti-reality. In fact, a verse play may have a greater, a more fundamental reality than a play of realism, since it exposes, in T. S. Eliot's words, "the underneath, or the inside, of the natural surface appearance." Many playwrights are returning to poetic drama as a truer way to present the subconscious mind of man. Excellent for study in verse drama are Yeats' *Purgatory,* Eliot's *Murder in the Cathedral,* Lorca's *Blood Wedding* and *Yerma,* John Synge's *Riders to the Sea,* and Christopher Fry's *The Lady's Not for Burning.*

DISCOVERING A PLAY

Seldom will the disparity between the dramatic or surface experience of a work and its true meaning be more sharply contrasted than in plays from the theatre of the absurd. Eugene Ionesco's short, one-act play *The Leader* belongs to this genre and illustrates many of the concepts and techniques that characterize avant-garde theater of this century. Read the play, which follows, and try to discern its true subject and the means the playwright uses to achieve his effects. After you read the play, read the discoveries that follow to test your comprehension.

THE LEADER [1]

Characters

THE ANNOUNCER
THE YOUNG LOVER
THE GIRL-FRIEND
THE ADMIRER
THE GIRL ADMIRER
THE LEADER

[*Standing with his back to the public, centre-stage, and with his eyes fixed on the up-stage exit, the* ANNOUNCER *waits for the arrival of the* LEADER. *To right and left, riveted to the walls, two of the* LEADER'S ADMIRERS, *a man and a girl, also wait for his arrival.*]

ANNOUNCER: [*after a few tense moments in the same position*] There he is! There he is! At the end of the street! [*Shouts of 'Hurrah!' etc., are heard.*] There's the leader! He's coming, he's coming nearer! [*Cries of acclaim and applause are heard from the wings.*] It's better if he doesn't see us . . . [*The* TWO ADMIRERS *hug the wall even closer.*] Watch out! [*The* ANNOUNCER *gives vent to a brief display of enthusiasm.*] Hurrah! Hurrah! The leader! The leader! Long live the leader! [*The* TWO ADMIRERS, *with their bodies rigid and flattened against the wall, thrust their necks and heads as far forward as they can to get a glimpse of the* LEADER.] The leader! The leader! [*The* TWO ADMIRERS *in unison:*] Hurrah! Hurrah! [*Other 'Hurrahs!' mingled with 'Hurrah! Bravo!' come from the wings and gradually die down.*] Hurrah! Bravo!

[*The* ANNOUNCER *takes a step up-stage, stops, then up-stage, followed by the* TWO ADMIRERS, *saying as he goes: 'Ah! Too bad! He's going away! He's going away! Follow me quickly! After him!' The* ANNOUNCER *and the* TWO ADMIRERS *leave, crying: 'Leader! Leeeeader! Lee-ee-eader!' (This last 'Lee-ee-eader!' echoes in the wings like a bleating cry.)*]

[*Silence. The stage is empty for a few brief moments. The* YOUNG LOVER *enters right, and his* GIRL-FRIEND *left; they meet centre-stage.*]

[1] Eugene Ionesco, "The Leader," *Rhinoceros and Other Plays,* translated by Derek Prouse. Copyright (©) 1960 by John Calder Publishers, Inc. Reprinted by permission of Grove Press, Inc.

YOUNG LOVER: Forgive me, Madame, or should I say Mademoiselle?

GIRL-FRIEND: I beg your pardon, I'm afraid I don't happen to know you!

YOUNG LOVER: And I'm afraid I don't know you either!

GIRL-FRIEND: Then neither of us knows each other.

YOUNG LOVER: Exactly. We have something in common. It means that between us there is a basis of understanding on which we can build the edifice of our future.

GIRL-FRIEND: That leaves me cold, I'm afraid. [*She makes as if to go.*]

YOUNG LOVER: Oh, my darling, I adore you.

GIRL-FRIEND: Darling, so do I! [*They embrace.*]

YOUNG LOVER: I'm taking you with me, darling. We'll get married straightaway.

[*They leave left. The stage is empty for a brief moment.*]

ANNOUNCER: [*enters up-stage followed by the* TWO ADMIRERS] But the leader swore that he'd be passing here.

ADMIRER: Are you absolutely sure of that?

ANNOUNCER: Yes, yes, of course.

GIRL ADMIRER: Was it really on his way?

ANNOUNCER: Yes, yes. He should have passed by here, it was marked on the Festival programme . . .

ADMIRER: Did you actually see it yourself and hear it with your own eyes and ears?

ANNOUNCER: He told someone. Someone else!

ADMIRER: But who? Who was this someone else?

GIRL ADMIRER: Was it a reliable person? A friend of yours?

ANNOUNCER: A friend of mine who I know very well. [*Suddenly in the background one hears renewed cries of 'Hurrah!' and 'Long live the leader!'*] That's him now! There he is! Hip! Hip! Hurrah! There he is! Hide yourselves! Hide yourselves!

[*The* TWO ADMIRERS *flatten themselves as before against the wall, stretching their necks out towards the wings from where the shouts of acclamation come; the* ANNOUNCER *watches fixedly up-stage his back to the public.*]

ANNOUNCER: The leader's coming. He approaches. He's bending. He's unbending. [*At each of the* ANNOUNCER'*s words, the* ADMIRERS *give a start and stretch their necks even farther; they shudder.*] He's jumping. He's crossed the river. They're shaking his hand. He sticks out his thumb. Can you hear? They're laughing. [*The* ANNOUNCER *and the* TWO ADMIRERS *also laugh.*] Ah . . . ! they're giving him a box of tools. What's he going to do with them? Ah . . . ! he's signing autographs. The leader is stroking a hedgehog, a superb hedgehog! The crowd applauds. He's dancing, with the hedgehog in his hand. He's embracing his dancer. Hurrah! Hurrah! [*Cries are heard in the wings.*] He's being photographed, with his dancer on one hand and the hedgehog on the other . . . He greets the crowd . . . He spits a tremendous distance.

GIRL ADMIRER: Is he coming past here? Is he coming in our direction?

ADMIRER: Are we really on his route?

ANNOUNCER: [*turns his head to the* TWO ADMIRERS] Quiet, and don't move, you're spoiling everything . . .

GIRL ADMIRER: But even so . . .

ANNOUNCER: Keep quiet, I tell you! Didn't I tell you he'd promised, that he had fixed his itinerary himself . . . . [*He turns back up-stage and cries.*] Hurrah! Hurrah! Long live the leader! [*Silence*] Long live, long live, the leader! [*Silence*] Long live, long live, long live the lead-er! [*The* TWO ADMIRERS, *unable to contain themselves, also give a sudden cry of:*] Hurrah! Long live the leader!

ANNOUNCER: [*to the* ADMIRERS] Quiet, you two! Calm down! You're spoiling everything! [*Then, once more looking up-stage, with the* AD-MIRERS *silenced.*] Long live the leader! [*Wildly enthusiastic.*] Hurrah! Hurrah! He's changing his shirt. He disappears behind a red screen. He reappears! [*The applause intensifies.*] Bravo! Bravo! [*The* ADMIRERS *also long to cry 'Bravo' and applaud; they put their hands to their mouths to stop themselves.*] He's putting his tie on! He's reading his newspaper and drinking his morning coffee! He's still got his hedgehog . . . He's leaning on the edge of the parapet. The parapet breaks. He gets up . . . he gets up unaided! [*Applause, shouts of 'Hurrah!'*] Bravo! Well done! He brushes his soiled clothes.

TWO ADMIRERS: [*stamping their feet*] Oh! Ah! Oh! Oh! Ah! Ah!

ANNOUNCER: He's mounting the stool! He's climbing piggy-back, they're offering him a thin-ended wedge, he knows it's meant as a joke, and he doesn't mind, he's laughing.

[*Applause and enormous acclaim.*]

ADMIRER: [*to the* GIRL ADMIRER] You hear that! You hear? Oh! If I were king . . .

GIRL ADMIRER: Ah . . . ! the leader! [*This is said in an exalted tone.*]

ANNOUNCER: [*still with his back to the public*] He's mounting the stool. No. He's getting down. A little girl offers him a bouquet of flowers . . . What's he going to do? He takes the flowers . . . He embraces the little girl . . . calls her 'my child' . . .

ADMIRER: He embraces the little girl . . . calls her 'my child' . . .

GIRL ADMIRER: He embraces the little girl . . . calls her 'my child' . . .

ANNOUNCER: He gives her the hedgehog. The little girl's crying . . .
Long live the leader! Long live the leead-er!

ADMIRER: Is he coming past here?

GIRL ADMIRER: Is he coming past here?

ANNOUNCER: [*with a sudden run, dashes out up-stage*] He's going
away! Hurry! Come on!

> [*He disappears, followed by the* TWO ADMIRERS, *all crying 'Hurrah!
> Hurrah!'*]

> [*The stage is empty for a few moments. The* TWO LOVERS *enter, en-
> twined in an embrace; they halt centre-stage and separate; she carries
> a basket on her arm.*]

GIRL-FRIEND: Let's go to the market and get some eggs!

YOUNG LOVER: Oh! I love them as much as you do!

> [*She takes his arm. From the right the* ANNOUNCER *arrives running,
> quickly regaining his place, back to the public, followed closely by
> the* TWO ADMIRERS, *arriving one from the left and the other from the
> right; the* TWO ADMIRERS *knock into the* TWO LOVERS *who were about
> to leave right.*]

ADMIRER: Sorry!

YOUNG LOVER: Oh! Sorry!

GIRL ADMIRER: Sorry! Oh! Sorry!

GIRL-FRIEND: Oh! Sorry, sorry, sorry, so sorry!

ADMIRER: Sorry, sorry, sorry, oh! sorry, sorry, so sorry!

YOUNG LOVER: Oh, oh, oh, oh, oh, oh! So sorry, everyone!

GIRL-FRIEND: [*to her* LOVER] Come along, Adolphe! [*To the* TWO AD-
MIRERS:] No harm done! [*She leaves, leading her* LOVER *by the
hand.*]

ANNOUNCER: [*watching up-stage*] The leader is being pressed forward,
and pressed back, and now they're pressing his trousers! [*The* TWO
ADMIRERS *regain their places.*] The leader is smiling. Whilst they're
pressing his trousers, he walks about. He tastes the flowers and the
fruits growing in the stream. He's also tasting the roots of the trees.
He suffers the little children to come unto him. He has confidence in
everybody. He inaugurates the police force. He pays tribute to justice.
He salutes the great victors and the great vanquished. Finally he re-
cites a poem. The people are very moved.

TWO ADMIRERS: Bravo! Bravo! [*Then, sobbing:*] Boo! Boo! Boo!

ANNOUNCER: All the people are weeping. [*Loud cries are heard from
the wings; the* ANNOUNCER *and the* ADMIRERS *also start to bellow.*] Silence! [*The* TWO ADMIRERS *fall silent; and there is silence from the
wings.*] They've given the leader's trousers back. The leader puts

them on. He looks happy! Hurrah! [*'Bravos', and acclaim from the wings. The* TWO ADMIRERS *also shout their acclaim, jump about, without being able to see anything of what is presumed to be happening in the wings.*] The leader's sucking his thumb! [*To the* TWO ADMIRERS:] Back, back to your places, you two, don't move, behave yourselves and shout: 'Long live the leader!'

TWO ADMIRERS: [*flattened against the wall, shouting*] Long live, long live the leader!

ANNOUNCER: Be quiet, I tell you, you'll spoil everything! Look out, the leader's coming!

ADMIRER: [*in the same position*] The leader's coming!

GIRL ADMIRER: The leader's coming!

ANNOUNCER: Watch out! And keep quiet! Oh! The leader's going away! Follow him! Follow me!

[*The* ANNOUNCER *goes out up-stage, running; the* TWO ADMIRERS *leave right and left, whilst in the wings the acclaim mounts, then fades. The stage is momentarily empty. The* YOUNG LOVER, *followed by his* GIRL-FRIEND, *appear left running across the stage right.*]

YOUNG LOVER: [*running*] You won't catch me! You won't catch me! [*Goes out.*]

GIRL-FRIEND: [*running*] Wait a moment! Wait a moment! [*She goes out. The stage is empty for a moment; then once more the* TWO LOVERS *cross the stage at a run, and leave.*]

YOUNG LOVER: You won't catch me!

GIRL-FRIEND: Wait a moment!

[*They leave right. The stage is empty. The* ANNOUNCER *reappears up-stage, the* ADMIRER *from the right, the* GIRL ADMIRER *from the left. They meet centre.*]

ADMIRER: We missed him!

GIRL ADMIRER: Rotten luck!

ANNOUNCER: It was your fault!

ADMIRER: That's not true!

GIRL ADMIRER: No, that's not true!

ANNOUNCER: Are you suggesting it was mine?

ADMIRER: No, we didn't mean that!

GIRL ADMIRER: No, we didn't mean that! [*Noise of acclaim and 'Hurrahs' from the wings.*]

ANNOUNCER: Hurrah!

GIRL ADMIRER: It's from over there! [*She points up-stage.*]

ADMIRER: Yes, it's from over there! [*He points left.*]

ANNOUNCER: Very well. Follow me! Long live the leader! [*He runs out right, followed by the* TWO ADMIRERS, *also shouting.*]

TWO ADMIRERS: Long live the leader!

[*They leave. The stage is empty for a moment. The* YOUNG LOVER *and his* GIRL-FRIEND *appear left; the* YOUNG LOVER *exits up-stage; the* GIRL-FRIEND, *after saying 'I'll get you!', runs out right. The* ANNOUN-CER *and the* TWO ADMIRERS *appear from up-stage. The* ANNOUNCER *says to the* ADMIRERS:] Long live the leader! [*This is repeated by the* ADMIRERS. *Then, still talking to the* ADMIRERS, *he says:*] Follow me! Follow the leader! [*He leaves up-stage, still running and shouting:*] Follow him!

[*The* ADMIRER *exits right, the* GIRL ADMIRER *left into the wings. During the whole of this, the acclaim is heard louder or fainter according to the rhythm of the stage action; the stage is empty for a moment, then the* LOVERS *appear from right and left, crying:*]

YOUNG LOVER: I'll get you!

GIRL-FRIEND: You won't get me! [*They leave at a run, shouting:*] Long live the leader!

[*The* ANNOUNCER *and the* TWO ADMIRERS *emerge from up-stage, also shouting: 'Long live the leader', followed by the* TWO LOVERS. *They all leave right, in single file, crying as they run: 'The leader! Long live the leader! We'll get him! It's from over here! You won't get me!'*]

[*They enter and leave, employing all the exits; finally, entering from left, from right, and from up-stage they all meet centre, whilst the acclaim and the applause from the wings becomes a fearful din. They embrace each other feverishly, crying at the tops of their voices:*] Long live the leader! Long live the leader! Long live the leader!

[*Then, abruptly, silence falls.*]

ANNOUNCER: The leader is arriving. Here's the leader. To your places! Attention!

[*The* ADMIRER *and the* GIRL-FRIEND *flatten themselves against the wall right; the* GIRL ADMIRER *and the* YOUNG LOVER *against the wall left; the two couples are in each other's arms, embracing.*]

ADMIRER AND GIRL-FRIEND: My dear, my darling!

GIRL ADMIRER and YOUNG LOVER: My dear, my darling!

[*Meanwhile the* ANNOUNCER *has taken up his place, back to the audience, looking fixedly up-stage; a lull in the applause.*]

ANNOUNCER: Silence. The leader has eaten his soup. He is coming. He is nigh.

[*The acclaim redoubles its intensity; the* TWO ADMIRERS *and the* TWO LOVERS *shout:*]

ALL: Hurrah! Hurrah! Long live the leader!

[*They throw confetti before he arrives. Then the* ANNOUNCER *hurls himself suddenly to one side to allow the* LEADER *to pass; the other four characters freeze with outstretched arms holding confetti; but still say:*] Hurrah! [*The* LEADER *enters from up-stage, advances down-stage to centre; to the footlights, hesitates, makes a step to left, then takes a decision and leaves with great, energetic strides by right, to the enthusiastic 'Hurrahs!' of the* ANNOUNCER *and the feeble, somewhat astonished 'Hurrahs!' of the other four; these, in fact, have some reason to be surprised, as the* LEADER *is headless, though wearing a hat. This is simple to effect: the actor playing the* LEADER *needing only to wear an overcoat with the collar turned up round his forehead and topped with a hat. The-man-in-an-overcoat-with-a-hat-without-a-head is a somewhat surprising apparition and will doubtless produce a certain sensation. After the* LEADER'S *disappearance, the* GIRL ADMIRER *says:*]

GIRL ADMIRER: But . . . but . . . the leader hasn't got a head!
ANNOUNCER: What's he need a head for when he's got genius!
YOUNG LOVER: That's true! [To *the* GIRL-FRIEND:] What's your name?

[*The* YOUNG LOVER *to the* GIRL ADMIRER, *the* GIRL ADMIRER *to the* ANNOUNCER, *the* ANNOUNCER *to the* GIRL-FRIEND, *the* GIRL-FRIEND *to the* YOUNG LOVER:] What's yours? What's yours? What's yours? [*Then, all together, one to the other:*] What's your name?
Curtain

1. DISCOVERING THE DRAMATIC EXPERIENCE

Reading *The Leader* or seeing it performed on stage constitutes a startling and bewildering experience. The play opens with three characters —the Announcer, the Admirer, and the Girl Admirer—waiting with tense expectation for the Leader, a great public figure, to pass along the street. The Leader fails to appear; energetically the Announcer and Two Admirers go in search of him. The Young Lover appears, and from the opposite side of the stage the Girl-Friend. In seven lines of dialogue they progress from initial encounter to avowed love and a proposal and acceptance of marriage. They rush offstage. The Announcer and Admirers reappear, and in increasingly ecstatic tones the Leader's off-stage actions are described: he holds out his thumb, and he receives a box of tools, a hedgehog, flowers, and a "thin-ended wedge" from the adoring crowd. He makes a speech, falls off a parapet, tastes the roots of trees, and "suffers the little children to come unto him." In the four sequences that follow, the Two Lovers appear, quarrel, and lose interest in each other, and as easily and quickly fall in love with the Two Admirers. They join the Admirers and Announcer who wait, excitement mounting. Finally the Leader appears, and he has no head. All—the Announcer, the Admirers and the Lovers —accept this startling fact and begin inquiring of one another their names. The play ends.

The absence of any standard plot, climax, character development, or discernible motivation for action and dialogue poses a puzzling ambivalence that cannot be solved by traditional methods of examining the play. Nothing makes sense except that the action and characters are amusing and absurd. Yet some tension, some meaning runs through the play, some sense of sadness, corruption, and truth that can be understood only when the true identity of the Leader is established, and when the stylized actions and meaning of the characters are translated into allegory or symbol. To find any significance deeper than farce requires a careful analysis of the techniques the author uses to dramatize his meanings.

2. DISCOVERING THE AUTHOR'S TECHNIQUES

The characters are not only nameless, but a careful examination of their actions reveals that they are too abstract even for types. They are symbols, representing ideas. Similarly, the play reveals that what the characters do is as unrealistic as the existence of a headless Leader. Actions therefore, like the repetitive dialogue, are stylized and made purposefully artificial so that they, too, represent ideas. Even the setting, the bare stage, becomes as abstract and representative as the off-stage action and the unseen crowds. As a result, the viewer or reader must approach the play with his intellect. He cannot identify with the characters or feel empathy with them because lack of characterization, situation, and story line make identification impossible. The audience is effectively alienated from the play and intellectually freed to study the ideas contained in the violent distortions of language, action, characterization, and structure. Such distortions, compressed and deliberately made bizarre, result in visual and auditory symbols.

Symbolism

The actions and visual and auditory images in *The Leader* convey ideas by embodying meanings more inclusive than the actual sight, sound, or action presented. Disguised as abstract thought, the meaning of the images is expanded by association until one image, distorted and stylized, suggests another, wider referent. The entire stage in *The Leader* is a visual experience in ideas.

LANGUAGE AS IDEAS.   Ionesco's language patterns, his use of concentrated banality coupled with rhythmical repetition, establish a stylized manner of speech that emphasizes and produces ideas. The language is devaluated not only to emphasize that what happens is more important than what is said, but also to promote characterization as abstract ideas, and to suggest what the character-ideas represent. The dialogue is simple, as if spoken by a child. The Announcer, rushing after the Leader, calls the same words over and over in his distress. To the Admirers, the Announcer reports each of the actions of the Leader as information of great importance. His description provides a method of highlighting the absurdity of the Leader's behavior and the equal absurdity of the crowd's unthinking adulation.

The repetitious cheering by the Announcer, the Admirers, and the unseen crowd and by the Lovers at the end of the play evokes in its mindless rhythms a sense of the absurdity of the crowd's devotion. Repetition in language underscores the unquestioning conformity of the crowd, and by extension, the automated conformity of society. Everyone has jumped on the bandwagon; no one understands or cares about the destination of the bandwagon.

The vacuous lip service paid to love (and by extension to human emotions and individual uniqueness and importance) is dramatized through understatement, clichés, and foreshortened dialogues. The Young Lover and the Girl-Friend, meeting for the first time, exchange stereotyped greetings; they neglect even to ask names before they fall in love. Their action is illogical and satirizes the concept of love at first sight. These characters function on the level of marionettes; the courtship game, its form frozen in clichés and custom, subsequently negates marriage and fidelity as each Lover—within minutes—tries to dominate his partner; this failing, they find new partners. Words, in the Lover episodes, symbolize the clichéd state of human emotions.

The same empty formulas and slogans fill the Announcer's and Admirers' speeches. The Announcer's report represents the methods used by pressmen to describe all celebrities. The irony of the broadcast's vacuous content is underscored by the Admirers' wild enthusiasm and cheering.

The effect of reducing language to cliché is to dissolve language as a method of communication. Language, passionless and automatic, reveals the pitiful human condition. Their thinking fossilized by convention, speaking banalities, people are shown to be divorced from what they say. Thus dialogue in *The Leader* reveals that language no longer communicates; it forms a barrier to understanding and ultimately alienates man from himself and from his fellow man.

ACTION AS IDEA.   Just as language reveals the triviality of man and his failure to communicate, so human action and motivation, complex in everyday life, are reduced in the play to body motions and elemental behavior. Action is exaggerated to make clear the puppet-like condition of modern man, and the stylistic rhythms of the characters represent ideas. The effect, like a dance, is a poetic image brought to life.

We see in the breathless, tense waiting of the Announcer and Admirers an ultimately ludicrous situation: people waiting for what they do not understand or perhaps even care about, but who are still held in the grip of mob psychology—of their own self-generated enthusiasm and hope that something significant will happen. The value of the eyewitness is personified in the Announcer and Admirers, and the entire play satirizes the basic premise that proximity endows authority. The Announcer fails to make a valid interpretation of the Leader's actions. The Admirers, seeing the Leader with their own eyes, fail to become wiser or more important. Primitive fetishism underlies the play: through contact, even eye contact, the qualities of the object are thought to be magically transferred to the beholder.

While the Announcer and Admirers rush about town, the Two Lovers, oblivious to politics, meet and declare their love. The rapidity of the courtship satirizes man's habit of constantly falling in and out of love. In ensuing episodes, time foreshortened, the Girl-Friend chases the Young Lover; he derides her possessiveness, then she his. Their emotion clearly does not withstand the pressure of association. Both exchange partners and, substituting personal involvement for impersonal group behavior, cheer the Leader. Thus another facet of the human condition is reduced to passionless automatism.

The actions of the Leader conceptualize his symbolic meaning as a famous celebrity and focus the play. The action centers on the appearance of the Leader, and in the indiscriminate reporting of the Announcer the great and the trivial receive equal attention. The Leader's "moving" speech is not recorded; what he represents or believes is never made clear. Instead, the Announcer describes each of the absurd actions that charac-

terize famous personalities during public ceremonies. The Leader entertains: he sticks out his thumb and sucks it; he dances with a hedgehog on
his hand. The behavior of the Leader and the crowd lining the streets reflects the stereotyped gift giving, tree planting, joke making, arm waving
conviviality required of all public figures on parade. The action satirizes
man's love of spectacle and his idolization of the famous. The Leader's actions, like those of the Lovers, the Announcer, and the Admirers, form an
elaborate and meaningless ceremony.

CHARACTERIZATION AS IDEA.   As a result of their actions and speech,
each character in the play represents an idea or concept about modern society. The Two Admirers, visual symbols of the off-stage crowd—in short,
of society at large—are personifications of accepted ideas and ready-made
slogans, of human conformity. They reflect the leveling of individuality; no
longer able to think or act independently, they represent the loss of identity in modern man.

The Two Lovers symbolize the loss of man's ability to be moved or
to care deeply. Neither can feel passion and both are indiscriminate. They
can exchange identities; therefore they can effortlessly exchange partners.
The Lovers represent the loss of the uniqueness of individual man, and as
a result the loss of a sense of man's mystery and dimension. Even love, the
greatest of emotions, has become commonplace and meaningless.

The Announcer is a simplified and caricatured symbol of the news
media; he promotes the Leader and all celebrities who make the news.
Awed by the power of his own words, the Announcer's description of the
Leader increases in reverence until he transforms the Leader into a Christ
figure. He says of the Leader, "He suffers the little children to come unto
him." He alone is not surprised that the Leader is headless, explaining the
absence of the Leader's head by declaring simply that genius justifies anything.

The Leader, clearly the dominant and centralizing force in the play,
is a symbol of all the lost and unworthy causes to which people have
blindly devoted their energies and beliefs. Caesar, Napoleon, Hitler: the
crowd becomes the babble of the streets and the blind fanaticism of Nazi
Germany, living reasons for the failure of reason and the cause of the rise
to power of dictators and totalitarian leaders. Deified in spite of their gross
limitations and ineptness (symbolized by the Leader's being headless) they
lack wisdom (the Leader never utters a word) but nevertheless succeed (the
"genius" the Announcer refers to) because man, eager to follow, fearful of
dissent and of standing alone, permits and even encourages leaders to assume power. Ironically, officialdom aids their rise by ceremoniously bestowing its legal stamp of approval.

STRUCTURE AND SETTING AS IDEA.   The bare stage in *The Leader*
represents all streets in all cities of the world. Setting therefore frees action

to exist as pure idea, applicable to countless specific events in history. The setting also holds up a mirror to the timeless void (see pages 70–73), which thematically further aids the concept of man's isolation and spiritual degeneration. Within the setting, and rhythmically emphasizing the abstraction of the characters, the structure operates with the precision of a carefully choreographed ballet. The structure consists of a series of accelerating tensions, dramatized in each scene by an increase in repetition in dialogue, by a decrease in the amount of time between the characters' exits and entrances, and by frantic movement alternating with frozen, motionless poses. Each scene visually represents the frenzy of modern life, and the gradual increase in tension expresses man's overwhelming task of facing the modern world, of coping with its frantic pace while still enduring the solitude resulting from his inability to communicate. The tension created by such dramatic devices in structure renders the play aesthetically whole. Its method contains and reveals its meaning. The comic reveals the tragic.

3. SYNTHESIZING SUBJECT AND THEME

A reading or interpretation of *The Leader* is subject to infinite variations. Plays from the theatre of the absurd use abstractions to create poetic images. The images may be interpreted as symbol, as allegory, as myth, as living metaphor. Their meaning is ultimately complex and ambiguous and it has been said that such plays transcend interpretation. Exploring meanings, however, proves rewarding, for it makes possible a final though still ambiguous synthesis of theme.

Two elements, seemingly divergent, control *The Leader*. The first is the fact that the play is based, structured, and dramatized as a work of total imagination. The second is the presence of unifying social and cultural criticism that dominates the play's content. The effect of comic exaggeration, of caricature of serious issues, results in black comedy or the absurd made horrible and tragic. Human existence, man's inability to control his destiny or avert death, is thus universalized through the creation of puppets who function in the play both as embodiments of ideas and as symbols for all men. Dehumanized by our conformity, our insincerity, our loss of identity in a highly mechanized, fast-paced world, the play indicates that we, the viewers, resemble puppets, and that the reality of the stage puppets exists on a level more real than ours. As a result each of us can see his own condition purified and condensed in them. This idea or truth is ludicrous. Seeing also that it is true, we experience the tragedy of our human condition.

The fact that the Leader, the Announcer, the Two Lovers, and the Two Admirers represent members of accepted society, members aspiring upward toward power, position, and society's approval, makes the play even more profound as a biting commentary upon modern man. Discovering that his aspirations are ludicrous, empty, and meaningless as answers to man's spiritual need is sad. It is more than that. It is tragic.

SAMPLE ESSAYS

SAMPLE ESSAY 15
USING GENRE

INSTRUCTIONS. Although "new criticism" (which advocates close textual examination of a work, to the exclusion of the author's intentions, biography, social conditions at the time of its writing, or response of the reader) does not believe that a consideration of genre is necessary to an analytical reading of a work, such considerations can sometimes prove valuable. To prepare for writing an essay using genre you must discover all the characteristics traditional to the particular species of literature with which you intend to work. For example, to write an essay in which you discussed *The Odyssey* in terms of its genre, you would have to research the characteristics of the epic. (Use the card catalogue at your library to find books on this subject, and also books on the novel, the short story, and other major kinds of literature.) Once you understand the genre you will be ready to apply your knowledge to an examination of a specific work.

Your purpose in an essay of this type will be to show how closely the distinguishing features of the species match those of the specific work. Your thesis will be to give what Coleridge called the "just distinction." As you write, justify the distinctive characteristics as they are employed in the work. *Why* does the work differ in the way that it does? Are the elements of difference justified by the nature of the subject matter? Are the elements of difference justified by the total effect of the work? Are the elements of difference justified by the meanings carried in the work? The essay that follows examines a play to show how the author's use of a particular genre to express his idea contributes to the play's effectiveness.

IONESCO'S *THE LEADER*
AS THEATRE OF THE ABSURD

Although it is an extremely short play, Ionesco's *The Leader* exhibits most of the outstanding characteristics of the theatre of the absurd. All plays in this genre are in revolt against the characteristics of the traditional theater—so much so that the theatre of the absurd has been called anti-theater. To understand how a playwright like Ionesco can bring out meanings in a play of this kind, we must first determine which characteristics of the theatre of the absurd *The Leader* exemplifies.

Like the traditional theater, the theatre of the absurd has its own conventions and characteristics. Characters, for example, are never presented as individuals. In *The Leader,* the characters are so stereotyped they do not even have names; they are simply the Announcer, the Young Lover, the Girl-Friend, the Admirer, the Girl Admirer, and the Leader. Plot, in the accepted sense of the term, has little importance in the theatre of the absurd. In *The Leader* there seems to be no beginning, middle, or end. Action does not follow a logical sequence, and there is no resolution (tragic or otherwise) to the situation. Instead, as is usual with this genre, the play is concerned with a static situation. The action of *The Leader* occurs as if in a vacuum. Characteristically, language in theatre of the absurd is shown to lack the power it has traditionally possessed for expression of emotion and thought. Language in *The Leader* is often nonsensical; it does not evoke sympathy; it delivers no "message"; it is, in essence, devaluated. With this devaluation of language, gesture and silence become other important characteristics of the genre. *The Leader* often uses the "pause" to suggest what we are to feel or think. In this play gesture and stance serve to implant ideas. Setting, as a functional element, is negligible in the theatre of the absurd since the action could take place almost anywhere. The use of sounds other than dialogue are also important in this genre, and in *The Leader* the cries of the characters and the off-stage cheers and noises of acclamation are used effectively.

It is apparent from the above that *The Leader,* like all plays of the absurd, has either dropped or distorted the prescriptive elements of plot, character, diction, and thought. Such complete anti-theater might seem to be revolt for revolt's sake. However, this is not the case. *The Leader,* by disregarding traditional elements, diagnoses the human condition in its own terms. Ionesco has said that his plays were in some ways a criticism of "the petit bourgeois," who for him is "a type of being that exists in all societies . . . a man of slogans, who no longer thinks for himself but repeats the truths that others have imposed upon him, ready-made and therefore lifeless." In *The Leader,* with its nameless, stereotyped characters, its illogical action, and its illogical language, he communicates the sense of a world that is absurd, a world peopled by those who do not think for themselves, who only repeat the lifeless slogans that have been imposed upon them. All the best plays of the absurd explore a particular area of life today. *The Leader* makes its point by exploring modern society's devotion to the cult of the leader.

The action of *The Leader* consists of the seemingly disconnected appearances of two sets of people: the Lovers and the Admirers. Excited by the Announcer, who continues throughout the play to announce in tones reminiscent of a circus barker the imminent arrival of the Leader, these couples impart a sense of confusion. The Admirers either flatten themselves against the walls or crane their necks forward to catch a glimpse of the Leader. Throughout, they obey without thought the exclamatory and contradictory commands of the Announcer. According to his barked orders, they shout, "Hurrah!" or are silent; they follow him or stand back. The nearer the Leader comes, the closer to hysteria they become. The Lovers at first seem oblivious to all but each other, declaring their love in a meaningless repetition of ready-made phrases. Because neither couple has real truths to guide them, they wait tensely for the appearance of the Leader. It is as though, knowing no inner surety, they await a magical being who will give direction to their lives.

The Announcer, whose function is to control the responses of others, reports throughout the play a hodge-podge of the Leader's activities, which the Announcer can see but the others cannot. These "activities" are symbolic of the trivia an overly eager mass media reports to an avid public about its various kinds of "leaders." The Announcer reports in a falsely enthusiastic tone that the Leader performs such unrelated acts as the following: he "changes his shirt" (The Leader is obviously a popular singing star), he "suffers the little children to come to him" (he is Christ), he "embraces a little girl" (he is a candidate for political office), and he "strokes a hedgehog" (he is irrational).

The Leader is never reported to be performing an action of real benefit to his followers. His imitation of Christ is· a blasphemous mockery; his embrace of the little girl is a hypocritical gesture; his recitation of a poem is a desecration of art.

The final absurdity of the play occurs with the entrance of the Leader. He is, shockingly, headless. The wily Announcer, however, cries out that he does not need a head because "he's got genius!" With ludicrous haste, the people who awaited the Leader's arrival agree that he does not need a head. The proclivity of the unthinking to accept any idiocy if it comes from a "leader" makes the reader see, shockingly, how absurd it is to accept slogans as truth. The play ends with all asking one another, "What's your name?" "What's yours? What's yours? What's yours?" This melange of inquiries caps the play's absurdist point: after all the slogans have been uttered, the world is still leaderless, peopled by nameless beings in search of identities that they long ago destroyed by their childish game of "follow the leader."

SAMPLE ESSAY 16
USING ALLUSION

INSTRUCTIONS.   You will recall that in literature an allusion is a reference made to something outside the work (reread pages 14–15). Authors allude to persons, places, objects, and events (real or fictitious) in order to suggest richly significant connotations in some aspect of their works. Allusions are made most often to other literature, to mythology, and to the Bible. Because the use of an allusion allows an author to share with his reader a common cultural experience, he can communicate on a level above other meanings of his words. Similarly, when you write an essay to show the value of allusion to a work you have a double opportunity to clarify for your reader what a work is saying: you can clarify the context, and you can point out associations that give even wider implications to the context.

In preparation for writing the essay using allusion your first step is to look up those references you do not recognize. Good sources for this research are dictionaries, encyclopedias, and bibliographical reference books (your library contains a bibliographical study for almost all the important writers and such studies list all the writer's works and most of what has been written about both the writer and his work). Your next step is to determine what relationship each allusion bears to the context. Decide at the end of these discoveries whether, taken as a whole, they seem to point to a dominant body of reference. The recurrent allusions to things ecclesiastical in Joyce's short story "Araby," which definitely point to the church's influence upon the lives of characters in that story, are a good example of such a case; so, too, are the allusions to the myth of the Fisher King in T. S. Eliot's long poem *The Waste Land,* which provide a framework that universalizes the experience of the poem. If you discover such dominant references in a work, your thesis will be to show the controlling function of the allusions. If, on the other hand, you discover only nonrelated allusions, your thesis then will be to show how each enriches the work. Avoid the pitfalls inherent in this last type of essay. Do not allow your organization to become a mere listing of the allusions with their meanings; instead, develop a controlling idea, which shows how the associations serve to communicate with the reader in a meaningful way. The essay that follows deals with a set of dominant references in Ionesco's *The Leader,* which point to a theme.

THE END OF HOPE IN IONESCO'S *THE LEADER*

In his book *The Theatre of the Absurd* Martin Esslin suggests that *Le Maitre,* the original French title of Ionesco's play, points to *The Leader* as a literary figure. This suggestion is richly connotative, but, considering the many Biblical allusions in the work, we may also see the Leader as the Master. This essay will concentrate upon a cluster of references, noticeable throughout the work, which rather insistently suggest that to the characters of the play the Leader is Christ. On the contrary, however, the headless creature who finally appears is the antithesis of Christ, a mindless, soulless being who puts an end to the hopes of the people. The Biblical allusions, when assembled, form a decided indication of the Leader's identity, not for us, but for the people of the world of *The Leader,* who must clutch at hope for alleviation of their despair.

In this play, which has no individuals, but only representations of types of people, the Announcer takes a dominant role. He manipulates the other characters, controlling not only their actions but their thinking. In the opening scene, with his back to the audience, the Announcer reports the Leader's movements off-stage and excitedly announces his imminent arrival. It is particularly appropriate that one who hails a false Messiah does not show his face to the people. At the close of this short scene, the Announcer cries out that the Leader is "going away." His strategy is to keep the people in suspense—to make them think the Leader is coming, make them think he is leaving. The Announcer and the Two Admirers run after the Leader, crying, "Leader! Leader! Lee—ee—eader!" The stage directions inform us that this last word echoes in the wings like a "bleating cry." Here we have the richness of ambiguity, for we immediately receive two ideas: the people, like sheep, will blindly follow anyone; spiritually, they are lost sheep crying after the Master to feed them.

The entire world of *The Leader* is a lost, desolate one. The faceless, nameless Young Lover and Girl-Friend, and the Two Admirers, are indeed lost. They long desperately for the appearance of one who can relieve their forsaken condition. They will grasp at any vouchsafement of hope. Allusions are made in the play to other beings or ideologies that people will follow—the dictator (at one moment the Girl-Friend calls the Young Lover "Adolphe"), the entertainer, the politician—but it is the hope of a *savior* that appeals most to their confused imaginations. The world of Ionesco's plays is invariably one that pictures man as devoid of spiritual life. The individuals of this world fill the void with meaningless talk, the clichés made by disseminators of political and religious ideologies. The commitment the Lovers and the Admirers feel toward the Leader as the Master is not based on deeply felt truth. They have not experienced inwardly the assurance of His ability to save them from their despair; rather, they follow blindly because they have been *told* that He can save them. Individuals who try to find their way without the inner experience will remain lost, and so it is with the people of *The Leader*.

It is with deliberate awareness of their condition of inner want that Ionesco continues to invoke by associations an ironic apprehension of the world that opposes the world of *The Leader*. As the Announcer continues throughout the play to describe the actions of the Leader, he uses phrases that are richly suggestive of this opposing world, the spiritually alive world. "Silence," the Announcer orders. "The Leader has eaten his soup. He is coming. He is nigh." The Announcer, who likes his self-appointed role of dictator to the sycophantic Admirers, has intermingled the sort of trivial information considered interesting if it concerns public figures ("The Leader has eaten his soup") with overtones of the prophecy in Joel 2:1 of a new day: "The day of the Lord cometh, for it is nigh at hand." The Apocalypse is at hand; the Lovers and the Admirers scramble in wild confusion to witness the revelation.

Earlier the Announcer had said that the Leader "tastes the flowers and the fruits growing in the stream. He's also tasting the roots of the trees." The allusion could well be to Revelation 2:7: "To him that overcometh will I give to eat of the tree of life." This Leader is touted as a Messiah, but he is not the Messiah, for we hear that he performs actions antithetical to a true saviour. As an example, he is "stroking a hedgehog." The allusion is to a kind of battle formation: the hedgehog formation is one which is woe to the enemy and to the user. This Leader's coming heralds, not salvation, but destruction. We are reminded of Luke 21:20: "And when ye shall see Jerusalem compassed with armies, then know that the destruction thereof is nigh."

As the Leader enters, the illogical Lovers and the sheep-like Admirers are close to hysteria. The Leader is headless. But the Announcer cries out, "What's he need a head for when he's got genius!" All agree, "That's true." Recalling the Announcer's words regarding the "thin-ended wedge," accepted by the Leader as a joke, we make the traditional associations with the bitterness of the "two-edged sword" of Proverbs 5:4, and see the woe that results for all, as we did with the "hedgehog"—it is death to the adversary and to the wielder.

The people of the world of *The Leader* are left as we found them. Lost, they had hoped for a savior on this day of the "Festival"; the false prophet has brought them instead a Hitler, a movie star, a political demagogue.

SAMPLE ESSAY 17
USING STRUCTURE

INSTRUCTIONS. Finding the structure in a work, determining how the structure embodies or aids meaning, and writing an essay analyzing the function of structure as a vehicle for the work's theme is at best difficult. But it is also important, and for this reason, your instructor may assign an essay requiring you to analyze the structure in a work. He will want to know if you comprehend the "bones," the essential layout that gives the total work its shape and form.

On pages 80, 132, 145, 161, and 187 we discussed the characteristics and function of structure in fiction, poetry and drama, pointing out that each genre has its own rules, its own conventions, and in many respects its own vocabulary and theories for critical approach. If by structure we mean, in poetry, the poem's paraphrasable argument in one work and its developing imagery in the next; if in fiction we mean the internal movement separate from plot in one work and a psychic time arrangement in the next; if in drama we refer to the five-act structure one moment and scenes developed through symbolism in the next—so be it. Structure has more than one meaning, and the essential framework or method of development will vary with individual works. Structure, like theme, must be discovered in each work because structure, like theme, expresses a particular world different in each work.

As you review structure in the various literary genres, remember that structure involves the arrangement, relationship, and development of the parts of a work. The arrangement and development may be logical or associational; the plan of a work may focus on imagery, symbol, idea, or character evolution. In fixed forms like the sonnet, tradition leads us to anticipate an argument or an elaborately developed series of related images. In long works you will seek some final change in character or situation. When you discover what that change is and what it means, look to the ways that the author accomplishes that change and you will have found the work's basic organization. In the Ionesco play, the structure is found in the work's increasing tension visually rendered through shortened scenes and culminating in the appearance of the Leader. The structure is stylized, but organic; much of the play's meaning is to be found in the structure itself.

Study the essay below to better understand how to write an essay using structure. Note that the essay focuses first on defining the structure then on demonstrating how structure thematically dramatizes Ionesco's ideas about modern man. When writing about structure make a statement about the work's theme in your opening paragraph. Identify the structure and summarize its effectiveness. In the body of your essay show point by point how the structure embodies and clarifies theme, how it dramatizes ideas, and how it lends form and, in some cases, inevitability to the work.

INTENSIFICATION: STRUCTURE IN IONESCO'S *THE LEADER*

Conventional plays often achieve much of their aesthetic form and structure through the playwright's arrangement of plot to accommodate the rhythms necessary to opening and closing scenes and acts. Many unconventional plays from the relatively new theatre of the absurd lack plot and are structured as circles; the characters return at the end of the play to the same point at which they began, and the zero effect indicates the futility of man's condition. Ionesco deviates from both patterns. He structures his plays as dramatically visualized ideas that progress through a series of increasing tensions to an abrupt and explosive final action. His is theatre of exaggeration, and escape or catharsis lies in laughter as the audience sees the absurdity of the human condition dramatized, and as it then soberly realizes that man's absurd condition is also deeply tragic. In *The Leader,* a short one-act play first produced in Paris in 1953, Ionesco abandons conventional plot, and the play achieves aesthetic form through a structure based on repetition, accelerating action, and increasingly shortened scenes.

The Leader is actually a sketch, and in the characters' actions, entrances, and exits the play resembles a rigidly choreographed dance. The characters' movements are stylized and purposefully mechanical. The play opens with the Announcer standing motionless, back to the audience, eyes fixed on the up-stage exit. Two other characters, the Two Admirers, stand "riveted to the walls" and when the Announcer begins cheering the approach of the Leader, the Two Admirers, "bodies . . . flattened against the wall, thrust their neck and heads as far forward as they can." Following a burst of cheering the three characters rush off stage. The stage is empty for a moment, then Two Lovers appear. They meet center-stage, engage in the mechanics of first meeting, then suddenly embrace and declare their love. They leave. The entrance and exit of both groups alternate, each group performing a series of stylized actions before rushing off stage. This essential rhythmical pattern is repeated to the end of the play and is compounded by irony when the two groups meet, dissolve allegiances, and regroup into newly formed love pairs. In the comical and totally absurd finale, all characters on stage reinforce the geometrics of moving patterns. The effect is choreographic; it lends a repetitive rhythm to the action and forms the basis of the play's structure.

The dialogue of each mechanized character is as repetitive, abrupt, and satirically stylized as the action. The Announcer shouts over and over, "There he is! Hurrah!" "Long live the Leader!" "He's going away!" The rhythmic cheering of the off-stage crowd orchestrates his shouts. The Two Admirers echo the Announcer. They say in unison, stamping their feet, "Oh! Ah! Oh! Oh! Ah! Ah!" When the Two Lovers meet the Two Admirers there follows a series of "Oh, sorry, so sorry, sorry, sorry"—lines that clearly parody the meaningless, unthinking phrases of polite society. Repetition in the Announcer's description of the off-stage actions of the Leader also provides the play with its dramatic suspense. The Announcer reports every action with equal seriousness, as if each were an immediate, momentous event. Each report opens and closes with cheers and authoritative commands to the Admirers, which adds to the rhythmical repetition of each scene. Thus, repetition in sound reinforces the play's stylized movements and, as each episode in the play is accelerated with shortened scenes and increasingly rapid action, the play realizes a fully developed structure.

The play moves essentially from the purely comic to the totally unexpected and surprising. The first episodes are paced slowly; with each succeeding scene the speed of the entrances and exits of the characters accelerates. The scenes shorten, become intensified by shouting and rapid regrouping of the characters on stage. An increasing tension results within the characters' and audience's growing desire to see the Leader. In the repetition in dialogue and action, and subtly, in the Announcer's mounting adulation as he describes the Leader, the play reaches its highest intensity. At this point the Leader appears. He is headless. The point of the play becomes clear: unthinking public opinion reaches epidemic proportions when man no longer thinks but acts in a mass as one brainless whole, blindly worshipping anything, or nothing.

Through structure Ionesco succeeds in visually creating a sense of the automation and artificiality in modern society that reduces man to the spiritual level of mechanical puppets. The structure is organic; in its rhythms it mimics its own theme.

SAMPLE ESSAY 18
USING SOCIAL BACKGROUND AND HISTORY

INSTRUCTIONS.   The essay using social background and history shows
that a work of literature is the product of a particular age. This method of
analyzing literature denies in a sense the view that a work of literature can
be studied as a work of art complete in itself, insisting as it does that investigation of the social milieu in which a work is created is necessary for
complete understanding of the work. Although we have taken the stand in
this book that a consideration of extrinsic factors is not necessary for an
understanding of a work of literature, we do agree that a special kind of
enlightenment often results from such an examination.

Before writing this kind of essay you will need to make a relatively
thorough search for information concerning the cultural background of the
era to which the work belongs. How thorough your research needs to be
depends, of course, upon your assignment. In most cases, you will be required to narrow your subject to one division of a broad category. For example, even though an essay using biography fits into the broader heading
of social and historical background, you would be required only to research information on the author. Another approach might be to study the
language of a work, not its metaphorical or stylistic aspects, but as representative of its linguistic traditions. This kind of essay can aptly point out
the appeal of a work by making clear the way in which language belongs
to a period in time but also retains interest for a later time. An example is
the scholarly work done on the epics of Homer in an attempt to establish
from dialect a more precise time of authorship. Another kind of essay in
this field authenticates the text of a work. The purpose of this essay is to
establish the reliability of a text that is very old, or that has an anonymous
author or is a work of collaboration, or from which parts are missing or
seem changed from the original. An example of this last kind of research
is the work done to authenticate the Dead Sea Scrolls, ancient manuscripts
not discovered until the late 1940's, which illuminate the religious background of Jesus.

Probably you will most often be asked to write the kind of essay in
this field that explains a work of literature in terms of its creation at a particular time. Your purpose will be to show that the work is representative
of the era in which it came into being. But even this more limited subject
requires still further narrowing.

As you write, be careful not to choose too broad a topic. In a short
essay you cannot trace the entire cultural and historical influences of an

era; therefore, limit your work to a single aspect of the background. For example, if you wanted to show the influence of a particular facet of contemporary life upon the shaping of Ionesco's play *The Leader,* you might choose any of a number of topics, including industrial developments, political thought, religious changes, wars, or new findings in science, sociology, psychology, or technology.

The thesis for your essay is inherent in the idea of this kind of approach: your essay will demonstrate that such factors do exert an influence upon the concerns of the work of literature you examine. In development show as many aspects of the work that have been affected by sociological or historical influences as your space allows. If you cannot show all the effects, organize your development around a specific core of effects (the essay that follows shows, for example, such effects upon the characterization, the action, and the dialogue of Ionesco's play *The Leader*).

SOCIAL CRITICISM IN IONESCO'S *THE LEADER*

Many contemporary writers have shown that people of the modern world fill their empty lives with meaningless activity and talk, but Ionesco has allegorized this social affliction in such a way that what we receive is a total impression of the automated frenzy of modern life. Ionesco's short play *The Leader* is a social allegory. The characters, the action, and the dialogue are not entities; instead they are symbols showing modern man as a being who possesses no inner resources, spiritual or intellectual, and who, as a consequence, expends much of his energy in the game of "follow the leader." With terrible accuracy, Ionesco pictures this spiritual and intellectual lack, creating in the process a penetrating criticism of one bit of contemporary insanity. A look at three prime elements of a play—the characters, the action, and the dialogue—will confirm the allegorical nature of his criticism.

The Young Lover and his Girl-Friend are symbols for Every Young Lover, acting out the stereotype of all popular love stories: boy meets girl, they fall in love, they agree to marry. Young love in this play, however, is distorted. We cannot see these lovers as fully realized characters and thus cannot feel sympathetic to their love; in addition, they neither demonstrate love for each other, nor indicate that their relationship will be a lasting one. One of the truths to which people cling, trying to fill the void, is thus present, but it is twisted. The Admirers are symbols for the somewhat older individuals who have gone beyond young love, evidently having found their version of it inadequate, and who are now trying to put admiration for some kind of leader in its place. They symbolize Every Admirer.

The Announcer is a more complex symbol; he is one who struggles with greater frenzy than the others to make his life meaningful. His method is to manipulate others, feeling that in doing so he assumes a power equal to the Leader he admires as frantically as The Admirers do. He is Every Announcer: the press agent, the reporter, the circus barker. Ironically, he succeeds only in devoting himself to a greater piece of foolishness than the others. He labors with great energy to make others follow him as he follows the Leader. The last symbolic character, the Leader, is less than a stereotype; he is only an amorphous creature, appearing briefly at the end of the play, a symbol to the others of what they would like to be; he is, however, the epitome of all that they themselves are: a complete nonentity with a "genius" for nothingness.

Action in *The Leader* is pointless. The physical attitudes of the characters lend a sense of confused excitement. At contradictory commands from the Announcer, the Admirers flatten their bodies against the wall or crane their necks forward to catch sight of the Leader; they cheer or remain silent; they follow the Announcer or stand back. They seem not to have wills of their own, but move like automatons, propelled by the Announcer's words. In their actions the Lovers also exhibit constant contradictions. They do not know each other; they will marry. They embrace each other; they suddenly shift and each embraces one of the Admirers. The Announcer displays no motivating force to account for his manipulation of the others nor for his deception of them. He moves forward; he moves backward. He runs; he stands still. He barks loudly his reports of the movements of the Leader; he remains silent. Action from all the characters shows these contradictions. They exit or enter without reason. Often the stage is empty, and the very emptiness seems to underscore the empty actions which take place when the characters are on stage. With his sudden shifts from one kind of action to another, from clamor to silence, from confused milling to an empty stage, and with the musical comedy effect of the exits and entrances from one side, then another, then a meeting of all in the center, Ionesco adroitly points up the emptiness of human action not intellectually or spiritually motivated.

Perhaps the most stringent social criticism of the play inheres in the dialogue. The characters do not communicate, they utter nonsensical words; they talk and their words never strike the consciousness of others. Their words glance off one another without leaving the faintest impression. And yet the sounds which come from their lips run the full gamut of emotions: cheers, bleating cries, terms of endearment, harsh commands, anxious questions. They react almost as though spontaneously from some hidden instinct rather than from logical motivation. Language, the playwright shows, has deteriorated to the point that one utterance cancels another. Human speech is thus shown to be useless.

The Announcer has by far the most to say. His flood of excited reporting displays the same contradictory quality that characterizes the speech of the others. He likens the Leader to such diverse kinds of persons as Christ, a popular singer, a military hero, an athlete. Even as these persons, the Leader is shown to have contradictory characteristics. As Christ, he "suffers the little children to come unto him," but he makes a little girl cry by handing her a hedgehog. As the political figure, he reports that the Leader "has confidence in everybody," but that "he inaugurates the police force." As the athlete he performs a feat of no consequence: he "spits a tremendous distance."

Ionesco handles his allegory so skillfully that each action and each bit of dialogue nullifies preceding ones. We are left with a totality that is null and void. But we should not suppose that Ionesco lacked a positive motive for showing this world. His very portrayal of a world where the actions and speech of men are worse than meaningless—where they are mutually exclusive—shows that he intends to provide a grim warning to a society that he sees as notable, so far as intellectual and spiritual truths are concerned, only for what it lacks.

SAMPLE ESSAY 19
USING ILLUSTRATION

INSTRUCTIONS. Illustration is effective when you want to describe or analyze the particularities of one subject and, by implication, simultaneously apply the same points to other, similar subjects. By this method your essay becomes both particular and representational, and your analysis gains in dimension because what you say describes not only your specific subject but all others like it. Your subject becomes, in other words, illustrative of a class; by describing a representational member you describe the whole class.

For example: if you discover that all of Ionesco's plays have common characteristics in theme or presentation (which they do), a description of these similarities as they apply to a specific work effectively describes not only the one work, but all Ionesco's works. The method for accomplishing this is simple: note the similarities in his works, then apply these similarities to a specific work. The one work becomes, as a result, representative or illustrative of his whole body of works.

The advantages of using this technique are many: first, you do not, in your essay, have to deal with each of his many works in order to comment about them; second, by using one work your essay becomes specific in reference; third, while being specific and therefore limited, the essay at the same time includes a broader reference and so achieves dimension and added importance.

The theory of illustration characterizes much fiction. When a writer uses a main character who is specific and individual on one level, and representative of all others in the world like himself on another level, the character is said to be universal. All universal characters are illustrations of their class. The young soldier in *All Quiet on the Western Front* is German and he fought and died in World War I, but his confusions, his bravery, his endurance and final, absurd death are timeless in application. Thousands of young men like him died in World War II and in Korea, and young men will continue to fight and die in future wars.

An illustration is a representation; it is an example from a class that typifies the common characteristics of that class. When writing an essay in which you use a specific subject to illustrate some larger group, make clear in your introduction that this is what you are doing. Words like "typical," "representative," "personifies," and even "illustrates" will make clear your plan or intention. In the body of your paper you simply discuss these specific points as they apply to your single subject, and as they apply to other, similar subjects. In your conclusion state again that the points made in the paragraphs in the body of your paper apply equally to other works or subjects.

Read the following essay and note how the writer has limited the subject to the Two Lovers in *The Leader;* note also how the characteristics of the Two Lovers are used illustratively: they are applied not only to the other characters in the play, but to a common theme running through all Ionesco's plays.

TWO LOVERS: CARICATURE
AND IDEA IN IONESCO'S *THE LEADER*

Ionesco employs the device of caricature in his plays to dramatize the spiritual sterility and conformity of modern man. He populates his plays with characters that represent, not individual human beings, but abstract concepts. Mechanized and inhuman, they resemble puppets, and Ionesco uses their stylized and exaggerated movements and speech to demonstrate truths about the absurdity of the human condition. The Two Lovers in his play, *The Leader,* are typical, excellent illustrations of Ionesco's technique of using characters as symbols to criticize the moral and spiritual degeneration of modern society.

One of Ionesco's dominant themes is that of the interchangeability of character. This concept is ambiguous, for it implies both universality in the shared condition of man and, conversely, man's loss of his own sense of uniqueness in a mechanized, impersonal world. The Two Lovers demonstrate this ambiguity. On the one hand they represent all mankind and on the other a leveling of consciousness that destroys love and fidelity and renders it an empty, vacuous act of self-gratification. In *The Leader* the Two Lovers meet, and in a parody of courtship, immediately declare their love. Subsequent scenes, however, show how shallow is their liaison. Their compatibility, satirically, centers on a mutual fondness for eggs, and as the play progresses, they become enemies, chasing not each other, but the idea of love. Their words, meaningless as their emotions, soon effect an easy exchange of partners for a new love-sex game. Thus, interchangeability evokes a sense of recognition of the Lover in all of us, and it simultaneously indicates that when individual man loses his own sense of uniqueness he loses it for all mankind; when any partner will do, all become facelessly the same.

Another dominant theme in Ionesco's works is his contention that language has become fossilized and clichéd and meaningless, that man can no longer effectively communicate in ordinary language. Ionesco dramatizes this belief by satirizing the courtship of the Two Lovers and by mechanizing their dialogue to show the basic absurdity of conventional language. He also dramatizes the truth of his statement by using visual symbols and silence rather than language to communicate his own meaning in the play. We understand the Two Lovers not by what they say but by what they do. The disparity between words and actions is made clear in *The Leader* through the Two Lovers, and we receive the full impact of Ionesco's contention by seeing this disparity dramatized. Dialectic is ridiculed; meaning is communicated in the visual, moving symbols of the Lovers.

Finally, the spiritual and moral vacuity of modern man posed in pathetic opposition to the inevitability of death, according to Ionesco, renders the human condition both tragic and absurd. In none of his plays is this fact made clearer than in this play, in which the Two Lovers, unaware of their own condition, play their empty, futile game. Unthinking, unfeeling, promiscuous, unawakened, they move toward death like puppets on a conveyer belt. The effect is complex, suggesting finally that man has no meaning except in his own mind; if he loses his consciousness of that, he becomes pitiful. The audience, seeing the Two Lovers parody love, realize this truth and so realize their own absurd, tragic condition.

These themes—man's changeability, the fossilization of language, and the absurdity of the human condition—are dominant in all Ionesco's plays. But none of the characters—Berenger in *Rhinoceros,* the two couples in *The Bald Soprano,* the professor in *The Lesson,* the two old people in *The Chairs*—more tersely demonstrate all three concepts than the Two Lovers in the short, one act play, *The Leader.*

SUGGESTED ASSIGNMENTS FOR WRITING ESSAYS ABOUT PLAYS

1. Compare a modern tragedy with a classical or Elizabethan tragedy (Shakespeare's *Othello* with O'Neill's *The Iceman Cometh;* Sophocles' *Antigone* with Anouilh's *Antigone*). Base your comparison upon some clearly defined criteria for what tragedy should be (Aristotle's "rules"; the presentation of a conviction concerning human nature; the high moral purpose of tragedy).

2. Some plays depend for their texture and scope on a dramatization of the past. Williams' *The Glass Menagerie* explores fragile people preoccupied with and doomed by the past. Compare Amanda in *The Glass Menagerie* with Daisy in Ionesco's *Rhinoceros* to determine what they have in common, wherein their grief and failure lies. Compare any two dramatic characters who are greatly influenced by past experiences and memories.

3. Write a character sketch of the protagonist of a play. Show how action and dialogue coalesce to reveal the inner working of the character's mind (Genet's *Deathwatch* or Behan's *The Hostage*).

4. Choose one of the many off-Broadway plays and discuss theme, characterization or audience. Use *Motel,* by Jean-Claude van Itallie, which reflects cynicism about American society; use LeRoi Jones' play *The Toilet* as theater of anger. Justify or condemn, in terms of theme or good theater, these or some other current play.

5. Choose a television play you have seen recently and determine its structure. Show how successfully (or unsuccessfully) the playwright unfolds his action and thought within the structure basic to drama (see pages 182, 189).

6. Discuss the function of a passage from a play (the passage between Oedipus and Teiresias in Sophocles' *Oedipus Rex;* the first scene between Hedda and Thea in Ibsen's *Hedda Gabler;* the opening scene of Shelagh Delaney's *A Taste of Honey*). How does the scene serve to reveal character? How does the scene aid the reader in judging the main character? Does the scene foreshadow coming action? As a thesis be sure to establish the principal function of the scene.

7. Power often becomes a major theme in drama. Analyze the effects of waning power in *Macbeth,* its destructive effects in *Medea,* its "puzzlement" in

The King and I. The drive for power, or its burden, or grief over its loss motivates many plays. Select a play of your own choosing and discuss power as theme or as complication.

8. Stage business and keys to directing and acting offer clues to understanding the way a character is to be interpreted or an act performed. Analyze the stage business in Shaw's *Pygmalion*, or Beckett's *Waiting for Godot*.

The bare stage is symbolic and requires audience participation and understanding. Define the meaning of the bare stage in a Greek tragedy, or in a modern play like Miller's *After the Fall*, or Sartre's *No Exit*, or the relatively bare stage of Albee's *The Zoo Story*. What is the significance of using few or no props?

9. Imagery often forms the basis of plays. Determine the importance and meaning of imagery in Strindberg's *A Dream Play* or in Yeats' *Purgatory*. Characters in plays from the theatre of the absurd are often used as images. Select a play and describe the function and meaning of its imagery.

10. Write an essay that analyzes the witty dialogue of a comedy. What is the quality of the wit? What function does the wit serve? Does it bring out thought, does it merely entertain, or does it present a "message" in pleasing form? Use Goldsmith's *She Stoops to Conquer*, Aristophanes' *The Clouds*, Garson Kanin's *Born Yesterday*, or Tom Stoppard's *Rosencrantz and Guildenstern Are Dead*.

GLOSSARY

The following is a supplementary list of literary terms not fully defined in the text. See the Index for page references to literary terms that are defined in the text.

Abstract and *Concrete:* Terms or words representing, respectively, indefinite qualities or tangible objects. **Abstract terms** or words represent ideas or generalities that cannot be perceived through the senses. They denote names of qualities: "beauty," "love," "honor," "green." Abstract terms describe concepts or attitudes, and **Abstract poetry,** first defined by Dame Edith Sitwell, refers to poetry that derives its meaning not from the use of concrete images but from words whose meanings (like the color and line of abstract painting) are produced through emotion and suggestion in the poem's tonal quality, rhyme, and rhythm. **Concrete** terms denote specific objects or entities (red apple, boy's flushed cheeks, pale moon) that have actual existence and can be perceived through the senses or can be directly experienced. Abstract terms, using particular instances to arrive at general truths, form the language of philosophy and science; concrete terms, emphasizing the vivid, the sensory, and the tangible, form the language of literature.

Aesthetic distance: A term used by critics to describe the objectivity or degree of independence between a work and the subjective feelings or experiences of the author. In one sense all literature derives from the emotions and experiences of the writer, but when the work is objectified and rendered complete and independent of its author, it is said to have aesthetic distance. Keats admired the quality (see **Negative capability**) and T. S. Eliot used a similar term (see **Objective correlative**) to describe the distance achieved when form and technique successfully separate a work from the writer and his emotions. Shakespeare's plays are considered to be objective; aesthetic distance divides the playwright from his works. Many of Wordsworth's poems are considered to be subjective and therefore without aesthetic distance; the poet acknowledged the speaker as himself, and the content as descriptions of his own feelings and personal experiences.

Affective fallacy: A term used in the New Criticism (see **Criticism**) to denote what the formalistic critics consider the error of judging a work by its emotional effects on the reader. Impressionistic critics advocate such an approach, but the new critics contend that the work must be considered independently of the reader's personal response, and further, that the work exists as a complete entity separate from the reader. W. K. Wimsatt, Jr., and M. C. Beardsley, new critics, introduced the term.

Allegory: An extended metaphor or system of dual meanings in a narrative or poem wherein objects and persons in their setting exist both on a literal level of realistic interest and a metaphorical level as objects and persons representing concepts or personifications of abstract qualities. The setting serves as the frame of reference or background within which the concepts function. Bunyan's *The Pilgrim's Progress* describes a Christian man's efforts to live a godly life by triumphing over inner weaknesses in faith. These weaknesses or obstacles take him through such places (or allegorical states of mind) as Vanity Fair and the Slough of Despond. Christian, of course, is the soul traveling through life toward heaven.

Allegory, unlike symbolism, is a system or structure of ideas that influences the formation or execution of the work. A symbol suggests other ideas or meanings but does not structure the work in narrative form.

Kinds of allegory include the fable, parable, and exemplum. The **fable** is a brief tale designed to dramatize a moral thesis. If its characters consist of animals that talk and think like human beings, it is a **beast fable.** Aesop's tales, Joel Chandler Harris' Uncle Remus stories, Rudyard Kipling's *Jungle Books* and George Orwell's *Animal Farm* are beast fables. A **parable** is also an illustrative story pointing to a moral, but it is structured by an analogy in which, detail by detail, the story parallels a situation the story calls forth. The story is told in concrete, everyday terms to make clear an abstract point or truth. Christ's parables of the Good Samaritan and the sower exemplify this form of allegory. The **exemplum** is also a moral tale, but one told by preachers to their medieval congregations to illustrate doctrines. Chaucer used exempla in his tales; for example, in the *Pardoner's Tale,* the Pardoner, to illustrate that avarice leads to an evil end, tells a story about three revelers who set out to find Death but find gold instead, and fighting for sole possession of it, kill one another.

Bathos: A Greek term for "depth," describing literary passages that are absurd or ridiculous because the author has overstrained to reach the sublime, or to achieve pathos. True bathos is wildly comic for the simple reason that the author tried so seriously to achieve the opposite effect (see **Pathos**). Pope made the word popular and in his "Martinus Scriblerus" quotes the following example of unintentional overwriting:

Advance the fringed curtains of thy eyes
And tell me who comes yonder.

Motion pictures and television dramas that try too hard to make the viewer weep and only succeed in making him laugh at their artificiality and triteness provide good examples of bathos.

Burlesque and *Parody:* Forms of comic art in which people, actions, or literary works are made ridiculous through exaggeration. Burlesque treats a literary *form* in grotesque or mocking terms; **parody** treats a literary *work* in grotesque or mocking terms. Burlesque is achieved through style; a **mock epic** uses elevated language to make laughable a common or trivial subject; a **travesty** uses grotesque or low language to make laughable a lofty subject. A **caricature** is a portrait of a person made laughable by exaggeration of features; a **lampoon** is a character portrait in which a person is made laughable by being described verbally in a biting manner. Caricature characterizes the theatre of the absurd.

Caricature. See **Burlesque** and **Parody.**

Carpe diem: A phrase meaning "seize the day." First used by Horace, it applies particularly to those lyric poems that thematically advocate the concept, "Let us eat and drink, for tomorrow we may die." Popular in English love poems of the seventeenth and eighteenth centuries, it expressed the idea of seizing life, of living fully by succumbing to love while still beautiful and young. Robert Herrick's famous poem, "To the Virgins, to Make Much of Time," epitomizes this concept; it opens with the line "Gather ye rosebuds while ye may." Saul Bellow wrote a novella on this theme and appropriately titled it *Seize the Day.*

Concrete. See **Abstract.**

Convention and *Tradition:* Any device, style, or subject matter recognized by time and habit as an accepted method or element of literary expression is called a convention. The **soliloquy,** the compression of time, or the use of scenery to suggest places the audience can imagine are real are all part of the convention of **dramatic illusion.** Coleridge described audience belief as the "willing suspension of disbelief." Conventions include the **heroic couplet,** the **sonnet, free verse,** the **novel, stock characters, tragedy,** the **drama** in **acts;** all forms we accept with time become conventions. Overused, they fall into disuse, perhaps to be revived, as the **ballad** was.

Conventions solve problems for artists in literature as they do in other arts, as, for example, perspective in painting was developed then consciously discarded by modern artists. The illusions of time and space are the most universal conventions in all the arts. When a convention is adopted by a group of artists it becomes a **tradition.** Pop art and op art, atonal music, the theatre of the absurd are traditions now. They were considered original and termed inventions when first introduced. Now they are traditions, and as single concepts and techniques, conventions.

Criticism: A term applied to the analysis, evaluation, and description of art. Schools roughly divide between the **Aristotelian**—analyzing and judging by formal standards—and **Platonic**—judging and evaluating works by

moralistic or **utilitarian** standards that lie outside the work. These represent basically a division between **intrinsic** and **extrinsic** interests (see page 24). Critical history since the seventeenth century makes a further division of approaches and schools: (1) **impressionistic,** in which the critic attempts to evaluate or explain the work by its effect upon him as an individual; (2) **judicial,** in which the critic attempts to explain the effects of a work through classifications of set standards; (3) **moral,** in which the critic evaluates by the standards of society; (4) **textual,** in which the critic studies the original manuscripts and subsequent changes; (5) **formal,** in which the critic evaluates the work according to its genre; (6) **mythic,** in which the critic looks to the original myth or the evocation of **archetype.** These overlap: some critics are **relativists;** that is, they believe in using any aid or method required to reach understanding. The classification above is valid for defining the **absolutist,** the critic who holds only one approach to be valid or correct. The **New Criticism,** arising in the 1940's in both England and the United States, advocates close textual analysis through *intrinsic* consideration.

Deus ex machina: A term meaning "god from the machine," referring to the convention in Greek theatre of lowering a god from the stage structure to intervene in the action and solve by godly edict a plot impasse. The term now refers to any device whereby an author extricates his story from a difficulty in plot by a forced or implausible solution. The hero's melodramatic, last-minute appearance with money or police to save the heroine from the villain, or in mystery stories, the introduction of knowledge into the resolution that is not feasible or that was not planted earlier in the story are both examples of *deus ex machina.* Farfetched or unmotivated solutions to plot complications marks the *deus ex machina* or "sell-out" ending of stories and movies.

Empathy and *Sympathy:* **Empathy** is the "involuntary projection of ourselves" or our identification with an object to the point where we feel we are part of its essence and existence. Seeing a photograph of violence, we may flinch or cringe; seeing a flower we merge with the flower and feel its physical sensations; we experience the animal's fear or its exultation as it runs across the countryside. Actively felt, empathy results in the creative process; passively felt, we appreciate. **Sympathy,** in contrast, denotes a feeling of emotional identification with another human being; we identify and seem to feel his joy or his sorrow.

Figurative language: An intentional departure from the normal use and meaning of words to achieve special effects. Figurative language is writing that uses various **figures of speech.** Divided into two categories, figures of speech become **tropes,** literally "turns," in which the meanings of words are extended, and **figures of thought** in which the arrangement and function but not the basic meaning of words are changed.

The following figures of speech are **tropes:** (1) the **simile**—a comparison between two things essentially unlike but having a resemblance in one respect, joined by the words "like" or "as." "Your nose is like a red, red rose" is a simile. The resemblance, we presume, lies in the size and color of both. (2) the **metaphor**—a comparison between two things in which one object is identified with another. "Your nose is a red, red rose" is a metaphor. For a further discussion of metaphor, particularly extended metaphor, see pages 151–152. See also **Allegory.** A species of metaphor, the **synecdoche** mentions an important part of one thing to signify the whole. In "All hands on deck," "hands" refers to sailors; in referring to the infantry, we say "foot" soldiers. **Metonymy,** another species of metaphor, uses one thing to refer to another with which it is closely associated. "The crown" refers to a king or queen; the "White House" refers to the President of the United States. (3) the **hyperbole**—a conscious exaggeration without the intent to persuade, as "He jumped on his horse and rode off in all directions." Southwestern humor is based in large part on hyperbole; so is Marvell's poem "To His Coy Mistress."

The following are figures of thought: (1) the **antithesis**—strongly contrasting words, phrases or sentences, balanced against each other for emphasis. "And wretches hang that jury-men may dine" is an antithesis. (2) the **apostrophe**—a direct address to some usually absent person, nonexistent person, or abstract quality. The apostrophe is used in patriotic oratory and invocations to the muse. Milton's line, "Hail, Holy Light, offspring of Heaven firstborn!" is an example of the apostrophe. (**Alliteration, assonance, onomatopeia** and **rhyme** are discussed in Section Four, pages 125–128.) See also **Irony.**

Form: A term that has many meanings in literary criticism. In one sense form refers to the literary types, or **genre,** such as novels, short stories, poems, dramas, and their subdivisions (drama, for example, may take the form of tragedy, comedy, tragicomedy, and so on). Also in this sense of the term, form means the molds into which types of literature traditionally have been cast, such as lyrics and narrative poems, or picaresque and historical novels. In another sense, form refers to the rhythmic organization of poems. Such fixed forms as sonnets, ballads, and *terza rima* are examples of poetic forms.

A third meaning of form makes a distinction between "conventional" form and "organic" form: conventional form refers to the ideal pattern or shape of a work, as in the fourteen-line sonnet; organic form refers to the internal development and thematic movement of a work, or to the shape a work assumes as a result of its content and meaning. In this last sense, form is sometimes referred to as the **structure** of a work. See **Convention and Tradition, Genre,** and pages 211–212.

Genre: The word *genre* is French, from the Latin *genus,* meaning kind, sort, species. In literature the term genre refers to the kinds of literature: tragedy, comedy, the novel, the short story, biography, and so on. In one sense, genre is closely allied to the term **form;** however, to designate a form of literature as a genre indicates that it is a major species of literature. Genre ideally indicates that technical characteristics exist in works of the same kind, although modern criticism denies that such characteristics exist, and the term now is most often used to describe major types of literature.

Hyperbole. See **Figurative language.**

Intentional fallacy: A term used in contemporary criticism to denote the error of judging or interpreting a work according to the expressed or supposed intentions of the author. Wimsatt and Beardsley, who introduced the term, write that "The author must be admitted as a witness to the meaning of his work." They suggest, however, that "the poem is not the critic's own and not the author's," that a work must be subjected to the same objective analysis, as a complete, separate entity, as any other "statement in linguistics or the general sciences." Their contention is that what a work means and what the author wanted it to mean may vary, and that ultimately the work must be examined as a complete entity, separate from the wishes or ambitions of its author.

Irony: A mode of speech in which the actual words express the opposite of the literal meaning. Irony is less harsh than **sarcasm** and traditionally speaks praise to impute blame. Anthony's speech over the dead Caesar, that "Brutus is an honorable man," is ironically spoken. **Understatement,** or **meiosis,** is a species of irony in which the speaker consciously makes light of something serious. If a person falls over a cliff, and an onlooker inquires whether he might not be hurt, he is using meiosis. **Socratic irony** employs a pretense to timidity and ignorance and a willingness to hear the other side, which is then shown to be ridiculous. **Dramatic irony** refers to information or knowledge the audience possesses but that is withheld from the actors. It also applies to actors' attempts to achieve one end, while unwittingly working to achieve its opposite. *Oedipus Rex* is based on this type of irony. See also pages 17–18 for additional comments about irony.

Lyric: Existing for thousands of years in all countries, the lyric, a personal and subjective expression of the poet's emotions, was first sung to the accompaniment of a lyre or other instrument, then later was written as poetry to be read. The lyric has no set form; it can rhyme or be composed in free verse. The lyric is melodic, imaginative, subjective; it is the genus, and the sonnet, ode, elegy, ballad, and other poetic verse forms are the species. In the broadest sense the lyric, as "song," is not a specific kind of poem but a manner of writing.

Meiosis: See **Irony.**

Motif: In medieval folklore, the term motif denoted a theme or subject about which many stories were told. (See **Carpe diem.**) In this sense, a motif is a theme, or major basis for a narrative structure and meaning. However, motif today carries a more subtle meaning. Motif refers to a recurring sound, image, color, figure, or character that lightly and rhythmically punctuates a work of art. Its presence, often unsuspected by the audience, helps unify the work and in some cases may suggest meanings. Richard Wagner used the "leitmotif" in his operas. His motifs were musical phrases, which came to be identified with the characters; each motif anticipated entrances and emotions. One of the most subtle uses of motif is to be found in E. M. Forster's *A Passage to India,* in which a wasp appears quite inconspicuously in all three of the novel's "symphonic" parts. As recurring images or repeated descriptions, like the wasps in Forster's novel or the motif of the "girls with big feet" in Thomas Mann's story, "Gladeus Dei," motif unifies and gives meaning in a work. Used in the modern sense, motif should not be confused with the theme of a work or with the heavier implications of major symbols.

Naturalism: A literary movement, which began in France in the late nineteenth century. The naturalists, seeing man as a product of his animal nature and his environment, believe that literature should present him in a scientifically objective manner. Naturalism, which often stresses the sordid and the depraved, demands the presentation of a clear, detailed picture of life, with no moral or aesthetic judgments placed upon the actions of men. The literature of naturalism offers a fatalistic view of man as entrapped by his hormones and genes and by his social surroundings. See **Realism.**

Negative capability: The ability of writers not to impose personal philosophy upon their works. The phrase was used by Keats in a letter to his brothers; he defined his phrase this way: ". . . when a man is capable of being in uncertainties, mysteries, doubts, without any irritable reaching after fact and reason." Keats said in the letter that Shakespeare possessed this capability enormously, that Shakespeare had "innate universality." Today the term refers to those qualities in an artist's work that allow him to avoid any direct expression of his own emotions or personality. The belief insists upon an objective view. See **Aesthetic distance.**

New criticism. See **Criticism.**

Objective correlative: T. S. Eliot, in an essay on *Hamlet,* first used and defined this term: "The only way of expressing emotion in the form of art is by finding an 'objective correlative'; in other words, a set of objects, a chain of events which shall be the formula of that *particular* emotion; such that when the external facts, which must terminate in sensory experience, are given, the emotion is immediately evoked." In Lady Macbeth's sleepwalking scene, Eliot says, the "state of mind of Lady Macbeth" is "communicated . . . by a skillful accumulation of imagined sensory impressions." The phrase has been defined to mean that a poet can control his reader's response by presenting in his work the objects and events to which he himself has responded.

Ode: A long lyric poem, of elevated emotion and elaborate metrical form. Pindar, a Greek poet, wrote odes modeled upon the songs of the chorus in Greek drama. In his odes stanzas were patterned in strophes and antistrophes, identical in form, with contrasting epodes, the three sets being repeated throughout the poem. Later odes lacked the strict stanzaic form and were not restricted to elevated themes. In the Romantic era odes were used for expression of personal emotion and thought (see Keats' "Ode on a Grecian Urn," and Shelley's "Ode to the West Wind").

Pastoral: Literally means "of shepherds." As a literary convention it refers to works which have a rural setting, and which extol the virtues of country life over city life. The convention originated with Theocritus, a Greek poet, who wrote about Sicilian shepherds, presenting the simplicity and goodness of the rural life. The form was used by later poets, including

Vergil, Spenser, and Milton. Usually pastorals are used for themes such as laments for the death of a friend, laments because of an unresponsive mistress, or praises of an existence like that of Paradise.

Pathos: From a Greek word meaning "suffering." It is used to describe the quality of a literary work that can evoke sympathy. In criticism the pathetic is distinguished from the tragic; the pathetic is evoked by scenes of suffering experienced by characters who suffer passively (that is, through no cause of their own); the tragic is evoked by the spectacle of the suffering of a character who brings disaster upon himself. See **Bathos.**

Primitivism: The belief in philosophy, literature, and all the arts that the "natural" is superior to the "artificial." The theory implies that natural, simple man possesses innate goodness and that educated, highly civilized man has corrupted that natural goodness. **Chronological primitivism** supports the belief that early cultures were superior to contemporary cultures. **Cultural primitivism** supports the belief that simple forms of social and political organization are superior to more complex forms. Blake and Wordsworth praised the virtues of the natural state, and such praise is implicit in the works of writers like Rousseau and D. H. Lawrence.

Realism: A literary movement that began with the novels of Daniel Defoe. Realism insists upon verisimilitude in presentation and prefers to show the commonplace experiences and situations of everyday life. The method uses a detailed manner of presenting events, reporting them in a matter-of-fact way. A work can be realistic in both subject matter and manner, or it can be realistic in only one of these respects. Handled skillfully, the realistic manner of presenting life leads the reader to feel that these events must have happened to real people. See **Naturalism.**

Satire: A literary work that ridicules a subject for the purpose of correcting human behavior. Satire may be only an element of a work that is not completely in the satiric mode. The method of satire varies, sometimes causing the reader to smile at the amusing foibles of human beings, sometimes evoking contempt and moral anger directed at the vices of men, and sometimes arousing a desire to crusade against a wrong. See **Burlesque.**

Stream of consciousness: Stream of consciousness is a technique used by writers of fiction to reproduce the inner working of a character's mind. Thoughts and impressions are presented as they occur in the mind of the character, with no rearrangement to allow for complete sentences, logical syntax, or logical order of narrative. The technique attempts to show the unending, irrelevant flow of the human mind at its different levels of consciousness. The last pages of James Joyce's novel *Ulysses* reproduces the fluid, kaleidoscopic interior monologue of the character Molly Bloom. Two other authors who used the technique effectively are Virginia Woolf and William Faulkner.

INDEX

Crane, Stephen (*continued*)
  "The Open Boat," 72
  The Red Badge of Courage, 122
Crisis:
  in drama, 185
Criticism: 225
cummings, e. e.:
  "next to of course god america
    i," 175

Dactylic foot: 129
Dante Alighieri:
  The Divine Comedy, 133
Defoe, Daniel: 230
Delaney, Shelagh:
  A Taste of Honey, 220
Denotation:
  definition, 7–8
Denouement:
  in drama, 184
  in fiction, 79
Deus ex machina: 226
Development scenes:
  in drama, 184
Dialogue:
  in *The Leader,* 202
Dickens, Charles:
  A Tale of Two Cities, 69
Dickinson, Emily:
  "A Bird Came Down the Walk,"
    65
  definition of poetry, 124
  "I Never Saw a Moor," 126
Diction:
  in style, 158–159
  in *The Leader,* 201
Didactic works: 37
Dimeter: 129
Dominant metaphor:
  instructions for writing about,
    150–152
  sample essay, 152–154
Donne, John:
  "Holy Sonnet X," 130
  "The Good-Morrow," 139
Dostoevski, Fyodor:
  Crime and Punishment, 69
Drama:
  closet, 188

Eighteenth-century, 188
Elizabethan, 187
Greek, 183
history of, 183–192
medieval, 187
modern, 189–192
Nineteenth-century, 188
Roman, 186–187
scenes, 184
Seventeenth-century, 188
types, 178–183
verse, 192
Dramatic experience:
  discovery of, *passim* 4–79
Dramatic monologue:
  definition, 138–139
Dryden, John: 29
  "Absolom and Achitophel," 132
  Aureng-Zebe, 188
  "Mac Flecknoe," 176
Durrell, Lawrence:
  Alexandria Quartet, 122

Eighteenth-century drama: 188
Elegiac stanza:
  definition, 134
El Cid: 136
Eliot, T. S.: 223, 229
  "Burnt Norton," 141
  Murder in the Cathedral, 192
  "The Love Song of J. Alfred
    Prufrock," 14, 139, 176
  The Waste Land, 175, 208
  on verse drama, 192
Elizabethan drama:
  history, 187
  structure and conventions, 187–
    188
  types, 187
Empathy: 226
Empson, William:
  Seven Types of Ambiguity, 18
End-stopped lines: 131
English (Shakespearean) sonnet:
  definition, 137
  "Sonnet CXLVI," 145
Enjambed (run-on) lines: 131
Epic: 73, 88
  catalogue, 136

Quotation:
  using in essays, 64—65

Raleigh, Sir Walter:
  "What is our life?" 176
Realism:
  definition, 230
  in drama, 230
Refrain:
  in the ballad, 138
Regional works: 71—72
Remarque, Erich Maria:
  All Quiet on the Western Front,
    75, 76, 218
  Arch of Triumph, 70
Repetition:
  in poetry, 127, 141
  in *The Leader,* 201
Retardation:
  epic flashback, 136
Richards, I. A.: 74
  metaphor, 152
Rising action:
  in drama, 185
"Rival, The" (Sylvia Plath):
  discovery of, 161—164
  reprinted, 160
  sample essays on, 164—175
Robbe-Grillet, Alain: 68
Rodgers, Richard and Oscar Ham-
    merstein II:
  The King and I, 181, 221
Roman drama: 186—187
Romantic comedy: 181
Rhyme:
  blank verse, 126
  definition, 125
  internal, 126
  masculine, feminine, 125
  partial or slant, 126
  sight or eye, 126
Rhyme royal: 134
Rhythm:
  counting syllables, 129
  definition, 128
  end-stopped lines, 130
  measurement, 129
  in "Sonnet CXLVI," 145, 156
  in *The Leader,* 212—214

in tragedy, 179
see Stanza
Run-on (enjambed) lines: 131

**Sackville, Thomas and Thomas Nor-
    ton:**
  Gorboduc, 187
Sartre, Jean-Paul:
  No Exit, 221
Satire: 125, 126, 133, 230
  in drama, 181
  in *The Leader,* 202
Satiric comedy: 181
Satyr plays: 181
Scansion:
  caesura, 130
  definition, 130
  end-stopped lines, 130
  run-on or enjambed lines, 131
  on "Sonnet CXLVI," 145, 156—
    157
  see Stanza
Scene:
  expository, 184
  climax, denouement, develop-
    ment, messenger, transition,
    184
Schmitz, Robert Morell:
  Preparing the Research Paper,
    63
Schorer, Mark: 7
Seneca:
  Medea, 186
  Thyestes, 186
Setting: 70—73, 76
  definition, 70
  instructions for writing about,
    107
  sample essay, 107—109
  symbolism in, 97, 98
  in *The Leader,* 203—204
Seventeenth-century drama: 188
Shakespeare, William:
  comedy, 182
  A Comedy of Errors, 181
  Hamlet, 29, 57
  Macbeth, 10, 220
  Othello, 220
  "Sonnet LXXIII," 151